ONLINE LANGUAGE TEACHER EDUCATION

"This is a welcomed collection. It makes an important contribution to our understanding of the complexity of online distance TESOL, addressing a range of issues that are pertinent to the development and implementation of online distance TESOL in the new digital millennium."
Honglin Chen, University of Wollongong, Australia

"The focus on online distance learning in TESOL makes this book stand out."
Lynn Henrichsen, Brigham Young University, USA

More and more, ESL/EFL teachers are required by their employers to obtain a Master's degree in TESOL. Thousands of ESL/EFL teachers are acquiring professional skills and knowledge through online and distance education instructional models. Filling a growing need and making an important contribution, this book is a forerunner in addressing some of the issues and problems for online distance learning and instructional delivery in TESOL and applied linguistics departments in universities around the world. Carefully addressing the complexity of the field, it includes primary research and case studies of programs where a variety of online distance models are used, organized in three sections:

- Learning in online distance TESOL
- Teaching in online distance TESOL
- Administration of online distance TESOL.

Readable and accessible, the volume represents the collected expertise of leading language teacher educators, bringing the reader a better understanding and ability to apply knowledge about online distance TESOL education.

Liz England is Professor and Chair of TESOL, School of Education and Human Development, Shenandoah University, USA.

ONLINE LANGUAGE TEACHER EDUCATION

TESOL Perspectives

Edited by Liz England

Routledge
Taylor & Francis Group

NEW YORK AND LONDON

First published 2012
by Routledge
711 Third Avenue, New York, NY 10017

Simultaneously published in the UK
by Routledge
2 Park Square, Milton Park, Abingdon, Oxon OX14 4RN

Routledge is an imprint of the Taylor & Francis Group, an informa business

Library of Congress Cataloging in Publication Data
Online language teacher education : TESOL perspectives / edited by
Liz England.
     p. cm.
    Includes index.
    1. English language—Study and teaching—Foreign speakers.
    2. English teachers—Training of. 3. Web-based instruction.
    I. England, Liz.
    PE1128.A2O66 2012
    428.0078′5—dc23   2011053477

ISBN13: 978-0-415-89450-0 (hbk)
ISBN13: 978-0-415-89451-7 (pbk)
ISBN13: 978-0-203-81326-3 (ebk)

Typeset in Bembo
by HWA Text and Data Management, London

Printed and bound in the United States of America on sustainably
sourced paper by IBT Global

CONTENTS

FOREWORD

David Nunan

Introduction

I first became involved in planning, delivering and evaluating a graduate TESOL program at a distance in the early 1980s. In addition to its regular face-to-face courses, the institution I worked at offered several, including the TESOL program, at a distance. While I appreciated the effort to take graduate level study to geographical areas where students would otherwise have been denied, as a teacher, I did not enjoy the experience. Packages of material—study guides, readings, and assignments—that colleagues and I had prepared would be dispatched by the distance learning administration unit. Weeks (sometimes months) would pass without any response from students. Some, in fact, were never heard of again. Expensive, overseas phone calls went unanswered. *This is not why I became a teacher,* I thought.

Fast-forward to the mid-1990s. It's a humid Saturday afternoon in Hong Kong. I sit in my home office in Hong Kong and log on to the Anaheim (formerly Newport Asia-Pacific) University website. AU is the first university in the world to offer a fully-online Master's degree in TESOL, and I'm about to conduct the very first synchronous tutorial in the inaugural module in the program. For several minutes, I sit staring at the screen and the blinking cursor, all alone in the virtual classroom. Then one of the students shows up, and another, and another. Within minutes, all but one of the students is in class and the tutorial begins. Ninety minutes later, I'm exhausted but exhilarated. I've seen the future, and, for the first time, am fully convinced that it will work. What a far cry this is from my initial experiences with distance education in the 1980s!

In her introductory chapter to this volume, editor Liz England wrote "Who knew where the world would take English language teacher education in the 21st century?" I certainly had no idea. I don't think that any of us did. As Steven Johnson

(2010) documents in his natural history of innovation, the Web has turned many of our preconceptions about the pace of change on their heads.

In 2011, the Anaheim University program is still going strong, although it's a very different entity from the one I started all those years ago. There are nine faculty members, three graduate programs and several hundred students. Content is delivered, not only through set reading and the discussion forum, but through video lectures and a residential program. The weekly synchronous tutorial is no longer conducted at a snail's pace through text chat, but through voice and video chat which are augmented by PowerPoint slides. Breakout rooms allow for group work and greater pedagogical flexibility. In terms of immediacy and human contact, technological advances have brought the online graduate study experience closer to that of the face-to-face classroom. Despite this, differences remain. Although there is evidence that distance learners have greater and more frequent contact than their face-to-face counterparts, the tyranny of distance dictates that this contact will be qualitatively different from face-to-face interaction.

What roles have evolved for technology in online learning? I believe that there are four major roles, and in the next section I shall give a brief description of each of these.

Roles of Online Technology in Learning

In instructional contexts, online technology has four major roles. These are:

- As a carrier of content
- As a practice tool
- As a learning management device
- As a communication tool.

As a Carrier of Content

The Internet brings content to the learner. In language learning, it provides a rich source of authentic listening and reading input. In teacher education, it also provides content in the form of audio and visual content. This can take the form of material prepared specifically by the institution offering the course, or through open sources that can be readily searched by the student such as You Tube, and Google Scholar. (Although a caveat is in order here. I advise my students to treat Google with caution and require them to read the article "How Google is making us stupid," which, ironically, is available through Google!)

As a Practice Tool

The computer provides the student an opportunity to practice the skills that the course he/she is undertaking is intended to develop. In language learning, this takes the form of spoken and written drills, comprehension questions, pronunciation and grammar exercises and so on.

As a Learning Management System

Online systems can carry out many, if not most, learning management functions more effectively than traditional "pen and paper" procedures. From initial needs analyses through to summative evaluation, as teachers we can administer, analyze and store data quickly and efficiently. Assignments can be administered and graded, student contributions to discussion fora and synchronous fora can be harvested and archived, and student evaluation of teaching can be administered and collated. I doubt that the management and administration of face-to-face teacher education programs could get by these days without the use of online management.

As a Communication Device

In an online learning environment, the Internet enables students who are studying in many different parts of the world to connect and communicate with their teachers and other students. This happens through asynchronous chat rooms, synchronous text, voice and video sessions, email, Skype and other emerging social networking sites such as livemocha.com, and other means.

Benefits and Challenges of Online TE

There are tangible benefits to graduate study at a distance. These include anywhere/anytime learning (up to a point), the convenience of being able to stay in situ for the duration of one's studies, access to some of the top professionals in the field, and membership of a scholarly community that spans the globe.

However, most benefits also bring challenges. Despite the attention given to community building in most distance programs that I'm familiar with, and the greater immediacy and contact afforded by online learning, distance study can still be an isolating and lonely way to learn. Access to resources, particularly library resources, is another major challenge for many learners. Another challenge is time. Not so long ago, I asked a group of online graduate students to keep a log of the amount of time they spent each week on their studies: activities included reading, watching videoed lectures, reading and making posts to the discussion forum, taking part in synchronous tutorials, participating in small group Skype sessions, completing assignments, having private Skype, email and SMS interactions with fellow students. Some students reported spending up to 50 hours a week on these activities—a staggering amount given the fact that all students were also in full-time employment. For my face-to-face students, who were taking the same course, and who kept a similar log, the amount of time spent on study was much less. (Any teacher who has taught online will also attest that this mode of instruction is much more time consuming than teaching face-to-face.)

These and other challenges in online learning, teaching and administration are documented in the 15 contributions to this collection. These are organized into the following sections:

- Learning in online distance TESOL
- Teaching in online distance TESOL
- Administration of online distance TSOL.

In the rest of this piece, I will provide a brief overview of the contributions to these sections.

Learning in Online Distance TESOL

Major benefits, frequently cited as reasons for choosing to study online, are access and convenience. By studying online, it is possible to remain employed while studying, rather than having to uproot self and family and travel halfway around the world in order to complete a graduate degree. In addition to the obvious financial benefit, there is a professional benefit as well. The student is able to contest the ideas prosecuted on the course against the realities of his or her teaching situation. As one of my own students so graphically put it, "I'm able to have one foot in the world of work, and the other in the world of ideas."

This benefit is particularly tangible for TESOL professionals who often find themselves teaching in remote areas of foreign countries where access to quality face-to-face instruction is either extremely limited or non-existent. This is true, not only for students working in remote areas of developing countries such as the Philippines, Thailand and Cambodia, but also in developed countries such as Japan.

Garton and Edge make this point in their contribution to the volume. They argue that

> practising English language teachers often have neither the time nor the money to take a year or more out of work in order to go to an institution to study full-time [and that] apart from such very practical reasons, online teacher education also has another advantage over more "traditional" on-campus programs: it can enable teachers to effectively bridge the gap between theory and practice.

One of the benefits of online learning in general is the potential for immediate, personalized feedback. With automated quizzes of various types, from closed (multiple choice, true/false etc.) to more open task-based formats, as soon as the student hits the "send" button, they will receive feedback on their performance with comments on what they got right, and explanations for why certain responses were incorrect.

Several contributions to this volume address the issue of online assessment. Contijoch-Escontria, Burns and Candlin use a sociocultural framework to discuss how feedback is mediated as part of an online course between online tutors and their language teacher learners. They highlight the transformative nature of online learning in general before focusing on formative assessment in online learning.

A major challenge when it comes to formal assessment concerns security. How does one know that a piece of work submitted for assessment was actually completed by the student him/herself? Accrediting bodies such as the U.S. distance Education and Training Council address this issue by insisting on proctored examinations. My own view is that these are a retrograde step. Most TESOL programs that I have been involved with abandoned formal examinations as a form of assessment many years ago in favor of more direct assessment measures. Proctored examinations also bring their own challenges, particularly for students who are working in remote areas. One such challenge is identifying an appropriate proctor who can vouch for the identity of the student.

Humphries and Mihai look at challenges and solutions in online assessment. Although the focus is on the assessment of second language learners, rather than the assessment of second language teachers in preparation, it offers perspectives and advice that are relevant to the concerns of this volume.

Legg and Knox frame their contribution in terms of contextualization and convenience, pointing out that online courses enable TESOL teachers to remain in situ, continuing to work while also undertaking graduate study (a point made earlier in this foreword). The chapter provides an interesting case study of graduate study at a distance from the perspective of the student and the teacher.

A perennial concern for distance education programs in pre-online days was the high attrition rate. With the advent of online learning, institutions have found a partial solution to this challenge by building communities of practice. This concept has emerged as one of critical importance in distance education and several contributions to the collection deal with it. Collaboration and communities of practice reduce the sense of isolation and the feeling that students are "facing the world of learning alone." They also enable students to enter a learning culture in which fellow students become important resources of learning.

In the final contribution to this section, entitled Life After Online Learning, Copland and Garton look at what happens to online learners after they have completed their course of study. Based on questionnaire data, the authors examine the benefits of online graduate study in terms of professional and academic development. The study is particularly interesting because it documents the advantages respondents perceive in online study in comparison with face-to-face instruction.

Teaching in Online Distance TESOL

Just as learning at a distance is quite different from learning face-to-face, so too is teaching. While some skills transfer from face-to-face to virtual classrooms, others do not. In addition to developing knowledge of, and mastery over the technical issues and challenges of teaching online (and these are constantly evolving), there are also critical issues to do with the management of the teaching–learning process at a distance as well as the social side of teaching and learning. Dealing with interpersonal conflicts, disciplining and counseling students are difficult enough in face-to-face instructional contents. In online teaching, they become exponentially more difficult.

Kaur's contribution highlights the fact that as an online community evolves a new online culture co-evolves, and those who identify with that culture embrace a new identity of shared values, relationships and interactional rules. Kaur comments that "Interactivity and learning from each other are the fuel for bonding and provide the reasons for sustainability of the community of practice." She sees, in the fostering of communities of practice, at least a partial solution to some of the challenges alluded to in the preceding chapter.

If any course is going to strike fear into the hearts of graduate TESOL students, it is almost certain to be quantitative research methods and statistics. The disquiet felt by students in face-to-face instruction is compounded in online courses. The course described by McAllister is designed to provide a rigorous introduction to quantitative data collection and analysis while allaying the fears of students who are allergic to numbers. The chapter provides concrete examples and suggestions, and articulates possible pitfalls in developing such a course.

In "Building An Online Community of Inquiry With Student Moderated Discussions," Shin and Bickel describe the use of course management systems to build communities through asynchronous discussion forums. They describe a study which uses the Community of Inquiry Model to identify those factors that made for an effective learning environment. Instructional strategies for enhancing the effectiveness of communities, such as word limits per message, starter-wrapper roles, and instructor modeling are described. Incorporating these strategies can "promote the social construction of new knowledge and increase the critical engagement of learners on the discussion board."

The contribution from Mann and Talandis takes the form of an action research study. Again, the substantive focus is on the creation of communities of practice. The researchers carry out a comparative analysis of two different initiatives designed to develop and maintain communities of practice in two teacher education programs. One of the initiatives was a relatively straightforward email list that evolved over time based on participant feedback. The other initiative involved a much more sophisticated web-based system. Mann and Talandis make the point that a more sophisticated system does not necessarily result in greater use and value, and point out that any system needs to develop in design terms if it is to be fully utilized and valued by participants.

Assessment is another substantive concern appearing in several contributions to the collection. Hall and Knox present a case study of peer assessment in online discussions. They raise a number of critical issues, most particularly whether online discussion should be formally assessable or not, and what difference this will make to either the quality or the quantity of online contributions. This parallels the concern in TESOL classrooms over whether students should be required to participate actively in a lesson, or whether they should have the right to opt out. In teacher education discussion fora, active contributors often resent fellow students who "lurk" in the chat room. I once had a very active student who referred to his reticent fellow students as "leeches." He, on the other hand, was criticized for having too much to say, and for dominating the forum even when he had little or nothing to say. The critical difference here between online and face-to-face instruction is that in online learning, we can only estimate the extent of a student's engagement with the course through their active participation.

Administration of Online Distance TESOL

In this foreword, I have already made the point that both learning and teaching online present challenges that are particular to the online medium. The same also holds for program administration. Challenges I have had to confront include hiring, evaluating and giving critical feedback online to faculty members I have never met face to face who are teaching in programs outside TESOL; arranging faculty meetings, and negotiating teaching schedules; dealing with accrediting agencies; setting up student record systems; marketing courses; assessing student admission applications; negotiating with partner institutions; assisting colleagues and students deal with technical failures and so on. These and other issues, along with suggested solutions are addressed by Opp-Beckman, Healey, and Hall and Knox in this section.

In her chapter, Opp-Beckman directs her attention to academic services. This, as she points out, is "an ongoing and integral aspect of an e-learner's journey." She identifies a range of issues that are specific to the online instructional medium, and makes suggestions for how to deal with these. She stresses the importance of knowing one's learners, of keeping abreast of the emergence of new e-learning tools, and ensuring that academic services reflect the dynamic and recursive nature of online learning and teaching.

Hall and Knox explore the rewards and challenges of online program administration. Their context is the traditional, face-to-face institution that, possibly in the face of increasing competition, turns to distance education to boost student numbers. They reinforce a point made throughout this collection that the planning, delivery, administration and evaluation of distance learning is different from, and cannot be conducted in the same was as face-to-face instruction. In traditional institutions, administrative procedures have been established to serve the needs of face-to-face teaching and learning, and these are not easily changed. For distance educators working within traditional structures, this is a source of enormous frustration. Despite the frustrations, the authors point out that administering a distance education program can be extremely satisfying, particularly in terms of student appreciation of the support that they receive.

In the final substantive contribution to this section, Healey's chapter takes the form of an elaborated checklist, as she lists the questions and issues that administrators need to consider as they plan distance education courses. She addresses administrative issues critical to the success of any online program including identifying the audience, marketing and attracting the right kind of learner to the program, assessing the competition, and technical issues, including the selection of an appropriate course management system. She also addresses the crucial issue of academic and technical human resources. The aim of the chapter is not to provide an exhaustive overview of all the choices that need to be considered by those who may be new to online education, but to set out the questions they need to address prior to embarking on a distance education venture.

The Future of Online Distance TESOL

In a concluding chapter, England and Hall look at future directions in online TESOL teacher education. For them, community building, a concept that appears in several of the contributions to the collection, is crucial. In this final piece, they consider how to build and maintain communities among students who are scattered all over the globe.

As a coda to the collection, all contributors provide brief summarizing remarks pertaining to the volume as a whole.

Reference

Johnson, S. (2010). *Where good ideas come from*. New York, NY: Riverhead Books.

1

ONLINE DISTANCE TESOL IN THE 21ST CENTURY— FROM THE TRENCH

Liz England

Who knew where the world would take English language teacher education in the 21st century? As the start of the second decade of the new millennium marches further along in the history of English language teaching worldwide, it is timely to consider a number of critical questions in online TESOL.

This chapter situates the remarkable growth of online distance TESOL preparation in the world today and provides readers with a clear and succinct description of the content and status of teacher education in online distance contexts worldwide.

With the explosion in the vast and diverse uses of technology to provide support for language teacher education in general, now there are more than 40 university-based TESOL master's level programs taught online and by distance worldwide, and more than 400 private institutions offering certificates in TESOL online.

Thousands of students enroll in these online teacher education programs in TESOL worldwide, and those who teach them are faced with remarkable and complex challenges in addressing quality online instruction.

In its effort to describe and clarify some of these challenges, this volume addresses the learning experiences for students in online TESOL programs, as well as the instructional and administrative tasks for those who lead them.

While most all face-to-face master's degree and certificate programs in TESOL include technology tools in their instructional programs, these "blended" models of teacher education are not the subjects of this book. Here, we focus on programs that rely on completely (or nearly completely) online instruction.

For the purposes of this volume, an early definition of online education is taken from one of the first publications on this topic. Paloff and Pratt (2001), defined online education as follows:

An approach to teaching and learning that utilizes Internet technologies to communicate and collaborate in an educational context.

So, with this definition in mind, several important questions in online TESOL are addressed in the current volume:

Who Takes Classes Online and at a Distance in TESOL?

Students enroll in online TESOL programs of study for reasons similar to their colleagues in face-to-face programs: in search of academic and professional education and experiences that will improve their classroom teaching skills and their ability to do research in TESOL (Lin, 2010). Individual universities establish their own admission criteria for prospective students to gain acceptance to study in their online programs. Most of those students who enroll in online programs do so for these reasons: program quality and reputation and convenience (Lin, 2010). In most cases, online distance students are unable to enroll in a traditional program of study locally (face-to-face) and if they want to do an educational program, they must do so in a distance (online program).

Why Do Students Choose Distance Models (Online) Over Traditional (Face-to-Face) Ones?

Students select online instruction in those cases where the degree they seek is unavailable in their geographical area or because they wish to complete their study in an institution with a reputation for excellence in instruction, and that also provides online options that suit students' personal or professional needs.

In the chapters in this book, contributors identify a wide variety of student profiles. It is important to know that unlike face-to-face programs, online TESOL programs welcome an extraordinary diversity of students. A majority of online distance TESOL students fit into one or more of the following categories: students who are located in rural areas or remote locations worldwide; those who are occupied with personal responsibilities such as child care, parent care or other priorities in their personal lives; those with professional responsibilities and limitations that require them to study in the evenings, at home, en route to a job, or other time-specific responsibility. Most online programs are asynchronous, allowing students to participate in their classes on a regular, but not fixed, schedule.

Online TESOL courses allow all students great convenience and flexibility in addressing other responsibilities, such as personal and work-related, no matter their location—a feature of online TESOL that is essential to the needs of 21st-century professional, worldwide education. In addition, online TESOL programs offer greater flexibility in terms of their freedom from visa requirements, thus providing access to those who are unable to leave home countries due to family or work obligations, or who lack the financial means to support a long trip, extended residence and living expenses in a foreign country, to study in other countries. The challenges and benefits of these realities are addressed below and in a number of chapters in this book.

It is important to note that the growing number of online TESOL programs in the United States and elsewhere use the flexibility and convenience of online TESOL as a factor in their promotional information and advertising. It is, in part, the goal of this volume to address the opportunities that face TESOL, as a profession and as an academic discipline, in maintaining high levels of quality in online distance programs of study leading to degrees and certificates in our field.

The content of this book offers opportunities for addressing unique features of online learning in TESOL, which we believe includes a different type of learner with different needs from those found in more familiar face-to-face programs.

What is Taught in Online TESOL Programs?

While factors influencing achievement in online TESOL programs may be different from those affecting achievement in face-to-face programs, goals and objectives in both online and face-to-face programs are similar (Nunan, 2002). A number of nationally and internationally recognized accrediting bodies now have identified the role of online instructional delivery in maintaining quality standards in TESOL.

Instruction in online TESOL includes the content of TESOL academic and professional preparation: the principles of language learning and teaching, second language acquisition, cross-cultural communication, methodology and materials in teaching speakers of other languages (various ages, proficiency levels and needs), research methodology, language testing principles, language classroom observation, and practical training experiences. It is the means of instructional delivery—online instruction—that is different from traditional, face-to-face teacher education in TESOL. While quality standards and some content may vary by geographical region, the content of online TESOL is generally the same as is the quality of instruction in face-to-face programs.

Who Teaches Online TESOL Courses?

While instructional skills for those who teach online TESOL are similar to many of those required for face-to-face courses, there are some differences that will be addressed in the chapters on teaching in online distance TESOL (see Part II, Teaching in Online Distance TESOL). A better understanding, offered in the chapters of this volume, is needed to describe clearly the skills needed for TESOL teacher education in online programs. These, combined with updated institutional requirements for faculty hiring, are addressed in the chapters in this volume.

What Electronic Communication Media and Devices Are Used in Online TESOL?

The extraordinary number of tools and devices now available for electronic communication provides a useful and timely analysis for TESOL online programs. The role and use of instructional packages and tools (such as Blackboard and other online instructional instructional systems) and the trillions of online resources in English and other languages are areas in need of analysis as to how and to what extent they contribute to effective language teacher education.

In addition, use of mobile phones for text messages purposes and telephonic communications is significant in the rapid growth of technology's impact on TESOL teacher education.

The role of video has also expanded with opportunities to make videotapes of classes or class segments (to be shown in its original form, edited or revised and viewed by oneself or others) and to view others teaching or providing other information for teachers—all on low-cost or free-of-charge web-based hosts. In years past, none of these tools was available when teacher education relied on face-to-face visual representations of concepts, classroom teacher training and evaluation, or for any other instructional purpose in TESOL.

What Are the Advantages and Challenges of Online TESOL When Compared With Traditional Teaching and Learning Contexts?

The major challenge for online TESOL in the new millennium is a lack of research to address the unique features of online TESOL and other language teacher education (Lin, 2010). This volume is a step in the right direction as we move forward with increasingly large numbers of offerings for those seeking TESOL professional and academic education.

1. Contributors to this volume generally agree that learning online appears to be a somewhat different process from learning in a face-to-face setting. Students write more and must master the use of more technological tools in their learning. Instructors provide different types of instructional materials. Interactions between instructor and student(s), and among students, are different from face-to-face classes in TESOL programs. Syllabi are different for online courses than from face-to-face courses. Materials are selected using different criteria. Assessment and testing is different. Professional developmental needs and opportunities for staying current in our field are all different for those learning with online TESOL content. Accreditation standards and compliance records and program quality assessment for online TESOL takes a different approach from those in face-to-face programs. This book addresses the challenges for innovation and change in TESOL, particularly as those relate to online teacher education.

2. Teaching online is a challenge to those of us who have learned to educate teachers in traditional, face-to-face settings. Course development, implementation and evaluation differ from traditional face-to-face courses taught online in TESOL. Identifying learner needs, addressing gaps in learner knowledge and skills and assessing student achievement—all of these are done differently in online settings as compared with traditional, face-to-face instruction. And, as addressed above, the skills and knowledge of effective online teacher educators will be somewhat different from those required of traditional, face-to-face TESOL faculty. In this volume, research is reported upon that will begin to identify knowledge and skills for effective instruction in online TESOL.

3. Administration of online TESOL programs: the focus of this volume has been on learning and teaching in online TESOL programs. In this final section, and in line with an effort to begin to develop standards in online TESOL, authors present a series of chapters addressing a variety of administrative issues in management of online TESOL programs: student services, planning a course, rewards and challenges of online program administration, and finally, a look at the future of online TESOL.

In reading the chapters of this volume, readers should find them individually enlightening, delivering a useful, insightful and unique description. Each chapter contains a list of references, all of which are worthy of follow-up for those who seek to know more on the topic of online TESOL work to date. In addition, discussion questions appear at the end of each chapter, and will be of use to those who want to focus his/her reading on one or another topic addressed in those questions.

While unique interests draw one to read any book, all readers of this volume will find the content of each and every chapter to be a unique and first-ever description of the remarkable and complex world of online TESOL—today and for the future. All contributors and the editor of this volume welcome reader feedback! Enjoy reading Online Language Teacher Education: TESOL Perspectives!

Discussion Questions

1. The content of this book is presented in three parts, reflecting different perspectives on the online language teacher education experience: Online Learning; Online Teaching and Administration of Online Programs. As a language teaching professional, what interests you about online language teacher education? Jot down three or four ideas now, as you begin to read this book. Refer to those ideas as you read the chapters that follow.

2. Describe an experience as a learner or instructor in an online course in the past. How did your experience differ from a class taken face-to-face? What challenges did you face as an online learner? Instructor? What rewards did you experience? Consider these possible pedagogical issues in online learning and

teaching: learner engagement, course assignments, class readings (textbook and other external readings), quizzes, tests and other assessment experiences, technology use, and interaction with instructor and fellow classmates.

References

Lin, L. L. (2010) Examining the effectiveness of TESOL master's programs to prepare graduate students for their current and future careers. Retrieved from http://www.eric.ed.gov/PDFS/ED510734.pdf

Nunan, D. (2002) Teaching MA-TESOL courses online: Challenges and rewards. *TESOL Quarterly, 36*(4): 617–621. Retrieved from http://www.jstor.org/stable/3588243

Paloff, R. M., & Pratt, K. (2001) *Lessons from the cyberspace classroom: the realities of online teaching.* San Francisco, CA: Jossey Bass..

PART I

Learning in Online Distance TESOL Settings

2

WHY BE AN ONLINE LEARNER IN TESOL?

Sue Garton and Julian Edge

Listen Up, This Is What It's About

Distance learning programs for teacher education are becoming increasingly popular, and for many good reasons, as England (this volume) notes. Practicing English language teachers rarely have either the time or the money to take a year or more out of work in order to go to an institution to study full-time. This is especially the case if such a move would involve leaving the country of which they are citizens, or in which they are long-term residents. These are facts over which it seems unnecessary to linger.

But that is not what this chapter is about. If that were the case, then we would not have moved on since the days of correspondence courses, when centers of learning sent out their bundles of information to be learned by those poor unfortunates who could not properly attend their classes, followed by tests on the extent to which they had digested this packaged wisdom.

In fact, a part of our problem in communicating about distance learning with many people in education, never mind those outside it, is that their understanding has *not* really moved on from those days. As one of the participants in Copland and Garton's study (this volume) noted:

> No problems in terms of institutions/jobs, but other teachers/acquaintances seem confused by the concept—perhaps thinking it's not a "real" Master's.

The need to move on from these outdated and restricted horizons is easy to demonstrate.

We can, for example, well imagine a convention of academics who could speak passionately, and from a variety of perspectives, about the situated nature of cognition, the sociocultural embeddedness of learning, not to mention the need to construct conceptual categories from a fully-contextualized, experiential database, but would have grave reservations about becoming involved in *distance* education. The ironies are almost deafening to those prepared to hear.

To put the same point another way, we see face-to-face TESOL programs, where teachers gather from around the world to study in prestigious academies at which they may expect to be taught the theories that they are meant to go home and apply, only to be instructed in the dysfunctionality of the theory/application discourse in TESOL (Clarke, 1994). They are told that what is important is for them to develop local understanding of what is particular, practical and possible (Kumaravadivelu, 2001) in their own educational cultures and contexts—contexts from which they are, unfortunately, currently *distant*. In other words, those who are undertaking professional development and choose to separate themselves from their professional context by going to a distant institution will sooner or later, if their development is to have any meaning, have to return to that context and move forward within it. This return represents a new and separate step in the learning process. In professional terms, there is *distance* between the context in which development can be realized and the site of formal learning. Seen in this light, the term "distance education" seems misleading when used to describe learning and development that is situated in the professional environment.

One part of what this chapter is all about, then, is a reconceptualization of what we mean by *distance* in this discussion, most particularly when we engage with cyberspace. And when we work on such a reconceptualization, it is important that we teacher educators take our course participants with us. Let us look at how we might do that. Here is some initial material that course participants[1] are asked to respond to with regard to what we want to be happening inside and around them (see Figure 2.1 and accompanying material).

Here, then, is one way of beginning an educational process which is not *distant*, but *situated*, and which we mean to be transformational in the ways alluded to above. Course participants must not see themselves as distant from where the learning is; they *define* where the learning is. Their role is less to apply theories than to explore their practice and theorize it, thus taking it forward into *praxis*—aware, informed, socially committed practice.

If You Don't Believe Us, Listen to This Lot

Both our programs have the explicit aim of guiding course participants to "*become theoretical*" as we wish them to understand the expression, where theory is defined (Edge, 2008, p. 653) as: "an articulation of the best understanding thus far available to investigators as to why things are the way they are."

As the materials extract above has shown, we introduce technical terminology (*declarative* and *procedural knowledge*), along with tips on academic practice (*analysis*

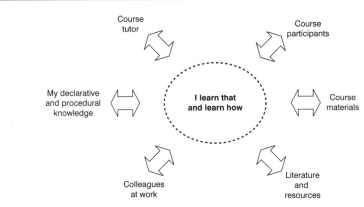

FIGURE 2.1 Inside and around you

Figure 2.1 is my attempt to represent my understanding of what is going on, or what *needs* to be going on if you are going to make the most of this MA experience. The *I* in the central oval is meant to represent you, the course participant, as you learn in (at least) two different ways: you learn new information (= "learn that" = declarative knowledge) and you learn new procedures (= "learn how" = procedural knowledge). The arrows are meant to represent some of the interactions involved. I say *some* of the interactions because a moment's thought will make clear that the interactions involved are much more complex than the diagram shows. Let us note in passing that this is a typical weakness of analyses and diagrams. In fact, in this world, everything is connected to everything else and it is a good idea not to forget that. We use analyses and diagrams in order to help us show specific relationships, or certain perspectives. Beware of diagrams that claim to do more than that.

So, what is going on is a complicated process. The extent to which it is a successful learning process will depend in great part on the extent to which you come to understand and influence the various aspects of the process in which you are involved. This matter of understanding and influencing will, in turn, depend on establishing a shared understanding with other people. You are called upon to be pro-active, to establish your own sense of agency, to make things happen.

At this point, I invite you to not only to look at the diagram, but to spend some time imagining what I might mean by its various parts. It could also be productive for you to think about which elements of *your* understanding of what needs to be going on are not shown here, as well as alternative ways of representing the MA process as you understand it. You might also want to go back to the home page of this course and look again at the documents there that deal with how the course is set up and how we communicate with each other.

and *diagrams*) implicitly through our ongoing communication. Right from the beginning of the program, our position on a theorizing role for our participants is made explicit in the course materials:

> The type of theorist which we want to encourage is the person who struggles to articulate statements which make sense of that person's own experience. *Theory*, in this sense, is the understanding which arises from practice, and the *theorist* is the person who gives voice to it. Theory is evaluated according to its usefulness in helping a person account for what is happening, and in planning future action. That is why we are interested in the specifics of a local situation, and why our participants need to be researchers in order to formulate local theory.
>
> At the same time, in order to appreciate the significance of what one comes to understand, one needs to know what others have said in other situations. And in order to formulate and communicate one's understanding, one needs to be in control of appropriate ways of speaking and writing. For both these reasons, one needs to be able to function at some level in the relevant discourse community.

While such a stance naturally elicits a variety of (re)actions and responses, as the following reflections clearly show, much of what we have said above finds confirmation in what the course participants themselves say. A task at the end of the Foundation Module (FND) module, from which the quote above is taken, asks participants to reflect on their initial course-related experiences and on what "*becoming theoretical*" means to them.

Ania, a participant working in the UK, explicitly compared her experience of "traditional" learning with her recent distance learning program:

> During my previous educational experiences [...] I was presented with many theories and concepts which I was then expected to know, but not necessarily apply in practice. What is more, frequently these theories bore no relevance to my professional life, which made identifying with them virtually impossible and which sometimes made me question the value of such knowledge. In contrast, the Foundation Module was an opportunity to begin to describe and analyse my actions and those of my students. Reading the Methodology unit in particular, followed by planning, researching, and writing the portfolio task required that I should observe and analyse my own classroom while also learning what some researchers had said about similar situations and drawing my own conclusions. I hope to be increasingly engaged in such attempts to provide a theoretical framework, not only for my classroom activity and interaction, but also beyond it.

Alan, based in Mexico, had a similar experience:

> Going through the module has made me reflect on the process of becoming theoretical. The great advantage of distance learning is the fact that we do not need to work on abstract contexts where everything has to be general and "theories" are never put into practice as happens in more traditional learning environments. Distance learning allows us to work in a situated learning environment, where our own, real context, together with our own experience, allows us to theorise our own practice. In other words, being aware of our situation and desired direction, and formulating our own method taking into consideration what others have said in similar situations, will lead us to a more realistic and local outcome.

Ania and Alan make a number of similar points. First, they both identify the abstract and general nature of knowledge acquired through more traditional means of program delivery and both underline the lack of practical application that such courses involve. Both point to using previous research to inform and develop their own responses to their classrooms and contexts.

In his comments, Michael in Poland also compares past and present learning experiences, but in his case, he focuses on how the transformational power of distance learning allows participants to get away from the idea of best method. He also picks up on the deep-rooted prejudice against distance learning that we mentioned above, that it is somehow second best (Garton & Richards, 2007), with his explicit realization that it is actually an advantage:

> I was pleased to see early on that through the concept of "situated learning" being a Distance learner could actually be viewed as an advantage in that it would allow me to theorize and base my work on my professional context. I found the notion of "emergent methodology" as discussed in unit 3 was both empowering and refreshing. The concept that appropriate methodology can only be defined in terms of a particular group of learners in a particular learning context is one that resonates strongly and represents a welcome contrast to the dogmatic insistence on a particular method that I have encountered elsewhere in the past.

Reflections on the nature of the relationship between theory and practice often challenge the received wisdom of superiority of theory. Caroline in Switzerland states:

> This process of exploring our own teaching situations combines practice, reflection and theory of learning principles and all three are important in "becoming theoretical". Looking at the well known adage that "theory

should inform practice" it should continue with "and practice, in turn can show the way for and inform theory."

Like Alan and Ania, Athina in Greece refers to awareness of her own classroom and of previous research, but she is also revising her view of the theory/practice relationship, coming to see theory and practice as no longer separate:

> The module has got me thinking that theory and practice can be the two sides of the same coin in TESOL; or the case may be that practice generates theory and vice-versa. If becoming theoretical means drawing and reflecting on my own professional and classroom experiences, or understanding how others have acted and what others have said in their situations and contexts, then yes, the expression "becoming theoretical" is capturing the mind processes which I am now starting to get involved.

Developing awareness is a key theme that runs through many reflections. Alison, based in Japan, underlines the idea of making the tacit explicit (Freeman, 1991), and thereby taking control of her professional development:

> van Lier (1996) describes language education as being founded on the theories of the teacher; theories which can be either explicit or implicit in nature. He suggests that, "if the theory is explicit, the teacher is potentially in control of his or her own professional life and progress ..." (p. 26). This is what I understand by the term becoming theoretical. I am being encouraged to take control of my professional development by making my ideas on teaching theories explicit. In turn, this will put me in a better position to make informed judgments regarding the needs of my students and classes.

The idea that becoming theoretical means becoming aware of what you are doing as a teacher and why you are doing it, and/or becoming aware of your beliefs about learning and teaching is perhaps the most common interpretation of the term in the reflections from participants. For example, Justin in Ecuador makes the point clearly:

> Through so much background reading, I have come to realize that a lot of what I do as a teacher is in fact unconscious. I don't feel that I have been an ineffective teacher, but much of what I've done has been done at a level of instinct, habit, and automatic responses to repeated stimuli.
>
> I find that I welcome and enjoy the process of becoming more conscious of my own teaching. Some would say that as long as it works, don't fix it. In this case, I disagree. Though my teaching may work instinctively, it is much more difficult to improve an unconscious process. Only by forming, and

testing, theories about why things may work, or fail to, is there a clear path to become more effective.

Becoming theoretical may or may not lead to changes in practice but it is almost certainly a source of motivation and development as a teacher, as Alina in Russia found:

> Even if I haven't made any specific changes to the way I teach, I have certainly started feeling different about myself as a teacher and teaching as an activity. In many ways, this reflection helped me come back to the beliefs I had about teaching when I started the job, but on a higher level. I can compare this re-assessment and audit of beliefs to cleaning the family silver: it never loses its beauty, but does get slightly grimy from everyday use and sometimes needs to be restored to its former glory. This is what reflecting throughout the module has done for me.

Becoming theoretical can be extremely empowering for teachers, a word, like Catherine working in Austria, they often use themselves:

> Back in March, in unit 1 of the module I noted on p. 17 in the box labeled "theorist": "This is definitely not me! I'm a practitioner, so theory doesn't really figure in my work at the moment."
>
> However, now I am definitely expecting to be (and no longer ruling out the possibility of being!) theoretical in the assignments and research that await me.
>
> So, that brings me right up to date as I finish this task and look back on these positive experiences following those first feelings of being overwhelmed back in March. I can safely say that I am looking forward to an enriching and empowering course of studies over the next couple of years at the heart of TESOL research and no longer on the periphery.

Catherine initially rejected the idea of being a theorist, an idea that can cause strong reactions among participants, underlining the rather negative connotations that such a term has and the sharp divide that has come to exist between "theorists" and "practitioners". Returning to Justin, he initially wrote:

> I sort of resent the feeling that I have, without prior consent, been membershipped as a theorist. This was not my plan, and I had not, prior to starting the FND, considered the term "theorist" to be a compliment. My attitude sprung from the experience of hearing all kinds of theories about teaching which seem to bear little relationship to the classroom realities with which I live.

This much is clear to me, however. My own growth as a teacher frequently springs from considering my experiences, forming ideas about what helped, or hindered, student learning, and trying them out. I certainly could call these ideas "theories." I guess that my resistance to the term is rooted in my experience of having read teaching texts, written by people who had not taught in my lifetime, and who yet had the impression that they should tell me how to do it. I guess that I am willing to call myself a "classroom theorist." What I mean by this is that I am happy to form, and share, theories about what happens in my classroom, and to learn from the classroom theories of others. I remain, however, deeply sceptical about theorists who no longer put in their classroom hours every week.

The outcome of this initial stage of the journey is almost always a sense of empowerment, potential for professional growth and excitement at the prospect of what lies ahead. Richard from Japan concluded:

It is not an exaggeration to say that has revolutionized my life. It has presented opportunities and, where I had not realized that I was standing still, at the outset, I am clearly aware now that I am moving forward.

Even Here, There Are Still Issues to Deal With

We have focused so far on the positive outcomes of what amounts to a deliberate and sustained assault on course participants' worldview, on what they have been used to seeing as their role in the production of knowledge, on their perception of their relationship to those teaching them, on their expectation of the level of risk that they are being called upon to take, and on their preparedness for the responsibilities that they are being urged to take on.

We should not, however, gloss over the difficulties hinted at above, especially, perhaps, with regard to the effect of participants being asked to achieve such a transformation in the relative isolation of a virtual learning environment.

Here is one initial response:

Subject: Lost and Confused
Author: Steve Gold
Date: 28 September 2010 12:38
Day 2 officially and while I worked all day yesterday some people are already leaving messages concerning Unit 5. Most of the discussion in the common room is techno-talk about different pdf readers and other things I don't understand. If I hadn't paid I would give up right now. I imagine one or two others are lost but the tone has been set in the common room now and its a tech-savy, "have you read this 125th extra article yet?" vibe, thus no-one in my situation dare break cover and scream "HELP!".

Steve, fortunately, was no quitter (and he had already paid!). An hour later, he posted the following:

> **Subject:** Re:Lost and Confused
> **Author:** Steve Gold
> **Date:** 28 September 2010 13:33
> What a difference an hour makes. Actually diving into something tangible, even just the first Teaching Text, and finding subject matter I can engage with has made me feel a whole lot better. The initial panic at seeing how many comments other participants had made and how many programmes they were using to download various documents has abated due to some reassuring words and guiding principles.

And then, under Course Evaluation, just over three months later, Steve posted:

> **Subject:** Feedback
> **Author:** Steve Gold
> **Date:** 04 January 2011 13:44
> Happy New Year!
> Firstly let me say the course exceeded my expectations, particularly after a daunting few days. Once the feeling of being overwhelmed subsided I found the format quite manageable and the content almost always interesting (there was just one article I found a hard slog) and often inspiring.
> Having said that I believe VERY basic instructions in the first week such as:
> • Read Teaching Text 1 then go the discussion space,
> • Read the digitized articles and return to discussion space,
> would take away the fear factor and soon students would be revelling in the online Master's experience. We all got there in the end but I always feel that a very simple guide, just to get people to dip their toes in the water, is helpful (all the more so with issues of technology!).

Here, we risk straying from our topic of, *Why be an online learner in TESOL?*, into the area of *how* to bring successful online learning about—a theme addressed explicitly by other authors in this collection. But we introduce Steve's contribution here as a reminder of the overlap between Ends and Means. Even shared goals between participant and tutor may be of no use unless the beginnings of a way ahead are indicated. Steve sees the road to autonomy beginning with the security of being given straightforward instructions in the imperative form. And, given the happy ending of his story, we are not minded to disagree.

Goals themselves, however, are not always shared. What, then, do we have to say to the participant who says, whether explicitly or implicitly, "These views are alien to me. I came to you in all good faith expecting to be given established knowledge to learn, keen to learn it, and well able to show you that I have learned it. Please be more clear about what it is that I have to learn."

Or, more subtly, what do we offer to the student who is well able to learn all the views on *empowerment* and *becoming theoretical* that we have put forward, and to repeat them accurately, but without ever taking on board the pragmatic significance of what they have learned to say? In other words, we have influenced their *espoused theory* without having affected their *theory-in-practice* (Schon, 1983)?

First of all, we note that the *espoused theory/theory-in-action* dichotomy haunts all approaches to teacher education, and the action-research oriented stance that we take is threatened perhaps less than others. Second, we need to acknowledge that the question, *Why be an online learner in TESOL?*, is susceptible to many answers. In addition to the reasons of cost, location and convenience with which we began this chapter, there is our preferred argument, which we believe to be very powerful, that being an online learner enables and facilitates professional development in ways that face-to-face programs simply cannot deliver, for all the reasons that we have outlined so far. However, we need to recognize that many participants may want to learn the *content* of our courses without going through the fundamental schematic changes regarding empowerment and responsibility that we are urging on them (cf. Argyris & Schön, 1974 on single-loop and double-loop learning). Indeed, they may object that for them to behave in such ways might get them into serious trouble with their employers, colleagues or students in their hierarchically organized teaching contexts. That is their right.

By the same token, it is our right to say that we will insist on assessing our participants' work in such a way that the re-presentation of content knowledge alone will not be well-rewarded. A part of our demand is that participants do indeed demonstrate an engagement with the exploration of their professional environments that leads to original experiential knowledge that they will articulate in the context of their increased intellectual awareness. We see learning as acquired through, and demonstrated by, action, and action must by its nature be situated. Just *how* this is to be done, with appropriate regard to contextual sensitivities is negotiable. *That* it be done, is not.

This is the case because it arises from our answer to the counter-question implicit in our title, the question: *Why be an online teacher educator in TESOL?* Why? Well, because these are the educational values that we bring to the table: a belief in the situated nature of learning, a commitment to exploration and to action as a fundamental element of learning, a respect for difference, and a desire for collaboration. We would not wish our insistence on flexibility, or on our own fallibility, to be mistaken for a lack of core values. Just as we demand of our participants, we do not set out to learn in order to be able to intervene; we intervene in order to be able to learn. Online teacher education offers our best chance of realizing these values in action *and* of creating a common ground on which teachers and teacher educators can gather, in order to move forward together (Edge, 2011).

Moving Forward

Our own belief in the transformational potential of online TESOL for both course participants and course tutors should by now be clear. Our conviction that such transformational potential is not available to those studying in face-to-face contexts should also be obvious. Equally obvious, however, is that such a conviction may not be shared, at least initially, by all participants.

The onus is on us as tutors to be more explicit regarding our approach, clearer regarding the double-loop learning that is required, and more convincing that our approach is one that can work. We ask participants to live with their unease for a while and trust that they will come to share our way of thinking. The following from Athina in Greece expresses the uncertainty, the desire for more guidance and support, but ultimately, the personal and professional development that such an approach brings.

> As regards the (methodology) task, at first I felt at a bit of a loss and finding a focus seemed really daunting to me. I thought I was presented with a task I could do nothing about and that I was previously not offered enough information on how to deal with. Having completed the task now, I still feel that prior to introducing it, it would have been extremely helpful to be provided with more explicit guidelines about drafting a proposal for action research. Of course, my reward was the sense of fulfillment and accomplishment I felt when completing the task.

It is our experience that the feelings of reward increase and those of uncertainty lessen as the course progresses. Moreover, the feelings of development and empowerment can continue to grow long after the progams end. Kaeko in Japan graduated in 2008. In 2011, she came to the university for the first time, not as a student but as a conference presenter, to talk about the beliefs and practices of Japanese primary school teachers. The theme of the conference was "Theorizing practice and practicing theory: developing local practices in language teaching." It was Kaeko's experience of becoming theoretical as an online TESOL course participant, investigating her own context that gave her the means and the confidence to continue to research, to obtain research grants and to present her investigations to an international audience at a conference with a theme that had empowered her in the first place. This was the first time that the physical distance from the institution had been closed; it is notable that it had never mattered and fitting that this should be the context.

> This July I had a chance to present my research at the BAAL conference, and it was my first presentation at a conference abroad. That presentation was based on my current work, supported by the Grant-in-Aid for Scientific Research (KAKENHI). This research is based upon my MSc TYL assignment module, so I can truly say that studying at Aston has opened many research opportunities to me.

Kaeko is not alone, as Copland and Garton (this volume) show. As well as presenting at conferences, course participants have taken on greater responsibilities for curriculum development in their institutions, become active in professional organizations, and published in international journals (e.g. Hancock (1997) on understanding the role of L1 in the English class, Boon (2005) on the use of IT in teacher development, de Sonneville (2007) on her collaborative innovations in teacher education, and al-Masri (in preparation) on micro-presentations in the building of a shared institutional culture among teachers). All of these, and many more such contributions, began life as assignments written for a situated Masters course, where participants are required not to write essays on topics, but to prepare either plans for, or reports on, action arising from the demands of their own environment. And, at the same time, indistinguishable from these efforts, the writers continue to strive towards "becoming the unique and best teacher it is in them to be" (Underhill, 1992, p. 71)

The epistemological position that we have espoused in this chapter is also explicitly ideological and we believe it is important that our courses are seen in this light. We do not see ourselves as distributing knowledge from the centre. We see ourselves as supporting situated teacher-learning through action and reflection. We do not have a preferred language teaching methodology that we wish to further through the exercise of the power that accrues to our status. Instead, we wish to exercise that power in scaffolding the development of hybrid approaches to language teaching as these are justified in the praxis of our course participants.

Other online teacher educators may have different views on, and different purposes for, the influence that they exert, and we believe that these should be equally explicitly expressed. In that way, potential participants will be best placed to answer for themselves the question at the head of this chapter, and to choose a program that best suits their own purposes and aspirations.

Discussion Points

In our early MA materials, we tutors make the following introductory points about our own reading:

> When we read articles in our field, it is not just a question of reading and learning what other people have to say, we interact with those texts in a variety of ways:
>
> - We evaluate them in terms of how useful they are to us with regard to our own purposes.
> - We see them as the source of ideas that we can investigate further or move on from.
> - We are critical of them, both with regard to their ideas and their presentation.

- We ask ourselves what difference the article has made to us with regard to pragmatic outcomes.

Following on from this, we suggest that course participants keep the following questions in mind in order to prepare themselves for further discussion.

Discussion Questions

1. What is the most striking/memorable/useful idea that I take from this text?
2. Is there one particular point on which I would like further clarification?
3. Is there one claim/suggestion/idea that I find questionable?
4. What statement would I like to make as a result of having read this article?

If you took the same approach to this chapter, what would the outcome be for you?

Note

1 We have decided not to differentiate between materials or participant voices with regard to which of our two institutions they come from. We write as colleagues in the field.

References

Argyris, C., & Schon, D. A. (1974) *Theory in practice: Increasing professional effectiveness*. San Francisco: Jossey Bass.

Boon, A. (2005) Is there anybody out there? *Essential Teacher, 2*(2), 1–9.

Clarke, M. (1994) The dysfunctions of the theory/practice discourse. *TESOL Quarterly, 28* 9–26.

de Sonneville, J. (2007) "Acknowledgement" as a key in teacher learning. *ELT Journal, 61*(1), 55–62.

Edge, J. (2008) Interested theory and theorising as goal. *TESOL Quarterly, 42*, 653–654.

Edge, J. (2011) *The reflexive teacher educator in TESOL: Roots and wings*. London: Routledge

Freeman, D. (1991) "To make the tacit explicit": teacher education, emerging discourse and conceptions of teaching. *Teaching and Teacher Education, 7*(5–6), 439–454.

Garton S., & Richards, K. 2007. Is distance education for teacher second best? *The Teacher Trainer, 21*(3), 5–8.

Hancock, M. (1997) Behind classroom code switching: layering and language choice in L2 learner interaction. *TESOL Quarterly, 31*(2), 217–235.

Kumaravadivelu, B. (2001) Toward a postmethod pedagogy. *TESOL Quarterly, 35*(4), 537–560.

Schön, D. A. (1983) *The reflective practitioner: How professionals think in action*. New York, NY: Basic Books.

Underhill, A. (1992) The role of groups in developing teacher self-awareness. *ELT Journal, 46*(1), 71–79.

3

FEEDBACK IN THE MEDIATION OF LEARNING IN ONLINE LANGUAGE TEACHER EDUCATION

María del Carmen Contijoch-Escontria, Anne Burns and Christopher N. Candlin

Technological advances have made an impact in most areas of knowledge and education has not been the exception. Among the various spaces that online learning has permeated it has become a genuine alternative for university learners, but also an option for university teachers pursuing professional development. As Goodfellow (2004) argues, online learning has changed the nature and delivery of university-level teaching and learning. Participants have had to take on new roles and adapt the way they interact in order to achieve efficient communication in the electronic environment. Within tutor–learner interaction, the construct of feedback is regarded as an essential component of any course since feedback is a fundamental means of supporting and mediating learning and has an impact on how participants learn.

This chapter illustrates research integrating three exploratory studies involving tutors' beliefs about feedback, the perceptions of learners towards feedback, and tutors' feedback practices through sociocultural discourse analysis (Contijoch, 2009). The micro context of the research is the Foreign Language Teaching Centre at the National Autonomous University of Mexico (UNAM).

Characterizing Online Learning

Recent studies in online tutoring have addressed aspects such as tutors' performance (Creanor, 2002), tutors' role (McPherson & Baptista, 2004), tutors' motivation and job satisfaction (Beyth-Maron & Harpaz-Gorodeisky, 2006), tutors' experiences with difficult learners (Bender & Dittmar, 2006), social presence of participants in online tutoring (Henninger & Viswanathan, 2004); and in conference environments (Gunawardena & Zittle, 1997). What is noteworthy is the comparative lack of studies into online feedback despite its crucial significance in determining the effectiveness of the teaching learning process (Clariana, 2000). Feedback is a complex interactive process, requiring time, effort and particular tutor abilities. However, although research studies recognize the importance and relevance of feedback, little is actually known about the social practice of feedback in the online environment. Accordingly, this chapter illustrates and critically discusses how feedback is mediated as part of an online course involving online tutors and their language teacher learners in Mexico. What we intend is to provide insights into the nature, characteristics, and purpose of online feedback so that course designers and tutors can be informed about the role that feedback plays in professional development and the quality of its delivery.

Defining Feedback

For Ramaprasad (1983) feedback is the "information about the gap between the actual level and the reference level of a system parameter which is used to alter the gap in some way" (p. 4). Despite its somewhat obscure expression, Ramaprasad's definition emphasizes that information must be *used* in order to modify the learning gap in some way. For Laurillard (2002, p. 55), more boldly, "action without feedback is completely unproductive for a learner," highlighting the need for feedback to be calibrated with action to enable learners to make appropriate and productive adjustments to their prior performance.

Feedback research has taken either a behaviorist or a cognitivist viewpoint (see Huet, 2004). From the former, providing and reinforcing correct answers is the key, presenting learners with two types of information: *verification* and *elaboration*. Verification refers to the judgment of a right or a wrong answer while elaboration refers to information provided to the learner with additional guidelines focused on achieving the right answer (see Kulhavy & Stock, 1989; Mory, 1992). From a cognitivist perspective, feedback is "a source of information necessary for verification, elaboration, concept development, and metacognitive adaptation" (Narciss, 1999, p. 3). Although the distinctions between these perspectives are grounded theoretically and differ in elaboration, from a practical perspective they can be said to present the same message.

What neither perspective emphasizes adequately is the social constructedness of online feedback provision. Here, the work of Higgings, Hartley and Skelton (2001), and Higgins and Hartley (2002) is especially relevant in suggesting that the process of feedback is never neutral: feedback as interaction always engages problematic issues of power relationships and how these are played out in feedback discourse. What is important, they argue, is to conceive of teaching, learning, and assessment as *social practices* involving the negotiation and construction of meaning, not least in the provision of feedback. As Brinko (1993) indicates, central to understanding these social practices are *inter alia* the tutor's subject knowledge, relevance, meaningfulness of content, focus, accuracy, timeliness, amount of positive feedback *vs* amount of negative feedback, and frequency.

Negotiating Feedback Online

As Bender and Dittmar (2006) argue, feedback is the necessary means by which learners obtain information about performance. The issue is whether online tutors (OLTs) provide sufficient and constructive feedback to show they care about their learners' efforts. For us, constructive feedback has to go beyond caring about learners' efforts: rather its focus should be on those pedagogical aspects which help learners organize thoughts and construct knowledge. Further, it should produce a positive impact encouraging learners to reflect and take action based on new information. Such action depends crucially on *interaction* engendered by learner–tutor feedback aimed at fostering productive academic relationships.

Characterizing Online Feedback

Following a traditional distinction in program and learner evaluation, Schwartz and White (2000) identify two types of online feedback (OLF): formative and summative. "Formative feedback modifies a student's thinking or behavior for the purpose of learning. Summative feedback assesses how well a student accomplishes a task for the purpose of grading" (p. 168). More interestingly, for this chapter, they identify several desirable characteristics of online feedback:

- Multidimensional: covering aspects such as content, presentation skills, grammar, and communication techniques.
- Nonevaluative: offering objective information about the participant's work, allowing participants to identify strengths and weaknesses.
- Supportive: offering information in such a way that the participant can see how he/she can improve his/her work.
- Student controlled: offering choices about how participants can respond to the information.
- Timely: providing feedback as soon as possible.
- Specific: describing specific observations and making recommendations.

We note here the lack of any reference to the importance of motivation. Motivation is ineluctably connected with learners' perceptions concerning feedback, as Higgins and Hartley (2002) and Lim and Cheah (2003) emphasize.

Contextualizing Online Tutors' Feedback (OLTF)

The ALAD (Applied Linguistics through Distance Learning) Diploma at UNAM, draws its theoretical base from social-constructivism. A major aspect of the student-teacher relationship is that the tutor plays the role of mediator and guide. Within this framework, feedback is intended to promote learners' construction of knowledge, guiding them towards successful completion of different pedagogical tasks. The tutor's feedback is based on specific tasks, activities, exercises, assignments or questions built into the pedagogical design of the course. The tutor offers feedback individually through the learner's personal electronic file or through the learner's personal e-mail. Group feedback is provided through the discussion forum when the tutor decides to summarize, to add questions, to provide input or to suggest resources to the whole group.

The Study

Participants

A total of 28 participants (12 online tutors and 16 online learners) took part in the study between 2007–2009. The 12 online tutors included 11 females and one male. Eight teach English as a foreign language, two teach French, one teaches German and one Spanish. All are experienced and qualified teachers and teacher trainers; most of them with a Master's degree. They all share understandings of the nature of the teaching-learning process in traditional campus settings. Their experience in online tutoring varies but can be considered to be at a developmental stage, ranging from three and a half years to more than six years at the time of the study. The online learners (OLLs), are foreign language teachers, aged between 35 and 44 years, who enrolled in the ALAD for professional development purposes. They include ten Mexicans, five French, and one Mexican-Argentinian; 10 are female and six are male. Their language teaching experience varies; some of them have taught for more than 19 years and some have only a few years of experience.

Research Strategy

This case study employs both qualitative and quantitative data. This combination was considered necessary so as to triangulate the study, enhance its trustworthiness, and accomplish the objectives of the research. Quantitative questionnaire-derived data offered a statistical dimension but they also involved translation of such data "into the qualitative language of ideas, concepts, and theories. Thus numbers cannot be divorced from words either conceptually or practically" (Schensul, Schensul, & LeCompte, 1999, p. 5). Qualitative data by means of interviews and discourse analysis represented the basis of the study, permitting in-depth analysis and interpretations of participants' voices and texts concerning their beliefs, experiences, feelings, and perceptions.

Sociocultural Discourse Analysis and Its Contribution to Understanding OLTF

Sociocultural theory (Lantolf, 2000; Pavlenko & Lantolf, 2000) contributes to understanding how knowledge is constructed and co-constructed in the classroom by means of the various interactions that take place. In this study, we utilize its explanatory potential for understanding how a sociocultural perspective on discourse analysis can provide insights into how OLTs provide feedback. Such a position is supported by a number of studies: Paltridge (2006) argues that one perspective is discourse as "social construction of reality" in that texts are "communicative units which are embedded in social and cultural practices" (p. 9). Paltridge acknowledges that discourse is shaped by the medium where it takes place, shaping also the potential for that medium. According to John-Steiner and Mahn (1996) sociocultural researchers highlight the use of qualitative methods that document cognitive and social change by exploring the nature of such processes and how these develop over time.

Sociocultural theory applied to the educational field contributes to understanding how the learning process develops in the classroom. In this study, understanding the way the OLT delivers feedback may provide insights about the learning development during an online course. Our data comprise the postings placed by OLTs and OLLs during the ALAD "Evaluation Processes in Language Teaching" course. The postings selected, analyzed, and interpreted are those related to group and individual feedback delivered by the two OLTs who taught this course (Pat and Victor). The corpus of selected postings was analyzed using a combination of genre analysis (Swales, 1990) and Mercer's socioculturally informed methodology (Mercer, 2004) focusing on the analysis of talk in social context. The usual way to exemplify the analysis is to select extracts of transcribed talk. The focus of the analysis is based on identification of the generic structure of the feedback messages and on the language functions that characterized the different moves or stages.

Description of the Module "Evaluative Processes in Language Teaching"

This module extends over 11 weeks and was designed in response to a need expressed by language teachers for courses on assessment and testing and their relation to language teaching. The course is taught in Spanish, the language in which the Diploma is conceived. It focuses on teachers' particular needs by helping them to identify and solve a problem related to their assessment of a particular language skill in their teaching context. Then, participants prepare an individual proposal to work on step by step as the course develops.

Data Analysis

Quantitative data exploring tutor and learner views on feedback, drawn from responses to closed questions and Likert scale items, were expressed in percentages. Qualitative data from open questionnaire items and semi-structured interviews were analyzed by means of Grounded Theory (Creswell, 2007) procedures (open, axial, and selective coding, categorizing different themes that emerged in the process). In relation to feedback, written messages provided by the OLTs were collected through the website (following consent from tutors and learners). A total of 1,261 postings were placed in the discussion room; online learners' electronic files, personal online learners' e-mails and work gallery formed the data corpus.

Outcomes of the Study

The recurrent themes that emerged in the studies involved OLTs, OLLs and the learning process, the methodology used and its characteristics, the relationship between feedback and assessment, and the relationship between feedback and psychological factors.

Overall, the study showed that online feedback is a process with distinctive features that are particularly determined by the medium, thus making it qualitatively different from that in the face-to-face feedback situation. As we indicated earlier, feedback is a complex process that develops over time involving key pedagogical and psychological aspects. Further, we may say that the beliefs expressed by the 12 OLTs derived from a combination of participants' personal and informed knowledge acquired through their experience as teachers, teacher trainers, and online tutors. Their views on feedback are of a formative rather than an evaluative nature. These beliefs can be said to be what Borg (2001) calls "espoused beliefs" and not "beliefs in action" (p. 187). On the other hand, the perceptions of the 16 online learners are the result of their initial experiences in an online course.

Online Tutors, Online Learners and the Learning Process

Tutors defined feedback as a means of guiding learners towards what they need to know and also as a way of assessing learning. The first view (66% agreement) coincides with the concept of "elaboration" (Kulhavy & Stock, 1989), namely the information the learner receives in order to lead him/her towards the right answer. The second view (83% agreement) has to do with the concept of "verification," also proposed by Kulhavy and Stock (1989), which refers to judgment of whether an answer is right or wrong. Online learners concurred with the way tutors view feedback and added that ideally feedback should be present throughout the course.

The OLTs were neutral towards what Huet (2004) calls the behaviorist view of feedback, suggesting that they do hold a more constructivist and cognitive attitude toward the learning process. They asserted that verification of an answer is needed, but should be expressed as a more qualitative judgment of the learner's work. This view was also confirmed when OLTs were asked whether feedback should stimulate dialogue and let learners know about their progress. There was a high percentage of agreement (83% and 91.6%) on these points, supporting Puccinin's view (2003), that

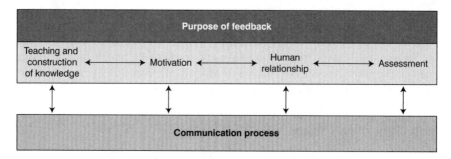

FIGURE 3.1 Purposes of feedback

tutors hold a more formative view of feedback. OLLs concurred, seeing feedback as a process where both tutors and learners participate, interact, and as one learner mentioned: "walk together in order to achieve a common objective" (OLL14). The tutors also agreed that OLF should encourage learners' self-evaluation (91.6%). While for Schwartz and White (2000), this is a key characteristic of feedback, for the tutors in this study such fostering is less a characteristic than a key objective of feedback.

Overall it can be said that tutors believe that feedback has four different purposes:

1. Constructing knowledge related to the pedagogical aspects of learning, including guiding, directing, facilitating, and teaching.
2. Motivating learners constantly to provide psychological support.
3. Promoting the relationships that inevitably develop in social interactions of this nature.
4. Assessing learners' performance.

Figure 3.1 illustrates how these relationships can be interpreted.

All four themes form part of the key processes of communication with the learner. Desirably, all are present when giving feedback which should be undertaken in an interrelated manner as Figure 3.1 shows.

The tutors' responses to statements intended to bring out their views on social-constructivist ideas about learning showed a high percentage of agreement (100% and 83.2%). Tutors clearly feel that feedback serves as an aid in the development of a learner's cognitive skills and also in the construction of knowledge. As such, they are in harmony with the basic principles of constructivist thinkers such as Vygotsky (1978). Note here that the OLTs provide feedback on a product which the learner has submitted. This product is based on a pedagogical task (a chart, a diagram, mental map, an answer to a question) and the tutor establishes communication with the learner, questioning, guiding, and fostering the kind of dialogue which Mercer (2000) calls "interthinking." Most participants described such interaction as one of the characteristics of "good" feedback; dialogue aims to foster critical thinking, and reflection, which are essential constructivist concepts (von Glaserfeld, 1991). To illustrate, we provide an example of group feedback where the tutor (Víctor) guides the learners when talking about formal and informal evaluation:

> I think there should be a clearer difference between the two. The difference between formal and informal evaluation is so subtle that one would think that they are the same as both share criteria and can become so precise that it´s easy for us to confuse them.

We can see here how the tutor guides by providing clues but not answers, inviting learners to discern subtle difference between formal and informal evaluation. Other characteristics of good feedback expressed by tutors and learners involved those related to pedagogy (positive and negative, specific, evaluative, interactive, multidimensional, relevant) and psychology (motivational, emotional).

OLLs' Perceptions of Tutors' Feedback and Methodology

Intimately related to the ideas expressed above is the role of the OLT when providing feedback. An aspect of the literature that has not been addressed is that of OLF strategies used by OLTs. This study showed that not all tutors are fully aware of the strategies they use, but do not seem to have developed a wide variety. Further research into OLF strategies would be valuable, as awareness of their usefulness and use are essential methodological aspects of an online course. The study found that tutoring strategies were cognitive (where the OLT serves as a mediator) or instructional (where the OLT guides, provides input and supports the OLL). Cognitive strategies as conceived by the OLTs are related to constructivist principles: the OLT acts as a mediator who helps the learner reach the Zone of Proximal Development (Vygotsky, 1978). This extract illustrates how OLTs expressed this concept:

> I try to encourage critical thinking, I try to encourage people to really [...] extend the analysis and to question things and to....yes, to [...] extend the discussion as much as possible.
>
> (OLT7)

As for the OLLs, they identified three teaching approaches, formulated as constructivist (guiding, questioning, promoting reflection), directive (asking for clarification, directing, instructing), and the combination of both (questioning, instructing, and motivating). Learners' comments indicate that OLTs are very direct when explicitly instructing as this learner (OLL7) describes: "Look for this article, go to this site, read this or that, reformulate this or that." This comment not only shows the OLLs' awareness of the tutor's imperative instructional style but also the authority that the OLT can display.

A characteristic of feedback which is not explained nor explicitly mentioned in the literature is that of relevance. The tutors stated that for feedback to be relevant it has to influence the learner; the OLT must be able to make use of personal feedback strategies and take into consideration the learners' individual and academic background and professional context. These last aspects are closely related to sociocultural constructivist views of learning (Lantolf & Thorne, 2006) in that they play a major role in the learning process. The OLLs in the study viewed the relevance of feedback in this light as one OLL expressed:

> It was relevant in the sense that it was adequate and necessary to help me improve my work.
>
> (OLL6)

Relevant feedback was also related to *timely* feedback; although the learner may find OLF meaningful, contextually appropriate, and useful, if it is not delivered promptly, it may become irrelevant. This last aspect coincides with Reid and Newhouse's (2004) findings that timely feedback turned out to be an essential factor for engaging students in the learning process.

The Textual Construction of Feedback

The analysis of the feedback messages allowed for the identification of different language functions used by the OLT in both group and individual feedback. In essence these language functions have to do with the role of OLTs and the way they mediate the teaching-learning process. OLTs organize their feedback in order to fulfill different communicative functions. Analysis of the data showed that it was possible to identify the generic and functional structure of individual feedback as shown in Figure 3.2.

Figure 3.2 shows that individual feedback consists of three obligatory stages: opening, body of feedback, and closing, and two optional stages: introduction to feedback and pre-closing. As Swales (1990) acknowledges these stages are relatively predictable.

In the opening stage, Pat and Víctor always greet the OLLs using: "Hi" followed by the OLL's name or just the OLL's name: "Hi Rebeca," and "Vanesa." This stage is always present in the messages, even in the short exchanges analyzed. Therefore, taking into consideration what Murray (2000) notes about optional openings and closings, greetings in the opening stage could be considered a common practice in this academic setting. In the next stage, the introduction to feedback, the OLTs inform, express wellbeing and/or make a judgment about the OLL's work. Sometimes they inform the OLL explicitly that the message contains feedback, stating the purpose of the message: "I've checked the evaluation activities you're proposing and I have some comments." Here, the tutor's statement is neutral. It does

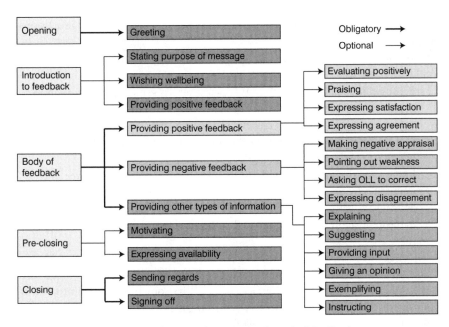

FIGURE 3.2 The generic and functional structure of invidual feedback

not anticipate whether the feedback that follows is positive or negative but simply informs and prepares the OLL. In other examples, the OLT uses this stage to wish the OLL well: *"Hope you're fine"* or provide a judgment about the work of the OLL: "It seems to me that your problem is well defined and you know the way you're going to evaluate." The statements are short and directly to the point. Omitting this stage does not create a drastic communication gap between the greeting and the body of feedback. It can be said that this stage is optional as it is the OLT's decision to include an introduction or to go directly to the body of feedback.

The body of feedback includes the provision of positive and negative feedback. Positive feedback is delivered by using the following functions:

a. Expressing satisfaction, "I enjoyed reading your summary." (Víctor)
b. Making an evaluative judgment, "I checked your summary and in general is OK." (Pat)
c. Acknowledging that the OLL understood something, "I think you understood the main idea of the article." (Pat)
d. Expressing agreement with the OLL's answers, "I agree with you that when correcting oral production one should be more flexible." (Víctor)

Most statements of positive feedback include an evaluative element either explicitly or implicitly. As seen in the statements above, these are short, direct and specific. Positive feedback is not, however, systematically present in the messages;

the literature suggests that positive feedback should be given in moderate amounts (Brinko, 1993).

Negative feedback is provided by using the following functions:

a.   Pointing out weaknesses of the OLL's work, "It has some typing errors and also some things here and there that aren't correct." (Pat)
b.   Asking the OLL to correct aspects of his/her work, "I'd like to ask you to be more succinct in your comments because you tend to write things that don't have to do with the task itself." (Pat)
c.   Expressing disagreement with the OLL's work, "I wouldn't agree that it's evaluation by process." (Pat)
d.   Making a negative appraisal of the OLL's work, "I think there's a lack of accuracy in the general objective and due to this, the activities are not that precise either." (Pat)

Pat uses very direct expressions such as: "It has some typing errors and also some things here and there that aren't correct," "It's sometimes difficult to follow your discourse." From the point of view of pragmatics theory, these are instances where the OLT threatens the positive face of the OLL. In examples a), c) and d) above, essentially Pat is saying to the learner "Your answer is not correct." In b) Pat also threatens the negative face of the OLL as she is telling him what to do. If one follows Brown and Levinson's (1987) view of politeness then these examples can be considered to be face-threatening acts (FTAs). However, if we consider Goffman's (1967) concept of "face-work," as "the actions taken by a person to make whatever he is doing consistent with face" (Goffman, 1967, p. 12), then it can be said that the actions undertaken by the OLT are consistent with his/her role. This role, amongst other aspects, entails the provision of feedback to his/her learners.

OLTF and Assessment

The tutors also believe that there is a strong relationship between OLTF and assessment. This relationship was highlighted by participants in the questionnaires and during the interviews and four types of processes were identified: a) instructional, b) evaluative, c) metacognitive, and d) critical thinking,. This relationship is interpreted in Figure 3.3.

The relationship can be viewed as an instructional and informative process where the OLT provides direct input or explicit information (A), or as an evaluative process when the OLT judges the OLL's work (B); it can be seen as a metacognitive process when the OLL is able to use self-evaluation and self-monitoring strategies (C), and finally, as a critical thinking process when the OLT questions and guides the OLL (D). This relationship also indicates that one of the purposes of OLF is precisely to trigger cognitive mechanisms which help learners to analyze, reflect, and evaluate

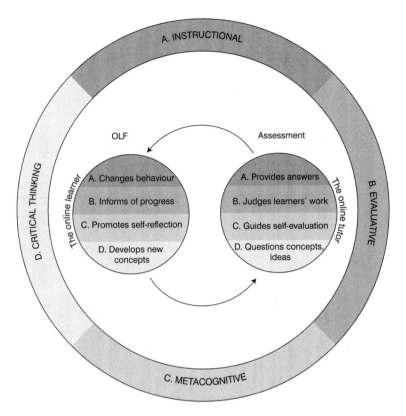

FIGURE 3.3 Relationship between OLTF and assessment

their performance. But there is also inevitable judgment of the correctness of learners' work, as noted by authors like Huet (2004), Kulhavy and Stock (1989) and Mory (1992) who view feedback from the behaviorist and formative points of view. This suggests that for feedback to be relevant it should include the assessing element to guide the learners towards the Zone of Proximal Development and to help them reach the course objectives. The tutors view the evaluative aspect of feedback as a strategy where tutor and learner negotiate the quality of the learner's work.

OLLs on their part, are aware of the judgmental element of feedback and are prepared to receive constructive criticism of their work. The following extract shows the view of one OLL:

> Yes, I remember that the tutor pointed out the positive things of my work and very subtly the tutor also pointed out what was missing or asked me about the relevance of a particular issue I had raised. The tutor always questioned me and asked me to work on aspects that I needed to expand.

(OLL5)

OLTF and Psychological Aspects

Two important psychological aspects come to light in the study: affective factors and motivation.

OLF and Affective Factors

The tutors all share a strong belief that it is essential to surmount the distance barrier when working online. This coincides with Wallace's (1999) research in relation to socio-emotional expression online. She notes that when people communicate online they are cooler, more task-oriented and more irascible than they are in person, because they are limited by the medium and because body language and facial expressions are not visible in asynchronous communication.

In relation to the role of emotions in the online feedback environment, OLLs revealed the state of anxiousness they experienced in the period between period of submitting assignments and receiving a message from the tutor as expressed by this OLL:

> At the beginning, I was fearful, (.) especially because when I do something I always demand a lot of myself. I'm not used to easily accepting when I make a mistake or when I'm wrong. So, (…) when I saw that I had mail I'd panic. When I read the heading of the message, I opened it and printed it (.) and then I took it with me to work and reflected upon the content. (…) I never answered back immediately. I digested the content (.) and then I replied to the tutor saying that I had received the feedback and that it was OK.
>
> (OLL8)

Anxiety may be exacerbated in the online environment, since time is a decisive element in asynchronous communications because of lack of immediacy. Värlander (2008) asserts that feedback situations are characterized by the presence of emotions on the learner's part. These emotions can overshadow the value of feedback, as Rice (1995) suggests, because they impact on the learners' reactions to it. Looking at the OLLs' comments and the literature related to emotions in feedback situations (e.g. Värlander, 2008), it can be seen that emotions are closely related to motivation and self-esteem. The way learners react to feedback is unpredictable. Strong feedback may result in even the most self-efficacious of learners becoming demotivated; on the other hand, positive motivation may be activated by criticism. Learners' attitudes to feedback are affected by individual differences and also their emotional states at the time of receiving feedback. Värlander too, notes that learners' motivational beliefs "depend largely on *how* tutors provide feedback" (p. 151). OLTs' feedback could be uncharacteristically strong and misdirected because tutors do not find what is expected from the learner or are themselves experiencing stressful periods such as work overload. Nevertheless, it is important to reduce the negative emotions that feedback may produce.

OLTF and Motivation

Both tutors and learners were well aware of the importance of motivation and felt very strongly that the learner needs to be encouraged throughout the learning process. They also felt that motivational messages have different objectives in an online environment. Motivation is one of the purposes of feedback and tutors stressed the importance of supporting and encouraging OLLs. Motivation was also related to assessment, as OLTs' messages usually contain judgments about the learners' work which informed them about their progress. This is similar to the goal-orientation theory of motivation (Dörnyei, 2001, 2009) where performance and success influence the successful completion of activities in the classroom. Further research is needed on how motivational messages impact OLL performance particularly in the context of the virtual classroom. Dörnyei (2001) further states that teachers who care for their learners and develop a good relationship with them are more likely to interest them in the subject matter than those who do not manage to establish rapport. The findings show that the tutors see this relationship from a methodological point of view (as a motivational strategy), but also from a more cognitive perspective, as they view motivation as a psychological aspect that is present alongside the learning process. For Williams and Burden (1997), and from a constructivist point of view, it is important to understand that each person is motivated in a different way and reacts differently to social, contextual, cultural, and personal factors. Since a variety of motivational messages operate for individuals or groups at different stages in a course, it seems logical that the participants should relate motivation to all the aspects mentioned above.

Redefining OLTF

During the study, the initial concept of feedback was redefined. Since OLTF is a dynamic process for triggering learning, the subsequent definition must also be seen as interim. It is presented here as a possible starting point for further research.

> OLTF is a multidimensional process of pedagogical online communication in which the tutor, after appraising the OLL's work, provides various types of information to the learner to help him/her develop, build, and acquire knowledge. The tutor achieves this process by guiding the OLL, by questioning him/her, by providing him/her with input, by supporting and motivating him/her and by fostering interaction and reflection. OLTF is an interactive, heuristic, and hermeneutic process where psychological and affective factors play a decisive role as they influence the way feedback is delivered and received in the electronic medium, and therefore, it also influences how communication takes place. This process implies a cycle that drives the overall process of learning where both OLLs and OLTs are co-participants and therefore co-responsible for the learning outcomes.

OLTF includes pedagogical and psychological aspects that interact with each other at different times depending on the nature of the pedagogical task at hand, the OLTs' strategies, methodology, and the OLL's individual needs, professional context and culture. The new definition we provide above is an attempt both to capture this dynamism but also to reflect the inherent complexity of feedback which this study has sought to illuminate.

Final Reflections

This study constitutes one of the few explorations so far in the field of TESOL of how OLT feedback mediates learning, and how, as Vygotsky suggests, mediational tools (digital tools, electronic environment) also act as mediators supporting the learning process. Within the relevant pedagogical aspects that emerged, it is necessary to reconsider the tutors' methodological procedures and assessment practices in order to provide quality feedback. The study suggests that if quality feedback is to be provided, tutors need to reflect critically on their methodological procedures and assessment practices within the online medium. It is particularly important to consider the way language is used in online feedback, precisely because of the nature of the medium. The OLT-OLL relationship depends critically on minimizing the possibility of misinterpretation, particularly of more negative feedback, and thereby jeopardizing the important processes of online learning. We end this chapter with some questions for further research.

Discussion Questions

1. What type of strategies can be used by OLTs to ensure successful communication with OLLs?
2. How can OLTs develop adequate methodological procedures to provide effective online feedback?
3. How important is it to maintain a balance between positive and negative feedback? Why?

References

Bender, S., & Dittmar, E. (2006) Dealing with difficult learners: Two perspectives, five best practices, and ten difficult learner types. *International Journal of Instructional Technology & Distance Learning, 3*(7), 55–59.

Beyth-Marom, R., & Harpaz-Gorodeisky, G. (2006) Identification, job satisfaction and work motivation among tutors at the Open University of Israel. *International Review of Research in Open and Distance Learning, 7*(2).

Borg, M. (2001) Key concepts in ELT: Teachers' beliefs. *ELT Journal, 55*(2), 186–188.

Brinko, K. T. (1993) The practice of giving feedback to improve teaching. What is effective? *Journal of Higher Education, 64*(5), 574–593.

Brown, P., & Levinson, S. C. (1987) *Politeness: Some universals in language use.* Cambridge: Cambridge University Press.

Clariana, R. B. (2000) Feedback in computer-assisted learning. *NETg* University of Limerick Lecture Series. See http://www.personal.psu.edu/faculty/r/b/rbc4/NETg.htm

Contijoch, M. C. (2009) Beliefs, discourses and perceptions: A study of online tutors´ feedback and learners' perceptions form an online diploma course in Mexico. Unpublished doctoral dissertation, Macquarie University, Sydney, Australia.

Creanor, L. (2002) A tale of two courses: A comparative study of tutoring online. *Open Learning, 17*(1), 57–68.

Creswell, J. W. (2007) *Qualitative inquiry and research design: Choosing among five approaches* (2nd edn). Thousand Oaks, CA: Sage Publications.

Dörnyei, Z. (2001) *Teaching and researching motivation.* Harlow: Longman.

Dörnyei, Z. (2009) The L2 motivational self system. In Z. Dörnyei, & E. Ushioda (Eds), *Motivation, language identity and the L2 self* (pp. 9–42). Bristol: Multilingual Matters.

Goodfellow, R. (2004) Key practices in e-learning across the university curriculum. Presentation at a seminar on elearning all' università. Centro dei Servizi Linguistici e Bibliotecari di Ateneo. Rome.

Goffman, E. (1967) *Interaction ritual: Essays on face-to-face behavior.* London: The Penguin Press.

Gunawardena, C. N., & Zittle, F. J. (1997) Social presence as a predictor of satisfaction within a computer-mediated conferencing environment. *The American Journal of Distance Education, 11*(3), 8–26.

Henninger, M., & Viswanathan, V. (2004) *Social presence in online tutoring.* Proceedings from the Knowledge Media and Research Centre Conference in Tübingen. Retrieved October 4, 2006 from http://www.iwm-kmrc.de/worshops/sim

Higgins, R., & Hartley, P. (2002) The conscientious consumer: Reconsidering the role of assessment feedback in student learning. *Studies in Higher Education, 27*(1), 53–64.

Higgins, R., Hartley, P., & Skelton, A. (2001) Getting the message across: The problem of communicating assessment feedback. *Teaching in Higher Education, 6*(2), 270–274.

Huet, J. (2004) Email as an educational feedback tool: Relative advantages and implementation guidelines. *International Journal of Instructional Technology and Distance Learning, 1*(6), 35–44.

John-Steiner, V., & Mahn. H. (1996) Sociocultural approaches to learning and development: A Vygotskian framework. *Educational Psychologist, 31*(3–4), 191–206.

Kulhavy, R. W., & Stock, W. A. (1989) Feedback in written instruction: The place of response certitude. *Educational Psychology Review, 1*(4), 279–308.

Lantolf, J. P. (2000) *Sociocultural theory and second language learning.* Oxford: Oxford University Press.

Lantolf, J. P., & Thorne, S. L. (2006) *Sociocultural theory and the genesis of second language development.* Oxford: Oxford University Press.

Laurillard, D. (2002) *Rethinking university teaching: A framework for the effective use of learning technologies* (2nd ed). London: Routledge.

Lim, C. P., & Cheah, P. T. (2003) The role of the tutor in asynchronous discussion boards: A case study of a pre-service teacher course. *Education Media International, 40*(1–2), 33–48.

McPherson, M., & Baptista, N. (2004) The role of tutors as an integral part of online learning support. *European Journal of Open, Distance and E-Learning, 1.* Retrieved November 25, 2006 from http://www.eurodl.org/materials/contrib/2004/Maggie_MsP.pdf

Mercer, N. (2000) *Words and minds: How we use language to think together.* London: Routledge.

Mercer, N. (2004) Sociocultural discourse analysis: Analyzing classroom talk as a social mode of thinking. *Journal of Applied Linguistics, 1*(2), 137–168.

Mory, E. (1992) The use of informational feedback in instruction: Implications for future research. *Educational Training Research and Development, 40*(3), 5–20.

Murray, D. E. (2000) Protean communication: The language of computer–mediated communication. *TESOL Quarterly, 34*(3), 397–421.

Narciss, S. (1999) Motivational effects of the informativeness of feedback. Paper presented at the annual meeting of the American Educational Research Association, Montreal, Quebec, Canada.

Paltridge, B. (2006) *Discourse analysis: An introduction.* London, UK: Continuum.

Pavlenko, A., & Lantolf, J. P. (2000) Second language learning as participation and the (re) construction of selves. In J. P. Lantolf (Ed.), *Sociocultural theory and second language learning* (pp. 155–177). Oxford: Oxford University Press.

Puccinin, S. (2003) *Feedback: Key to learning.* Halifax, NS: Society for Teaching and Learning in Higher Education.

Ramaprasad, A. (1983) On the definition of feedback. *Behavioral Science, 28*, 4–7.

Reid, D., & Newhouse, P. C. (2004) But it didn't happen last semester: Explanations of the mediated environmental factors that affect online tutor capabilities. Proceedings of the Australasian Society for Computers in Learning in Tertiary Education (ASCILITE), 791–797. Perth, WA.

Rice, P. (1995) The art of assessing. *New Academic 5*(3), 3–6.

Schensul, S. L., Schensul, J. J., & LeCompte, M. D. (1999) *Essential ethnographic methods: Ethnographer's toolkit.* Walnut Creek, CA: AltaMira Press.

Schwartz, F., & White, K. W. (2000) Making sense of it all: Giving and getting online course feedback. In K. W. White & B. H. Weight (Eds), *The online teaching guide* (pp.167–182). Boston, MA: Allyn and Bacon.

Swales, J. M. (1990) *Genre analysis. English in academic and research settings.* Cambridge: Cambridge University Press.

Värlander, S. (2008) The role of students' emotions in formal feedback situations. *Teaching in Higher Education, 13*(2), 145–156.

von Glaserfeld, E. (1991) An exposition of radical constructivism. In G. J. Klir (Ed.), *Facets of system science* (pp. 229–238). New York, NY: Plenum Press.

Vygotsky, L. S. (1978) *Mind in society: The development of higher psychological processes.* Cambridge, MA: Harvard University Press.

Wallace, P. (1999) *The psychology of the internet.* Cambridge: Cambridge University Press.

Williams, M., & Burden, R. (1997) *Psychology for language teachers.* Cambridge: Cambridge University Press.

4

ADDRESSING THE CHALLENGES OF ONLINE ASSESSMENT

Practical Solutions for TESOL Instructors

Steven Humphries and Florin Mihai

Introduction

The well-documented growth of online TESOL and the array of course management systems through which it is taught provide unprecedented opportunities for those TESOL teacher trainers who have the exciting opportunity to instruct and mentor a new generation of English as a Second Language (ESL) and English as a Foreign Language (EFL) practitioners. But with opportunity comes challenge. This chapter will address one such challenge—online assessment. In doing so, it will highlight many of the assessment issues that online TESOL teacher trainers inevitably face, and offer practical solutions for how to solve them.

The chapter is designed to address both formative assessments, conducted while students are still learning the skills they will need, and summative assessments, usually carried out at the end of a unit or course to summarize how well students have grasped the concepts taught (Brown & Abeywickrama, 2010). It also addresses both traditional assessments such as tests, and alternative assessments, such as portfolios, projects and discussions. The lines between these categories, formative-summative and traditional-alternative, are not always clear, but they serve as groupings from which to make distinctions and advance the discussion.

The overarching question is this, "In an online context, how do we know that students are learning the skills they need to be effective teachers; in other words, how can we best determine whether our assessments work?" In this chapter, these questions are answered through the lens of four invaluable and fundamental assessment concepts—validity, reliability, practicality, and authenticity.

Online Assessment: Definition and Characteristics

Before continuing, it is important to consider how online assessment has been operationalized, as well as to outline some of the research-based principles of online assessment. Generally, assessment has traditionally been associated with tests and exams. However, the educational environment has registered a change from the culture of testing towards one based on multiple assessments. Today, the focus of assessment includes not only individual assessment, but also group-process assessment, not only paper and pencil measurements, but also authentic assessments (Twigg, 2001). Angelo (1995) defines assessment as follows:

> Assessment is an ongoing process aimed at understanding and improving student learning. It involves making our expectations explicit and public; setting appropriate criteria and high standards for learning quality; systematically gathering, analyzing, and interpreting evidence to determine how well performance matches those expectations and standards; and using the resulting information to document, explain, and improve performance.
>
> (p. 7)

Moving from a face-to-face mode of delivery to a more web-centric or purely online type of instruction necessitates a re-evaluation of class materials, creation of new types of assignments, and the designation of new ways to measure student learning. In addition, the online medium affects student and teacher roles, communication styles, and teacher-student and student-student relationships. As the learning paradigm is fundamentally influenced and changed by the online environment, the assessment design and delivery models will undergo important transformations as well, as established techniques of traditional face-to-face classrooms are not always suitable for the new classroom format.

In spite of their clear differences, traditional face-to-face and online classrooms have at least one essential principle in common, which is the need to link assessment, teaching, and learning in a deliberate manner. Throughout their courses, instructors must make a concerted effort to include their students in the assessment of their learning. Moreover, they must use the information gathered to make positive changes in their instruction to facilitate learning more effectively. To ensure the teaching-learning-assessment connection, online instructors in TESOL programs need constantly to be aware of their teaching setting. Online instructional environments have several unique features that distinguish them from more traditional classes. One example is the possibility of both synchronous courses, in which students and professors meet together online at a specific time, and asynchronous courses, in which there is no one time that everyone is together as a class. Additionally, the use of technology is essential for accessing and communicating course information.

These characteristics require a conscientiously student-oriented and more technology-driven pedagogy, which, in turn, should be reflected in the design of the assessment practices. Assessment activities used in more traditional face-to-face teaching cannot and should not be simply transferred to online classes without taking into account the role of web-based technology in the learning process. Online assessment design and implementation should include the unique characteristics of online teaching environments and should be based on sound assessment principles, such as validity, reliability, practicality, and authenticity. Each of these principles is addressed below.

Principles of Effective Online Assessment Practices

Validity

Validity refers to whether an assessment, whether through an informal process such as an observation or through a formal instrument such as a test, actually measures what it is intended to measure (Brown & Abeywickrama, 2010). An online TESOL educator can help to ensure validity by taking some very practical actions. While some of these actions are based on techniques employed in face-to-face instruction, others incorporate the distinctive features of the online environment.

The first action goes back to the principle of both online and face-to-face TESOL classrooms, emphasizing the strong connection between teaching, learning, and assessment. This action is to teach what will be assessed and to assess what has been taught. In essence, it is a call to planning assessments when—not after—planning lessons, courses, or curricula.

For example, one of the core courses taught in TESOL preparation programs is Applied Linguistics, which concentrates on phonetics and phonology among the many sub-systems of English. One important aspect of phonetics is the description of how sounds are articulated, as well as their characteristics. During lectures and through class materials made available online, TESOL instructors must explain how meaningful sounds are produced in English, explain why this knowledge is important to ESL or EFL students, and illustrate methods to help those students articulate the sounds correctly. As discussed, instructors should ensure when creating these objectives that they simultaneously create assessments that measure all three as well.

First then, TESOL instructors would want to make sure their students know the places or manners of articulation of English sounds. In online classes, the use of technology allows for objective measurements of this type of knowledge, which can be assessed easily using quizzes and tests. These instruments can be summative but, in this case, they should be formative, thus allowing for the re-teaching of problematic areas. An example of a test item for this objective is provided in Figure 4.1.

TESOL students will also encounter circumstances in which they have to address particular pronunciation problems for a particular ESL or EFL student. For this reason, they will have to know how to apply the theoretical knowledge obtained in Applied Linguistics to their particular teaching situation. Therefore, an assessment

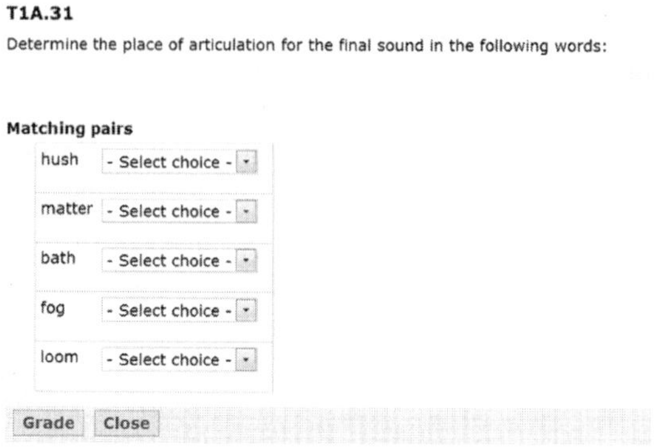

T1A.31

Determine the place of articulation for the final sound in the following words:

Matching pairs

hush	- Select choice - ▾
matter	- Select choice - ▾
bath	- Select choice - ▾
fog	- Select choice - ▾
loom	- Select choice - ▾

Grade   Close

FIGURE 4.1 Test item assessing phonetic knowledge

instrument for this purpose will measure, on the one hand, the ability of TESOL students to identify different phonetic characteristics of sounds in English and, on the other hand, to apply this knowledge to real-world classroom situations. An example of such assessment is illustrated in Figure 4.2.

To further foster validity, TESOL instructors should *emphasize* in the assessment what they have emphasized in class. For example, suppose that in an online Applied Linguistics class there has been a great deal of time spent on sound characteristics, as we illustrated in the previous example, and less time spent on elision, the omission of a final or initial sound in pronunciation. Consequently, assessment should concentrate more on sound characteristics as well. This same idea applies to study guides, for example. In short, the amount of time, text, and presentation assigned to a topic should be a strong indicator of how important the TESOL instructor believes the topic is to students' future success as ESL or EFL teachers, and therefore be reflected by a commensurate relative weight for that topic in the assessment.

In addition, also to help create valid assessments, TESOL instructors need to match the learning objectives to the test format. For example, again in the context of phonetics and phonology, TESOL students often are required to listen to and subsequently represent sounds by producing appropriate corresponding symbols from the International Phonetic Alphabet (IPA). Creating an online test in which students match sounds with symbols is certainly feasible, but not a valid measure of being able to *produce* the correct symbol for a given sound. Instead, this can be accomplished by providing the sounds and asking students to supply the symbols. This is simple in traditional face-to-face assessments, since instructors can say or play the sounds aloud and students can draw the symbols on paper to turn in by hand during the class itself.

However, in an online environment, TESOL instructors must consider alternative methods for both how to produce the sounds and for how to receive the symbols. Both challenges can be overcome easily since instructors can record and post the sounds, and students can draw or cut-and-paste the symbols and upload them back

Phonetics/Phonology Assignment

(This assignment can be completed individually or in pairs.)

Objective: To give students an opportunity to use phonetics/phonology principles in the analysis of non-native English language samples.

Tasks:

a. Please go to

http://accent.gmu.edu/browse_language.php?function=find&language=spanish

Listen to the following speakers: Spanish 3, Spanish 5, and Spanish 7. They are all female speakers from Bogota, Colombia. For each speaker, make a list of sounds they have problems with, including the word in which the sound occurs.

Example:

Spanish 3

Target Sound	Produced by the speaker as	Word where the sound has been identified
/s/	/z/	see

To insert IPA symbols in your please use one of the following websites:

http://www.e-lang.co.uk/mackichan/call/pron/type.html

http://ipa.typeit.org/

Important note: Please list sounds and not groups of sounds. Also, please remember that letters do not have a close sound correspondence in English. For example, the letter 'x' in 'six' is not the sound /x/. In fact, there are two sounds, /k/ and /s/. The phonetic transcription for six is /sɪks/.

b. Let's suppose you have these Spanish speakers you have analyzed in your class. How would you help them understand how the target sounds (or English sounds) they had problems with are produced? Apply the knowledge you have on organs of articulation and place/manner of articulation to the specific pronunciation problems of the three Spanish speakers you have analyzed.

FIGURE 4.2 Assessment combining the theory and practice of phonetics

TABLE 4.1 Validity do's and don'ts

Validity do's	Validity don'ts
• Assess what you teach and teach what you will assess • Emphasize in assessment what you emphasized in class • If you provide study guides, make sure your assessment covers the topics listed in a meaningful manner	• Don't mismatch learning objectives and test format • Don't make the time for taking the test too short

to the course management system. The point is this—though some creativity is required, instructors can and must use the technology available in online courses to match their learning objectives with their test formats if their assessments are to be valid.

The example in the previous two paragraphs also illustrates the importance of creating valid assessments when, not after, objectives are written. For instance, what would happen if the instructor did not have the necessary technological expertise, software, or computer hardware to record and post or otherwise create the sounds needed for students to demonstrate understanding of the objective? Clearly, he or she would have to either acquire the necessary expertise, software or hardware—or change the objective. Because the solution may be impossible, or at the least too impractical (see section on "Practicality" below), the time to do this is not when it comes time to assess an objective, but when that objective is created.

Finally, an assessment cannot validly measure what it is designed to if students, even if they know the material, do not have enough time to complete it. Learning how much time this is for any given assessment comes with practice, so new teachers or those teaching new courses should err on the side of giving too much time as opposed to too little. Depending on the nature of the assessment, course management systems can help, as they can record the amount of time each student takes to complete an assessment. Aggregating and averaging these data provides an ideal source of information for determining how much time students need to complete an assessment and to ensure that it does not become a validity issue. Table 4.1 summarizes several ways to ensure validity of online TESOL assessments.

Reliability

Reliability asks the question, "Does this assessment give consistent results?" If an assessment is reliable, a student who took the same test twice, or two groups of comparable students who took the same test, should get similar results (Brown & Abeywickrama, 2010). If this is not the case, the assessment is considered unreliable, any inferences drawn from it are questionable and, by definition, the assessment is not valid. Therefore, reliability for any assessment is extremely important.

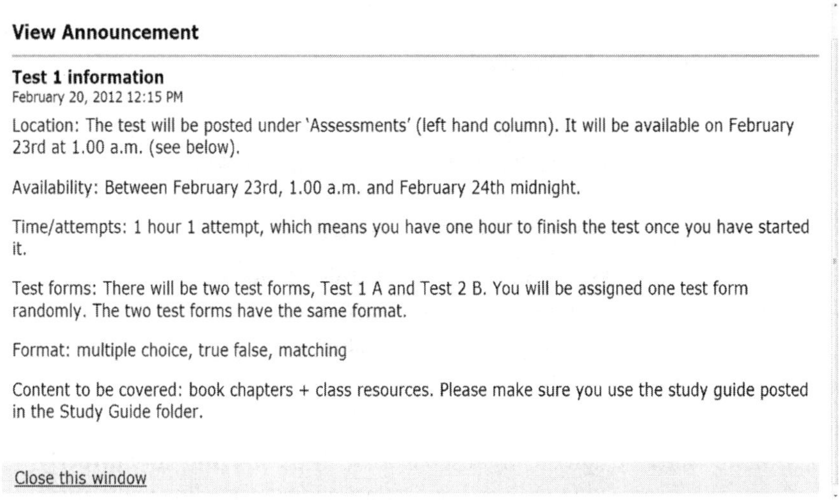

View Announcement

Test 1 information
February 20, 2012 12:15 PM

Location: The test will be posted under 'Assessments' (left hand column). It will be available on February 23rd at 1.00 a.m. (see below).

Availability: Between February 23rd, 1.00 a.m. and February 24th midnight.

Time/attempts: 1 hour 1 attempt, which means you have one hour to finish the test once you have started it.

Test forms: There will be two test forms, Test 1 A and Test 2 B. You will be assigned one test form randomly. The two test forms have the same format.

Format: multiple choice, true false, matching

Content to be covered: book chapters + class resources. Please make sure you use the study guide posted in the Study Guide folder.

Close this window

FIGURE 4.3 Test information

In a traditional classroom, reliability can be affected by the physical conditions under which students are assessed. For example, if one group of students takes a test while loud construction noise permeates the classroom, and another group takes the same test in quiet conditions, then this test is not going to give reliable results. This type of reliability concern does not occur generally in an online environment. Instead, questions of reliability for online courses more often revolve around student access to the test, how it is scored, and technology issues.

Online assessments are often available to students in a specified window of time. This is true for both synchronous and asynchronous courses. For this reason, it is extremely important that students know when a test (or other assessment) will be available, where to find it, what they will need to take it, how long they will have to complete it, and how they will submit it for grading and feedback. All of this information must be easily and equally available to all students *prior* to taking an assessment (see Figure 4.3). If, for example, some students know how to go directly to the assessment during the open window, while others spend time looking for it, they will have qualitatively and quantitatively different opportunities to successfully complete the assessment, and its reliability will be distorted.

Grading assessments online is similar to grading them in a traditional classroom, but there is perhaps more room for error. For example, course management systems can automatically grade fill-in-the-blank assessment items, but cannot know if an answer is correct but misspelled, or uses different words from those TESOL instructors have programmed in as acceptable, so instructors must check carefully to ensure consistency, i.e., reliability, in grading. Fortunately, grading multiple-choice items should take care of itself as long as TESOL instructors have correctly programmed in which answer is the correct one.

Online Discussions (25 percent)

- For each week that a reading is assigned, the instructor will post a question or set of questions and due dates on the Blackboard Discussion Board. Students should respond in between 500 and 600 words to these questions. **(Provide a word count with the posting)**.

- **Twenty-five (25) points will be deducted for each day that a Discussion Board posting is submitted late.** Points also will be deducted for failing to respond to questions to your posts from other students or the instructor.

- Grades will be based on quality of response and meeting length requirements. High quality responses are those that **fully and directly** answer the question or questions, reflect an understanding and critical analysis of the readings, and incorporate responses to other student postings for that assignment. These responses should be incorporated into your own thread.

Scoring Criteria **Each Response...**	**Percentage of Total Score**
Reflects Understanding of the Reading	20 percent
Directly Answers Question/s	20 percent
Thoroughly Addresses Topic	20 percent
Demonstrates Critical Analysis of the Reading	20 percent
Meets Length Requirements	10 percent
Incorporates Replies to Earlier Student Postings	10 percent
Total Possible	**100 Percent**

FIGURE 4.4 Example of a discussion board grading rubric

For more subjective assessments, one key to reliable scoring is to have clear criteria for acceptable responses. As in traditional classes, this is best done with a detailed and accessible rubric. Here again, accessibility is especially important for online assessments, so it should be clear to students where to find and how to apply the rubric. One way to do this is to post the rubric, as illustrated in Figure 4.4, require students to read it, and then monitor through the course management system who has at least opened it and who has not. This may not guarantee that students have read the rubric, or read it carefully, but it does provide a record that they have had an equal opportunity to do so.

There are other reliability considerations that occur in online courses that do not in traditional courses. One is that all computer networks require some down time for maintenance, and students should be notified when these are scheduled if an assessment window is open at that time. Few things are more frustrating than having the computer screen go blank in the middle of a test but, more importantly, this will change the assessment experience for students unfortunate enough to be taking it at the time, and again call into question its reliability.

Depending on the particular course management system used, it also may be necessary to block students from downloading the actual assessment. This can be an issue in at least two ways: 1) once downloaded, the assessment can be passed to other students who have not yet taken it, and 2) a dishonest student could download the assessment, claim computer or course accessibility problems, complete it offline, and then turn it in when given access again. We all like to think that our students are honest, and most are, but little good can come from having assessment instruments that may be used again floating around in cyberspace.

Another academic integrity issue, plagiarism, can be addressed through a program available in course management systems and commercially online called Turnitin. This program matches text from assignments with student papers, webpages, library databases and publications.. It works not only to ensure that students are doing their own work, but is also an excellent training tool to teach them the art of paraphrasing and to better understand the concepts and practicalities of academic integrity. As a tool to foster reliability, Turnitin can help to ensure that students work is consistently their own. Table 4.2 summarizes some of the practical solutions offered to TESOL instructors who want to increase the reliability of their online assessment instruments.

Practicality

Practicality in assessment has the same definition as practicality in its general sense. Brown and Abeywickrama (2010) list three ways in which an assessment should be practical—it should be financially viable, work within time constraints, and be relatively easy to administer, score and interpret.

In terms of cost associated with online TESOL classes, there is a cost for contracting for course management systems themselves, although there are some open-source

TABLE 4.2 Reliability do's and don'ts

Reliability do's	Reliability don'ts
• Make sure students know what is expected regarding procedures prior to the assessment, e.g., Is there a time limit? • Make sure students are clear about using the technology needed for the assessment, e.g., Where is the assessment? How do I submit it? • Prepare for correct but misspelled answers • Have detailed and accessible rubrics • Block students from downloading tests • Use Turn-it-In to check originality of written assignments (and as a teaching tool for students)	• Don't make the time window too short for taking the assessment • Don't ignore maintenance times

versions and other options for teaching online. However, there is no substantive additional expense for creating, administering, scoring or interpreting assessments online. In fact, in at least one aspect, online assessment can cost less because it can be done without the need to print out paper copies of various assessment instruments and student responses.

As with much of online teaching and learning, there are many time-related differences between online instruction and more traditional face-to-face modes of delivery. Because so much is best written that could be spoken in a traditional classroom, such as instructions for how to take a test, some aspects of online teaching require more time on the part of the teacher, but also on the student. This may be particularly true for formative assessments, which often consist of verbal classroom conversations between the teacher and students, or among the students themselves, but are commonly done through written Discussion Boards in online environments. For example, a conversation about second-language acquisition theory that could cover 30 minutes in a traditional classroom might take participants collectively several hours to discuss in a synchronous online environment, or several days in an asynchronous one. It is also important to note that any instructions for assessments (or other aspects of online teaching and learning for that matter) must be written very clearly so as to avoid any confusion or ambiguities that could cause a reliability question (and more work for both teacher and student).

The good news is that not all aspects of online assessment require more time and, in some cases, take less. There are also several tips that TESOL instructors who teach online can implement to minimize the time required to create, administer, and grade tests and other assessments. One such tip is that most course management systems allow teachers to copy assessments from one course to another so they do not have

In this online course, you will be graded on two discussion tasks. One is co-leading a discussion. The other is co-summarizing what happened in a module (a different discussion from the one you co-led). In other words, you will be randomly assigned to co-lead one discussion and you will be randomly assigned to co-summarize another discussion.

(A) Co-Leading a Discussion: You will be randomly assigned to lead 1 discussion with a co-leader for which you will be graded. Your job is to keep the discussion moving and keep it focused on the topic. Just as in any class discussion, maintaining this discussion may require asking questions, drawing people out, adding other points, etc.

(B) Co-Summarizing a Discussion: You and your co-summarizer will write a short summary of the top items brought up in another discussion and post it to the Discussion Summaries. Remember that some of the class members are not in your group, and though they started with the same prompt or topic, the odds are that each group's discussion will include different topics. At this point, people not in the discussion may have questions and can post them in the same place.

FIGURE 4.5 Assigning roles in dicussion boards

to create them anew each time they teach a particular course. Another is that course management systems allow instructors to create online test banks from which to build new assessments from items they have already created.

There are also ways that are not necessarily technology related that online TESOL educators might employ to save time with assessments. For instance, in larger classes, they can have students work in pairs or groups, which has the added benefit of creating a more collaborative learning environment. In online discussions, one strategy that works well has been the assignment of specific roles to students to facilitate communication, e.g., Opener, Closer, Facilitator, Summarizer. Figure 4.5 exemplifies how the discussion is set up in an MATESOL Vocabulary course taught online, while Figure 4.6 depicts a discussion in a TESOL Classroom Observation Skills course.

In addition, for discussion groups, essays, research papers, and other more open-ended and subjective assignments, it is important to determine and enforce a word limit. The number of words instructors choose will depend on the assignment, and they will fine-tune those numbers as they gain experience in the online pedagogy environment. Both of these ideas are common in traditional classes, but they work extremely well and are almost essential in online environments from a practicality perspective.

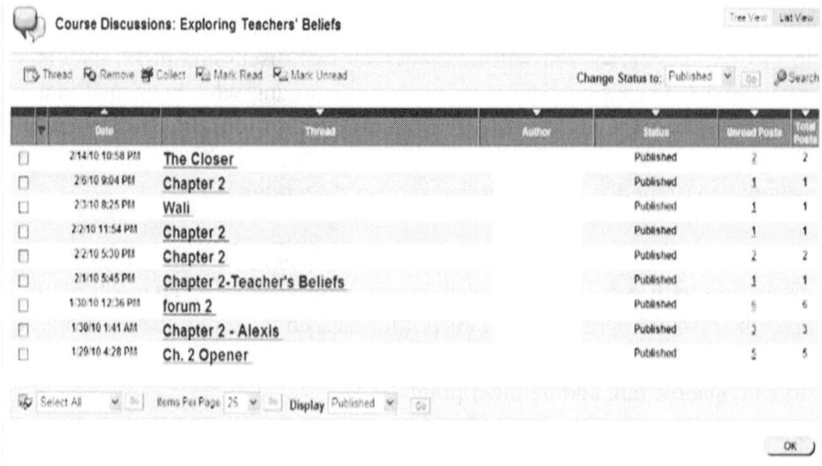

FIGURE 4.6 Discussion screen shot in a TESOL classroom observation skills course

One last word about practicality in online assessment is worth mentioning. There will always be technology concerns with any computer-based system, and TESOL instructors should make sure that their institution provides sufficient technical support to address them. This is true not only for general computer issues, but also for whatever course management system is used. Unfortunately, tech-support personnel do not always have all the answers and are not always available when needed. For this reason, it is critical that online TESOL instructors familiarize themselves as much as possible with how their systems work. This will bring them a sense of accomplishment and ownership, while also allowing them to be pro-active by anticipating and solving many technical issues before they have a chance to affect assessments in a negative manner. Table 4.3 lists several ways that can make TESOL online assessments more practical.

Authenticity

Authenticity in assessment asks the questions, "How does this test, quiz, project, discussion relate to the outside world?" and "How real is it?" These questions are often asked when assessing language learning, but they should apply when designing effective language-teacher training as well.

The most effective way to ensure that online assessments, or any assessments for that matter, are authentic, is to create original, practical, real-world teaching activities and then to assess what has been taught in a similar way. This is best done through task-based activities such as individual and group projects, including portfolios of original work. TESOL instructors in online environments should resist depending on assessments from course texts unless they meet these criteria.

TABLE 4.3 Practicality do's and don'ts

Practicality do's	Practicality don'ts
• Use the course management "Copy" function to carry over assessment (or entire courses) from one term to the next • Use the course management "Test Bank" function to create a pool of questions to pull from • Create a hypothetical student account to see what students see (already available in Webcourses course management system) • Have students do projects in pairs or groups to create a more collaborative learning environment and save grading time • For discussion groups, assign specific roles to students to facilitate communication, e.g., Opener, Closer, Facilitator, Summarizer • For discussion groups, essays, etc., determine and enforce word limits	• Do not recreate each assessment every term • Do not expect tech support to solve all your software issues

For example, instead of giving a test on language teaching methods and materials, TESOL instructors can require students to create and explain the rationale for original methods and materials for a particular group of students in a specific education setting—a public sixth-grade class with ESL students, a university conversation class in Japan, a walk-in adult education program at a local community center. Instead of asking students to define and explain the steps in evaluating a language program, TESOL instructors should have their students evaluate an actual language program. If no program is available, students might develop a hypothetical new one to include determining needs, defining resources, setting goals and objectives, developing content and materials, and creating methods for assessment.

One positive aspect of such assessments is that students can gather and share information and complete their work collaboratively—all online. They can search databases and share articles from the university library; upload materials for group members to evaluate; discuss strategies in blogs, wikis, and discussion boards; converse about progress in chat rooms, and literally co-create authentic materials or evaluations to be assessed through tools such as Google Documents, all while sharing in the writing and editing through cyberspace. The result will be assessments that reflect the skills that students will use during their professional careers as ESL and EFL educators. They may also include them in electronic portfolios to share with prospective employers at home or abroad.

TABLE 4.4 Authenticity do's and don'ts.

Authenticity do's	Authenticity don'ts
• Create your own task-based assessments for individuals, pairs, or groups • Have students create their own assessments and select those that will be used for the class	• Do not rely too heavily on assessments from the course text or texts

In many ways, the online teaching and learning environment can foster authenticity in ways that a traditional class might not, such as by grouping students with different resources to work together toward a common goal. Using one example above, TESOL instructors might pair a student physically in Japan with another in the United States to create materials for a Japanese university conversation class or an American intensive English program writing class. There is no reason that a virtual learning space should ever by its nature limit authenticity in assessment.

Each of these four concepts—validity, reliability, practicality, and authenticity—contributes in some way to ensuring that all assessments, including those done online, are effective in the meeting the needs of teachers and students. Considering each one when developing a new course will help to ensure that assessments will truly measure whether students meet course goals and objectives and, as a result, become more effective ESL and EFL practitioners. Table 4.4 summarizes several directions TESOL instructors might follow to design authentic online assessments for their classes.

Conclusions

This chapter addresses assessment for online TESOL, though many of the concepts discussed can be applied to any online pedagogical environment. The examples might be different, but any field of study can include both formative and summative and traditional and alternative assessment instruments and methods. Further, all meaningful assessments, regardless of field, must demonstrate validity and reliability, and best serve both educators and students by being practical and authentic.

The chapter does not address any particular course management system. Though these systems are all similar, they may vary slightly in their capabilities and details for the practicalities of use. Nonetheless, the concepts discussed should apply in general to all such systems. It therefore falls to individual teachers, departments, programs, or schools to determine which particular course management system works best for their needs.

Finally, no individual chapter can address all of the challenges an educator will face in teaching and assessing students online. It is hoped that this one provides a start for those who have the rewarding opportunity to do so.

Discussion Questions

1. What are the primary assessment challenges facing online TESOL educators today? How might these challenges change as new technologies are developed?
2. Define *validity, reliability, practicality,* and *authenticity* in the context of assessment.
3. What is the relationship among the assessment concepts discussed in this chapter? In practice, can you see ways that implementing one would effect implementation of others? Explain.
4. How does the online environment affect the application of these concepts for TESOL courses?

References

Angelo, T. (1995) Reassessing (and defining) assessment. *The AAHE Bulletin, 48*(2), 7–9.
Brown, H. D., & Abeywickrama, P. (2010) *Language assessment: Principles and classroom practices* (2nd edn). White Plains, NY: Pearson Education.
Hill, J., & Hannafin, M. J. (2001) Teaching and learning in digital environments: The resurgence of resource-based learning. *Educational Technology Research and Development, 49*(3), 37–52.
Twigg, C. A. (2001) Innovations in online learning: Moving beyond no significant difference. Retrieved September 28, 2011, from http://www.thencat.org/Monographs/Mono4.pdf

5

REFLECTIONS ON LEARNING TESOL AT A DISTANCE

Miranda Legg and John S. Knox

Language-teacher education by distance is a prevalent practice, with well over 100 institutions offering TESOL qualifications by distance, and a large increase in the numbers in recent years (Hall & Knox, 2009a). Volumes such as those by Holmberg, Shelley & White (2005), Richards & Roe (1994), and the current one, attest to the rise in interest of the distance education of TESOL teachers as an important site of professional practice, and therefore an important area for research in Applied Linguistics.

At the same time, the field of Applied Linguistics has seen a recent interest in the status of introspection and reflective narratives. This is evident most notably in the volume by Nunan & Choi (2010a), where experienced scholars in Applied Linguistics and related fields share and explore narratives of their own learning journeys. As Nunan & Choi argue (and as their collection demonstrates), narratives of participants in social sites can make an important contribution to the overall knowledge of any set of social practices. And to date, the narratives of learners are under-represented in the literature on language-teacher education by distance.

In what follows, we wish to give accounts of our experiences as distance learners of TESOL/Applied Linguistics, in order that a focus on particular aspects of our own experiences might uncover issues that resonate with the growing community of former and current learners in our field who have studied/are studying by distance. In sharing these experiences, we have adapted the guidelines in Nunan & Choi (2010b), and have included:

> a brief [distance] learning history; one or two narrative events or critical incidents that occurred while learning [TESOL by distance] ... and that highlighted some aspect of [learning TESOL by distance] or the interconnections

between [aspects]; and a commentary on the narratives. ... [E]ither present the background, narratives and commentary separately, or ... weave these elements together.

(p. 1)

In writing our individual sections for this chapter, we did not consult or share our contributions until each one was basically complete. Rather than editing them to attempt to make them conform to one another, we decided they should stand, as their differences say things about us as individuals, just as their similarities say things about us as members of the community of former and current students who have studied TESOL by distance.

Miranda

My first experience of distance learning was as a part-time distance learning student on the MA in Applied Linguistics at Macquarie University in Australia. When I first started the MA I had been teaching English as a Second Language mainly to adults for five years—two and a half years in Slovakia and two and a half years at the British Council in Hong Kong. I had moved from Slovakia to Hong Kong to do the RSA DELTA and had stayed on in Hong Kong as a full-time teacher. After completing the DELTA and taking a rest for a year and a half, I felt ready to start an MA. Even though I had some reservations about studying through a distance learning program, I had heard good reports about this program and liked the idea of doing an Australian qualification (as an Australian myself). In the following, I would like to share some of the challenges I experienced as a distance learning student and I believe that these challenges are common for most distance learning students. These include the importance of meaningful scaffolding activities, the difficulty of developing an academic voice and the lack of a supportive community.

The Importance of Meaningful Scaffolding Activities

Most of the courses on the MA program I took required us to participate in online discussions. Discussion topics were set and we were asked to post a reply and reply to the posts of others. However, almost all of these discussions failed in that many students did not participate at all, and those that did, rarely if at all, replied to the posts of others. Biggs (2003) highlights the educational value of discussion. "Good dialogue elicits those activities that shape, elaborate and deepen understanding." The discussions that were happening in the online classrooms that I attended did not tend to shape, elaborate or deepen my understanding of academic concepts. I suspect that this was largely because of the way that the tasks were written, and also because students did not understand the educational value of active participation.

As a teacher, I know that writing challenging and engaging discussion questions is not easy. Bloom's taxonomy attempts to categorize different activity verbs according to their level of cognitive difficulty and this can be a useful starting point for analyzing discussion topics. At one end of the taxonomy you have verbs which ask students to display knowledge ("tell", "list", "describe"). A little more cognitively difficult are comprehension verbs ("explain", "discuss", "describe"). Next on the spectrum are application verbs ("compare", "classify"). The most cognitively difficult are analysis ("analyze", "investigate"), synthesis ("create", "propose") and lastly evaluation ("justify", "judge"). The discussions that I participated in were far more effective when students were given tasks from the more cognitively difficult end of the spectrum. Yet this was rare and the result was that there were few opportunities for meaningful scaffolding of learning (see Vygotsky 1978 for the concept of scaffolding of learning).

As mentioned above, my experience has also been that students didn't seem to understand that real learning can take place through these discussion activities, evidenced by the lack of active participation by the majority of students. This was the case, even though a percentage of the final mark was usually given for "active participation." Students seemed to believe that displaying knowledge was sufficient for active participation and no guidance was given to explain that active participation is actually more than this.

Now, I can see that introducing us to the concept of transactivity (Berkowitz & Gibbs, 1983) could have helped us to understand what kind of participation is valued in a scaffolding activity such as discussion. Transactivity is the way in which students build on the contribution of other students and teachers. Discussions that have high scaffolding potential are those where there is a high level of transactivity. Any assessment of online discussion must be able to identify different levels of transactivity and explain these to students.

Understanding is deepened through interaction with other students and teachers. The theory of social constructivism (Berger & Luckmann, 1966) is a useful one to foreground here. Knowledge construction is more effective in learning settings where students and teachers negotiate academic arguments together. For this to happen, there needs to be interaction in some form between teachers and students. Discussion forums, chat rooms, video conferencing all promise interactivity. Can these distance learning tools be used effectively to promote the social construction of knowledge? My personal experience has been "no" but I believe that it does have the potential to achieve this. I also found that there were certain classes which would have benefited greatly from the integration of collaborative completion of online tasks. I took one compulsory class on Systemic Functional Linguistics. This course came with an extensive set of notes along with a course book. However, Systemic Functional Linguistics, I soon found, was a challenging form of discourse analysis. It required a certain level of subjective analysis and I struggled greatly with the text analysis assignment. What I was missing were those group-based scaffolding tasks often found in a classroom setting—where students work on the completion of a task together. I wanted an opportunity to work on an analysis of a text with a small group of students, try out my ideas, get feedback, and attempt to negotiate a final interpretation of the text with fellow students for eventual feedback from the teacher. Although this might be difficult to set up online, I believe that this would have been a very valuable experience for me and would have saved me a lot of time struggling by myself with text analysis.

Developing an Academic Voice

One other challenge for me was developing a writing style that was appropriate for an MA student. It took me some time to acquire an academic voice. My only other postgraduate learning experience had been the DELTA. I had learned a lot in this course. I had refined my pedagogical skills. However, it was much more of a practical qualification than an academic one, and the type of writing that I did for the DELTA, I quickly learned, was not appropriate for an MA.

To write this chapter, I went back and read the feedback I gained on assignments from my MA course. One of the first assignments I did was on Language Teaching Methodology. Looking at the comments on the assignment for this course was very revealing. They show a student who was not yet able to express her academic voice. Here are just some of the comments that I was given:

> In several places you need to tighten your arguments. There are quite a lot of sweeping statements that are unsupported by evidence e.g. reference to the literature, to research or to theory relevant to the topic. When this happens it makes the writing look too personal and subjective"
>
> People who get A grades always do this [tie their arguments to theoretical ideas]. The practical, concrete and specific things you are explaining are not clearly "framed" and located in the theoretical ideas in the literature.

I owe a lot to the teacher who took the time to write this feedback (two sides of A4 paper in total). She clearly spent a lot of time explaining this to me. Developing an academic voice takes time, I would argue, it is harder and probably takes more time in a distance program than a face-to-face program. Much of the development of academic communicative competence happens in the classroom, through feedback with teachers and interaction with other students. Just hearing other students and teachers voicing academic ideas, listening to the reaction of others to these ideas, practicing voicing these ideas is very valuable. It is through this interaction that students start to get a sense of the standards, of what is valued and not valued in an academic context. It is through interaction that enculturation happens. If this kind of enculturation happens in the face-to-face classroom, we need to find a way to achieve this online as well. This is difficult without establishing real connections online—a sense of community.

Establishing a Community

The last challenge that I would like to discuss, is that of the need for distance students and teachers to establish a real sense of a community somehow online. Any type of scaffolding activity is a lot more difficult and, I would argue, less effective, when one does not feel part of a community.

At the beginning of every online discussion forum on the MA course we were required to "introduce" ourselves online. We shared our names, where we worked, what country we were from, a bit about our past teaching experience, and so on. However, that was not sufficient to really build a supportive and collaborative community. The lack of interaction online was evidence of that. Throughout the MA course I felt that I was missing out on a chance to engage in academic discussion, academic debate. I felt that I could have been pushed more in an academic community of peers than I could push myself.

Because of this, I tried to create a community for myself. I tried to set up a writing group amongst my colleagues who were also studying distance postgraduate qualifications. There were three of us at my workplace. However, this felt unsatisfying as we were always studying different subjects and the discussions became largely knowledge exchange rather than cognitively challenging discussions. I audited some MA classes at a university in Hong Kong; yet again, I didn't feel like I was able to really engage with fellow students about the concepts that I was studying at that time. What I really needed was to be able to establish a supportive community with the students on my course, even though they were scattered around the world. To be honest, I am at a loss for how to solve this problem and I believe this to be the biggest barrier to effective learning online.

I am now working at the University of Hong Kong and doing a PhD, yes, distance learning through Macquarie University. I still feel that I am missing out in some respect by doing my study in distance mode. However, it has probably made me a more independent learner, more reflective, and maybe even a better teacher who understands the importance of interaction, scaffolding and rapport building in the classroom.

John

I had been teaching in a Thai university on the northern edge of Bangkok for almost two years, when I saw an advertisement in the *Bangkok Post* to study for a master's degree in Applied Linguistics by distance. The timing was good. I was not viewing Applied Linguistics as a lifelong career at this point, but I was teaching language and enjoying it, learning language and enjoying it, and figured that a master's degree earned while living and working abroad would probably serve me well in years to come. I was already looking at possibilities for postgraduate study, and the advertisement was offering the right thing in the right place at the right time. I contacted the local representative, sent my letter (there was no email or website then), completed my application, and was in the first distance intake of the program beginning August 1994.

I have a number of recollections from that time that have stayed with me— some of them anecdotes, some of them short flashes of memory. I have a strong recollection of struggling to "re-acquaint myself with my native language," as I liked to put it then. The struggle to read, write, and be fluent in academic English, while surrounded by no one who was sharing my study experience, took some time to come to terms with. Years later, I realized that I had not been re-acquainting myself with anything. I was, in fact, learning a new register, a functional variety of language with typical meanings related to a specific contextual configuration (Halliday & Hasan, 1989), and this understanding, gained with hindsight, has helped me in selecting readings for my own students (distance and on-campus), in developing materials for my learners, and (I like to think) in my own writing.

The social aspect of distance learning is key to a number of my important recollections from that time. I remember talking with other (former) distance students, and sharing our impressions of our teachers. It was fascinating that we could come to such consistent conclusions about people whom we had met only through course notes, and handwritten feedback on assignments.

A related recollection has to do with assignments and the learning process. I was studying a course on Systemic Functional Grammar, which turned out to be very influential for me. As I worked through the course, there were aspects I did and did not understand, and a particularly challenging aspect of the theory was presented towards the end of the course (where, pedagogically, it belonged). As I neared the end of the course, and the deadline for submission for the two text analyses on which I was to be assessed, I realized that an intense and uninterrupted period of work was going to be necessary. I still remember closing the curtains and pulling the telephone out of the wall (we used to physically plug them in to the network, back then), literally cutting myself off from the world for a number of days in order to do what needed to be done to understand the content, analyze the texts, and get the assignments submitted.

The feeling of sealing and posting the envelope containing those assignments is difficult to verbalize. There was some relief, some sense of achievement and even excitement at what I felt I had accomplished, but the overwhelming sense was of walking blindfolded along the edge of a cliff, and not being certain whether the next footfall would land on *terra firma* or thin air. In fact, much of my early experience of distance study felt like this, and it is something easily recalled when dealing with enquiries from students who are unsure of what is required (cf. Hall & Knox, 2009a, p. 73).

In later semesters, I had much greater confidence and understanding of what I was doing: I had the benefit of feedback from earlier courses, a wider knowledge of the literature from earlier reading, and a better system for working through materials. Also, in later semesters, I had become quite used to exploring the relations between the theories of Applied Linguistics I was learning, my personal pedagogical philosophy, and the day-to-day realities of my teaching context; and the way these relations played out in the development and implementation of curricula (Knox, 1999, 2007), and in the broader context of the education system in Thailand (Knox, 1996, 1997).

Over the course of my distance studies, I developed academic independence. But in the early semesters, I was largely unsure of myself, my understanding of the concepts I was studying, and the quality of my submitted work. With no fellow students to talk with, and no affordable way to have fast communication with my teachers, I just had to deal with this and get on with it. I think it made me a better learner.

When I started studying by distance, I could not use a computer, and the Internet was just becoming publicly available in Thailand. My early assignments were handwritten, and my partner taught me to use a computer in my second semester of study. The popular operating system we used then had no graphical user interface, and I learned to type the appropriate DOS commands at the C:\ prompt to get into my word processor. In 1995, we were among the first users of email in Thailand, and our Internet account gave us text-only access to the world wide web. I still recall our amazement as we typed in commands, watching the delay as they registered and controlled actions on computers on the other side of the world.

Reflecting on these experiences (and others they bring to mind), a number of key issues are raised for me. The first has to do with my identity (cf. Nunan & Choi, 2010a), as a distance student, and later as an applied linguist: an identity that evolved as I participated in the discourse (connected stretches of language that make sense in context) and "played" the Discourse (ways of acting through language that are ideological and identify the language user as a member of a certain group or groups) of each role, (Gee, 1990, p. 142). My distance studies brought me membership of what Swales (1990, pp. 24–7) would identify as the discourse community of applied linguists (who have a broadly agreed set of goals, established mechanisms of communication, specific genres and lexis, and expert membership). But it was years later, working in a university where my identity changed to "applied linguist" instead of "English teacher," that the social bonds of a workplace (more akin to Swales' "speech community," with socialization, group solidarity, and a tendency "to absorb people into that general fabric"—Swales, 1990, p. 24) allowed that identity to take hold.

The second key issue, obviously related to the first, is the social aspect of teaching and learning. One of my clearest and earliest lessons in this regard was in humility and flexibility. As a teacher, I had been incredibly strict on deadlines with submitted work. By the end of my first semester "at the other end" of the distance classroom, I had remembered my own predilections as a student, and the familiar sound that deadlines make as they fly by. And I was strongly reminded in my studies of the value of teachers who were flexible enough to grant extensions.

More fundamental, perhaps, was my experience of developing academic independence discussed above. This process was productive and valuable for me, but, as with everything, there was a cost. And the cost was a strong sense of isolation and uncertainty, something which is discussed in the literature on language-teacher education by distance (Hall & Knox, 2009b, p. 222). I was fortunate that, at a later point in my studies, two work colleagues also became distance students in the same program, and the sense of camaraderie and support that we developed became an important source of academic and social sustenance.

But my early experience of isolation, coupled with my positive experiences of support from my distance teachers, had a strong impact, later, on my own practices as a distance teacher. Online discussions, which became much more readily available between the time I stopped studying (in 1997) and started teaching by distance (in 2000), represented to me (and still do) a forum where much of the interaction I missed in my early studies could take place (cf. Biesenbach-Lucas, 2003; Kamhi-Stein, 2000).

I am still excited by advances in technology and the social potential they create. I have reservations about individual privacy, and the collection and use of massive quantities of personal information by commercial, governmental, and criminal organizations. But the growth of email, the world wide web, and social networking media mean that distance learning is very different from what it was when I studied by distance. Learners can and do form social networks online, within and without their classes. Collaborative projects can be done on wikis; debates held in online discussion forums; questions about assignments and course content asked by email; content delivered by video. Technology, for those who have access to it, has greatly reduced the kind of isolation I first experienced as a distance student, and also opened pedagogical possibilities that were not possible at that time, but that are now widely used in both face-to-face and distance programs (cf. Hall & Knox, 2009a, pp. 74–75).

The care and professionalism I experienced in the way that feedback was provided to me as a distance student had an immediate impact on my own teaching in the face-to-face language classroom, and a lasting impact in the way I give feedback in my own distance teaching. Putting "the interpersonal" into written feedback is time consuming: it takes longer to write personalized and "tempered" comments than it does to write, for example, a single question mark in a margin; it takes longer to comment on the positive aspects of a piece of writing than to work on the assumption that the student knows "no news is good news." But as a distance learner, something I discovered is that much of the teaching is done in the marking, and in a teacher-learner relationship mediated across long distances, the construal of the relationship between teacher and learner is also of great importance.

My experience as a distance student has also had an impact on my subsequent work in relation to administration. The resources available on the world wide web when I began teaching by distance were exponentially more plentiful, and more useful than those that had been available when I finished my distance studies, and I was involved with a number of colleagues in collecting and maintaining links and information on such resources in a single place for distance students. On committees, I found that it was constantly necessary to advocate for "equal rights" for distance students, who often represent a "forgotten cohort" when university practices and policies are designed and implemented. Fortunately, there are many colleagues in my department and in other parts of the university who are similarly aware of the needs of distance students, but we are still a minority.

In sum, largely as a result of my personal experience as a distance learner, I am a strong believer in the benefits of distance education and its value for TESOL teacher education. Further, I believe that the role of the teacher educator in distance TESOL teacher education programs includes a strong degree of responsibility for developing practices and opportunities for social relations to develop. At the same time, as adult learners and practicing or trainee teachers, (prospective) TESOL teachers studying by distance can benefit from the independence that comes from distance study, and the sense of achievement brought by the hard work, independent study, and self-reliance that distance study requires.

Discussion

As stated in the introduction, we wrote our accounts of our experiences as learners of TESOL by distance separately. As graduates of the same program, and colleagues who have shared distance-learning experiences in a number of roles, it is perhaps unsurprising that we raised similar issues in our respective pieces (though the degree of similarity did surprise us). These similarities include our experience of assessment feedback, the challenges of studying detailed theory in isolation from other students, the formation of communities among distance learners, and the technological possibilities for making this happen. At the same time, we differ in the potential we see for technology in community building.

In conclusion, we would like to highlight one factor that, in retrospect, runs through both our pieces: the role of the teacher-learner relationship in distance TESOL programs. For both of us, the *teaching* we received as distance learners—both positive and negative—had a significant impact on our learning experiences and our recollection of the program. The process of personal reflection on our journeys has highlighted the impact that the pedagogical practices of language-teacher education mediated across distance—practices that include task development and implementation, assessment and feedback, materials development, use of technology, and development of effective teacher-learner relationships—has had on our lives as students and teachers. The pedagogical practices of language-teacher education are in many ways amplified in importance for distance students, whose need for community in the learning process, and for quality *teaching*, is no less than for students studying face-to-face.

Discussion Questions

1. How might learner narratives be employed as a pedagogical tool in a course you are familiar with? What kind of reflection would be most productive? How much guidance and direction would be most effective in directing the learners to produce narratives?
2. How important is it for a language teacher to learn to "develop an academic voice"? Is this something that gives distance learners access to a broader community of practice, or distracts them from their development as a practitioner?

3.   What are the qualities of a good distance student of TESOL, and a good distance TESOL teacher educator? How can these qualities best be developed?

References

Berger, P. L., & Luckmann, T. (1966) *The social construction of reality: A treatise in the sociology of knowledge*. London: Allen Lane.

Berkowitz, M., & Gibbs, J. (1983) Measuring the developmental features of moral discussion. *Merrill-Palmer Quarterly: Journal of Developmental Psychology, 29*(4), 399–410.

Biesenbach-Lucas, S. (2003) Asynchronous discussion groups in teacher training classes: Perceptions of native and non-native students. *Journal of Asynchronous Learning Networks, 7*(3), 24–46.

Biggs, J. (2003) *Teaching for quality learning at university* (2nd ed.). Buckingham: The Society for Research into Higher Education and Open University Press.

Gee, J. P. (1990) *Social linguistics and literacies: Ideology in discourses*. London: The Falmer Press.

Hall, D. R., & Knox, J. S. (2009a) Issues in the education of TESOL teachers by distance education. *Distance Education, 30*(1), 63–85.

Hall, D. R., & Knox, J. S. (2009b) Language teacher education by distance. In A. Burns & J. C. Richards (Eds), *Cambridge guide to second language teacher education* (pp. 218–229). Cambridge: Cambridge University Press.

Halliday, M. A. K., & Hasan, R. (1989) *Language, context, and text: Aspects of language in a social-semiotic perspective* (2nd edn). Oxford: Oxford University Press.

Holmberg, B., Shelley, M., & White, C. (Eds) (2005) *Distance education and languages: Evolution and change*. Clevedon: Multilingual Matters.

Kamhi-Stein, L. D. (2000) Looking to the future of TESOL teacher education: Web-based bulletin board discussions in a methods course. *TESOL Quarterly, 34*(3), 423–455.

Knox, J. S. (1996) Choice in English testing methods: A case for communicative language testing in Thailand. *Studies in Language and Language Teaching: Occasional Papers, 6*, 1–8.

Knox, J. S. (1997) Standing at the portals of power: English language education as a foreign gatekeeping encounter. Unpublished Master of Applied Linguistics dissertation, Macquarie University, Sydney. Available online at: http://www.ling.mq.edu.au/about/staff/knox_john/knox_1997.pdf

Knox, J. S. (1999) Culture and language: What do our students need? *ThaiTESOL Bulletin, 12*(1), 41–52.

Knox, J. S. (2007) Foreign eyes on Thailand: An ESP project for EFL learners. In A. Burns & H. de Silva Joyce (Eds.), *Planning and teaching creatively within a required curriculum for adults* (pp. 119–142). Alexandria, VA: TESOL, Inc.

Nunan, D., & Choi, J. (Eds.) (2010a) *Language and culture: Reflective narratives and the emergence of identity*. New York and London: Routledge.

Nunan, D., & Choi, J. (2010b) Language, culture, and identity: Framing the issues. In D. Nunan & J. Choi (Eds), *Language and culture: Reflective narratives and the emergence of identity* (pp. 1–13). New York and London: Routledge.

Richards, K., & Roe, P. (Eds) (1994) *Distance learning in ELT*. London: Macmillan.

Swales, J. (1990) *Genre Analysis: English in academic and research settings*. Cambridge: Cambridge University Press.

Vygotsky, L. S. (1978) *Mind in society: The development of higher mental processes*. Cambridge, MA: Harvard University Press

6

LIFE AFTER ONLINE LEARNING

Fiona Copland and Sue Garton

Introduction

Aston University is a relatively small institute in Birmingham, UK. It has been conducting distance-learning TESOL programs (often called online programs in other countries) since 1988, when materials were sent through the post and communication was by phone and fax. Today, the program, like most similar programs, is delivered online via a virtual learning environment, and communications are generally by email, Skype and Elluminate. During its existence, the program team has developed an ethos of distance-learning whereby Aston sees itself at a distance from the course participants rather than the other way around (see Garton & Edge, this volume and Garton & Richards, 2007). Tutors at Aston believe that course participants are at an advantage by being in their research sites (their classrooms/schools) and have developed the concept of "situated learning" to explain the relationship between participants, research site and tutors and the focus is on theorizing from practice. Although such an approach might be followed by other universities for similar reasons, there have been no attempts, as far as we are aware, to ascertain whether this belief that participants are advantaged by staying at their research sites is actually beneficial. In particular, there appears to be little information as to the long-term benefits of such programs after participants have left the course. In this chapter, we aim to address this gap by drawing on data from three questionnaires administered to distance-learning students in 2000 and 2010 and on-campus students in 2011. We aim to look at the skills that distant learning students acquire from the program and the long-term benefits to their careers and professional development. The data from the on-campus students' questionnaire will provide a point of comparison between "traditional" program delivery and online learning.

Background

Distance education has become increasingly popular. According to the U.S. Department of Education National Center for Education Statistics, in 2007–2008, nearly 4.3 million undergraduates took at least one distance education course (http://nces.ed.gov/fastfacts/display.asp?id=80). A similar trend can be identified for language teacher education with an increase from around 23 programs in the early to mid-1990s to over 120 in 2009 (Hall & Knox, 2009). The increase has led to a plethora of studies investigating various aspects of distance learning. These studies have recently tended to focus on pedagogy and good practice (for example, Salmon, 2000; Tam, 2000; King, 2002; Parvan et al., 2003; Rovai and Barnum, 2003), cultural aspects of distance-learning provision (for example, Wilson, 2001 and Fay & Hill, 2003) and student support (for example, Hyland, 2001; Motteram & Forrester, 2005; Forrester et al., 2005). Within these general areas of research a number of advantages of distance learning in TESOL, from both an educational and professional point of view, are identified. However, to our present knowledge, no study has performed a follow-up with participants to investigate the advantages that distance-learning programs may have on learners in terms of their professional development as teachers once the program is over. This chapter represents an initial step towards filling that gap.

Professional Advantages of Distance-Learning TESOL Programs

Although the advantages of distance learning in TESOL are well documented, it is worthwhile to briefly review the main claims made.

First of all, as Hall and Knox (2009) note, distance learning is a particularly appropriate mode for the mobile population of English language teachers. There are good practical reasons for this in that few English language teachers can afford to give up their jobs for a year and study full-time on-campus. What is more, teachers of English, particularly from English-speaking countries, often change their place, or even country, of work. By enrolling in an online program, they can continue their study despite changes in their professional circumstances.

Second, distance learning allows teachers to become part of the global TESOL community through the interactions they have with colleagues around the world who are also simultaneously engaged in similar studies (Nunan, 2002).

However, perhaps the biggest advantage claimed for online programs in TESOL lies in the possibility afforded for situated learning (Garton & Edge, this volume, Hall & Knox, 2009; Nunan, 2002). One of the problems with an on-campus program of study is that the work done there is separate from its point of application, i.e. the teacher's local context. New ideas are encountered but cannot be applied or investigated until the course is over and the teacher returns to his/her institution. At that stage, there may be some discontinuity since the teacher has little time to experiment with new ideas due to teaching commitments. Employers may not be amenable to the idea of classroom investigations, something returning teachers may wish to undertake. What is more, expert advisers from the university are not on hand to discuss issues and outcomes of this research. As Widdowson (1990, p. 65) put it:

> With such programs there is, however, a persistent problem of renewal of connection with the classroom ... What happens very often here is that participants are inspired by the social and professional intensity of the event but find they have little to carry home with them except a heady sense of general enlightenment which is often quickly dispersed on its contact with reality.

Distance learning, on the other hand, encourages teachers to investigate new ideas and approaches as part of their course of study, in the context of a supportive online community and with a reliable link to an academic centre.

It could be assumed, therefore, that distance-learning courses give teachers an advantage over teachers studying in on-campus programs in a number of areas. These include identifying key issues in their contexts, developing a research agenda, acquiring research tools and strategies, designing and implementing research projects and evaluating research. Moreover, it is hoped that such knowledge and skills will continue to be of use in ongoing professional development, even after the program of study is over. Results from our surveys seem to corroborate this claim, but also reveal further benefits of distance learning.

Data and Participants

Data for the study were collected from three questionnaires. The first was a paper questionnaire, sent out to distance learning alumni in 2000 (at that time, online survey tools were less readily available). A similar questionnaire, with many of the same questions was sent via Survey Monkey to alumni in 2010 (a maximum of 10 alumni may have answered both questionnaires). Finally, a questionnaire was sent to alumni of on-campus TESOL programs in 2011. This survey was slightly adapted to take into account the fact that the mode of delivery was different. Altogether, 41 alumni answered the 2000 survey, 44 answered the distance learning survey in 2010,[1] and 16 answered the on-campus survey in 2011 (out of a possible 58). It should be noted that the on-campus program first enrolled students in 2007.

All three questionnaires focused on the following areas: current job situation; perceived benefits of higher qualification for career progression and financial reward; learning experiences on the different masters' programs; and participation in the wider TESOL community via publications, conference presentations and involvement in professional organizations. The questionnaires comprised a combination of open and closed questions in order to obtain both quantitative and qualitative data about graduates' post-learning experiences.

TABLE 6.1 Career prospects of DL students

	2000		2010		
	Yes	No	Yes	No	
Get/retain job	26	14	34	10	
Financial gain	26	9	31	10	
Promotion	32	6	30	8	5 maybe

Findings

In this section, we will first discuss the data from the surveys to distance learning students before comparing the findings with the small on-campus data set. The purpose of the comparison is to investigate whether the benefits identified by the distance learning students seem to be particular to this mode or whether on-campus students identify the same benefits.

Career Benefits

The majority of respondents work in universities (24 out of 41 in 2000 and 24 out of 44 in 2010), with much smaller numbers working in secondary schools, private language schools, companies or freelance. No respondent either worked or works in a primary school.

To examine the effects of the MSc on career progression, respondents were asked whether the course had helped them to get or retain their current position, whether they are financially better off as a result of the MSc and whether the qualification had helped them gain promotion or develop their careers. Table 6.1 shows that around two thirds of alumni believe that the course had helped their career prospects in all three areas.

A higher percentage of participants in 2010 felt that the MSc helped them to get or retain their job (77.3% as opposed to 63.4% in 2000). This seems to confirm anecdotal evidence that, in institutions such as universities for example, a master's level qualification is now a requirement.

When the 2000 and 2010 respondents were asked how the qualification helped career progression, they indicated a number of factors, which do not appear to have changed over time. These concerned:

1.   The need for a master's qualification to get a job, particularly though not exclusively in universities as already mentioned. For example:

Without a Master's degree, this position would simply not have been open to me (2000).

I need an MA/MSc for my current university job. This was only possible after completing my Master's (2010).

2. Gaining promotion or being given greater responsibility as a direct result of the qualification:

    Requirement of promotion into management (2000).

    Now EAL coordinator in the school (2010).

3. Gaining research skills and/or the confidence leading to publication and/or conference presentation:

    I had already embarked on a writing career when I started at Aston. However, I feel that it would have stagnated very quickly without the confidence and capability which I gained doing the Master's. Barely a working day goes by in which I don't refer back in some way to the books, materials and ideas which I first came across during the course (2000).

    In some cases, publication led to promotion. This was the case with the extract below, for example:

    It taught me how to do research and write papers on the field, which I needed to get a promotion. People at work wanted to give me the promotion, but they would not have been able to do so if I hadn't written a couple of papers (2010).

4. Being part of a network, having developed contacts as part of their program. In some cases, knowing fellow graduates also led directly to being hired for a new position:

    I'm more fully engaged in the field of TEFL; have more professional contacts (2000).

    The national and international networks I participated in helped me to develop professionally (2010).

5. Knowledge and skills needed to be a better teacher:

    Develop as a teacher, most certainly (2000).

    At a practical level it helped me to question the teaching materials I used/ use (2010).

Participation in the TESOL Community

Although previous research points to the participation in the global educational community as a key advantage of distance learning (see, for example, Nunan, 2002), our data, as indicated in comments about publishing above, show that such participation may extend to the much wider professional TESOL community as well.

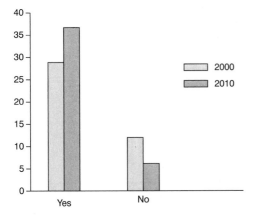

FIGURE 6.1 Number of MSc TESOL students who have presented at a conference

Figure 6.1 shows that a large majority of graduates from the MSc TESOL programs have presented at conferences. These range from international conferences such as TESOL, JALT and IATEFL to local conferences, with some respondents presenting as many as 15 or 20 papers (and in one case, more than 40).

The number of respondents who have published in either journals or books is also high, with just over half having done so in 2000 with an increase to two-thirds in 2010 (Table 6.2 shows the types of publications achieved by the 2010 respondents). Again, the increase in the figures from 2000 to 2010 could be due to the growing pressure on university staff to publish, as the quote above seems to indicate.

However, the 2000 cohort included some prolific writers who had published a very high number of papers (around 40 in two cases). The 2000 respondents included graduates from as long ago as 1988 with the majority from the mid-1990s, therefore making the time period referred to much longer than that of the 2010 questionnaire. These results may be an indication that graduates from the program continue to publish long after their studies have concluded, possibly due to continued job pressures or because such writers maintain their commitment to the TESOL profession over a period of time. Whatever the reason, these figures offer some evidence of the enduring nature of a professional developmental process that begins (or at least gains momentum) with a distance learning TESOL program.

Further evidence of participation in the wider TESOL community can be seen in responses to the open question, "What else do you think you have achieved professionally since completing your MSc?" Four respondents in 2000 and five in 2010 pointed to involvement in professional organizations such as JALT and TESOL Arabia. For example, one 2010 respondent wrote:

> I have become more active in the TESOL Arabia community as a member of the TESOL Arabia Conference organizing committee.

TABLE 6.2 Types of publications achieved by respondents in 2010

Publication	Number
Book chapters	10
Internal/institutional journals	9
Country-specific journals	9
Conference proceedings	8
Peer-reviewed international journals	7
Course books	7
Professional magazines	3
Edited collections	2
Books	1

Further Qualifications

It is noticeable that a number of graduates from MSc TESOL programs have gone on to further study. Of the 2000 survey, 34.1% said they had continued with their professional studies, the number increasing slightly in 2010 to 37.5%. Out of the number of respondents, 12 were either taking or had completed a doctorate both in 2000 and 2010. One person indicated explicitly that the MSc had prepared him/her for a PhD study.

Confidence

Many of the respondents in both 2000 and 2010 indicated that they had gained more confidence as a result of their MSc studies. This seems to be an important aspect of such studies and yet it has been generally neglected in the literature. This confidence was linked to many different aspects of professional and academic identity. Some respondents simply pointed to their increased poise as teachers:

> I could gain some confidence to teach English (2000).

> To be more confident in my own judgments about how and what I teach (2010).

Others linked their classroom confidence to their knowledge about the language as a result of the master's program:

> To know the theory of language is as important as developing practical ideas (gives confidence) (2000).

> I now have much more confidence in answering questions from learners about the intricacies of English (2010).

Others pointed to their increased confidence in their dealings with others:

I can give my opinions to other teachers confidently (2010).

Confidence to present my own teaching agenda (2010).

A number of respondents linked confidence to their participation in the wider community as writers and presenters:

Gave me the confidence to make my 1st JALT presentation (2000).

It gave me confidence to try my hand at writing EFL books (2000).

Writing and presenting are important and I have the confidence and desire to do them which I didn't really know about before Aston (2010).

Becoming a Researcher/Reflective Practitioner

Alumni from both surveys highlighted the value of the MSc TESOL program for developing as a researcher, although this aspect seemed to have greater importance for the 2010 cohort. For some, the research skills they learned were particularly beneficial, for example, in terms of learning appropriate methods for researching their own context. One participant wrote in 2010, in response to the question about the two most significant things learned on the MSc, that he/she had gained the knowledge to:

Research [effectively] and how to be reflective of my own practice so that classroom outcomes improve (2010).

A number of respondents pointed to the value of doing research and how research can be empowering as the following extract, responding to the same question, reflects:

I learned that academic research can be an effective vehicle for effective public service (2010).

Research skills were certainly present in the 2000 survey, with one participant saying, for example:

I gained a "compass" for orientation in the world of TESOL research (2000).

while another said one of the best things he/she learned was an:

Enduring interest in researching my own context (2000).

However, there was less emphasis on research skills in the earlier survey. This could be due to updates that were made to the program materials in 2004 where greater *explicit* emphasis was placed on the development of such skills, possibly making participants more conscious of this aspect of their studies. This is a potentially interesting difference between distance learning and on-campus study, where indirect messages may be more likely to permeate discussions in which students participate (see below for the comparison with on-campus students), thus underlining the importance of explicitness in distance learning materials.

Developing Knowledge and Skills, Including Study Skills

Respondents indicated a number of areas where they thought the program had helped them to develop their knowledge of the field, either generally:

> A greater awareness of my craft from a variety of theoretical perspectives (2010).

> It gave me an excellent foundation in applied linguistics (2000).

or in specific areas:

> My worst grade was in the Analysis of Written Discourse module. But ironically I found it fascinating, and the module led me to read several books on grammar that completely changed my previous ignorance on the subject (2010).

> About evaluating course books for the course and syllabus design assignment: Obviously doing this and designing courses is a key part of setting up a new language school (2000).

The identification of specific areas of knowledge, and especially knowledge about language, was particularly prevalent amongst the respondents to the 2000 survey. Such knowledge was seen to inform and improve teaching:

> It introduced me to discourse analysis, conversation analysis, the importance of lexis, all of which have proved valuable in my teaching (2000).

Development of study skills was also highlighted, particularly by the 2010 respondents. This aspect included academic writing, citations and bibliographies, time management, independent study and thinking critically which these comments illustrate:

> Rediscovering the discipline of academic writing and citing sources (2010).

> I learnt how to work hard independently (2010).

> I can write, i.e. express myself fairly well in writing (2000).

Although numerous participants separated learning and research from knowledge and skills of the field, the two were linked by some participants:

> A set of skills (or even a mind-set) that enabled me to research into and make informed decisions about everything from whole curricular down to specific help for a specific individual.

A Comparison of Distance Learning and On-Campus Study

The results from both surveys of distance learning students suggest that teachers accrue a number of benefits from their studies. Chief amongst these are improvements to career prospects, developing a research profile and improvements in personal and professional confidence in a number of areas ranging from teaching to presenting. In order to investigate if such benefits are the result of the mode of delivery rather than the content, we decided to survey alumni of our on-campus TESOL Studies programs. These programs are still in their infancy and only have a small number of alumni (58 at the time of writing), and so the results cannot be seen as statistically significant. All the same, they are of interest and tend to suggest that modes of delivery can affect the long-term benefits perceived by teachers.

In terms of careers, nine of the 16 on-campus alumni who answered the questionnaire are currently working in TESOL. All nine believe that the master's helped them to get or to retain their position and six say that the MA[2] has helped to get promotion or develop career. However, only four of nine believe they are financially better off.

A comparison between distance learning and on-campus responses in terms of career prospects in all three areas is given in Table 6.3.

The data suggest that on-campus students may obtain similar benefits (if not greater benefits) than distance learning students in terms of getting work and/or promotion. However, fewer teachers reaped financial rewards as a result of their program of study. The reasons for this are not immediately apparent and need further investigation, perhaps through an interview protocol. We surmise, nonetheless, that as the on-campus students generally come to the program with less experience than their distance-learning counterparts, it is likely that the jobs they are obtaining as a result of their studies are probably "lower" in status and with less pay. One respondent said:

> My MA degree has helped me change my career. Currently I feel that I will be able to secure a long-term career in TESOL. However, I need to find a full-time job so I can gain classroom experience.

As shown above, distance-learning alumni have contributed to the TESOL community in a number of ways, most notably through presentations and publications. In contrast, none of the on-campus alumni had published material, and only one had given a paper, at a state teacher's conference in Greece. This is despite the fact that several of them cited developing research skills as the most important skill they learned during the program.

This finding is of particular interest since it seems to suggest that teachers on the distance-learning program benefit from their studies in ways not afforded to on-campus alumni. It seems likely that the situated learning aspect of the distance-learning program, whereby teachers investigate their own classrooms and educational

TABLE 6.3 Comparison of responses from distance learning and on–campus alumni

	2000		2010		2011 On campus	
	Yes	No	Yes	No	Yes	No
Get/retain job	26	14	34	10	9	0
Financial gain	26	9	31	10	4	5
Promotion	32	6	30	8	6	3

contexts for their assessed work, signifies that they not only develop research skills but gain practice in writing about research. They also receive constructive feedback from course tutors. By the time they reach the dissertation stage, some may have conducted up to four research projects and have plenty of data from which to draw information for presentations and publications. In contrast, on–campus students are often required to produce work for assessment that displays knowledge and understanding of theoretical constructs and that requires them to analyze classroom practices against remembered contexts, rather than actual ones. They have therefore developed fewer skills in designing and writing up research and have collected fewer data for potential publication. Moreover, while both distance learning and on–campus alumni both repeatedly cited "confidence" as an attribute gained from the master's study, for distance learning alumni this confidence seems to develop into a belief that they have something worthwhile to contribute to the field by finding an outlet to share their work with the TESOL community.

In terms of which aspects of the program were most significant, the on–campus students gave both similar and different responses to distance learning students. Unsurprisingly, learning about approaches to teaching and the teaching practice element of the program were identified as important by a number of respondents:

Learning about teaching methods and gaining teaching experience.

Academic and study skills were identified as a key area, with one respondent saying:

I have developed my critical thinking, and analysis that are crucial for any language teachers personally and professionally.

As with the distance learners, specific areas of knowledge, which were linked to the practice of teaching, were seen as significant, as this respondent notes:

I have learned how to evaluate textbooks, which is very important in real classrooms. As such I became more confident in selecting, modifying and adapting the most appropriate materials for my learners.

It is notable how *confidence* again figures into this group of responses, as with the distance learners.

The biggest difference in the "most significant things learned" from the course seems to lie in the area of research. While three on–campus respondents mentioned research skills, this tended to be in terms of learning *about* research skills rather than their application, with students just writing *research skills* or *action research* and *learning how to research effectively*. No respondent linked knowledge of research skills to investigating their teaching or to developing their practice. This finding seems to confirm Widdowson's (1990) observation concerning the difficulties of connection with the classroom in on-campus programs, a difficulty that distance programs based on situated learning are specifically designed to overcome (Garton & Edge, this volume).

Finally, it seems that distance learning alumni are more likely to go on to further programs of study than on-campus alumni. More than a third of all alumni surveyed in 2010 (37.5%) stated that they had gone on to further study, the most popular program being a doctorate. In contrast, none of the on-campus alumni had taken other courses, although three stated that they intended to apply for doctoral study.

Discussion

Before we conclude that distance learning leads to greater professional opportunities once the program is completed compared with on-campus study programs, some caution is necessary. There are a number of reasons that the findings from distance-learning teachers and on-campus teachers are so different.

First, there are issues with the design of the study. The contact details available for alumni are limited, and the questionnaire respondents are therefore a convenience sample and may not be representative of the overall population of alumni for the programs. Moreover, it is likely that those who chose to respond are those who had the most positive experiences.

Second, students on the on-campus and distance-learning programs tend to have very different characteristics. It is a requirement of entry for the distance-learning programs that teachers must have at least two years' experience. In effect, many have many more years than this and so they are not grappling with the basics of teaching methodology but are looking to better understand their practice as well as to improve it. As for the on-campus program, experience is not a requirement, and most applicants have much less experience than their distance-learning counterparts. What is more, the distance-learning program is a well-established program with a reputation for academic rigor. As a result, it attracts applicants who are extremely serious about their course of studies. The on-campus program, while equally rigorous, is still young and has not, as yet, built a strong reputation. Finally, distance-learning students are balancing a number of demands on their time simultaneously. All have jobs along with familial responsibilities and personal obligations. They invest a great deal when they sign on to a distance-learning course and recognize that using their classrooms as a site for research is one way in which their studies can be aligned with their work. The on-campus students do not have this affordance: although teaching practice is included in the program, it is performance and reflection on it which is assessed—students do not need to research their classrooms in addition. These realities could all affect the findings from the surveys.

However, it is clear from the surveys that for the two groups of respondents in 2000 and 2010, the distance-learning program was successful in its goal of promoting professional development through situated learning. Moreover, the survey responses indicate that alumni acquire the skills and knowledge from their programs to ensure that life after online learning can be rich and rewarding in terms of continued professional development.

Discussion Questions

1. According to the questionnaire data from the 2000 and 2010 surveys, the only area that having an MSc did not seem to improve was promotion opportunities. In fact, promotion opportunities decreased over the 10 years. What could be the possible cause(s) of this? List a few possibilities that could contribute to this decline. Does your answer lie inside or outside the realm of Professional TESOL studies?
2. Part of this study focused on the differences between the affects of distance-learning programs versus on-campus courses of study. As stated, on-campus learning programs are still "in their infancy." What crossover aspects could be taken from the distance-learning courses to the on–campus programs to improve the positive effects for students?
3. What do you understand by the concept, "situated learning" and to what extent does the concept apply in either your own study program or one which you know well?

Notes

1 It is difficult to obtain accurate figures for graduates from the distance-learning programme as methods of record keeping have changed over time. However, we estimate approximately 360 people have graduated from the distance-learning programme since 1988.
2 At Aston, distance-learning programmes are given the title 'MSc' while on-campus programmes are given the title 'MA' to facilitate distinguishing between them for administrative purposes.

References

Fay, R., & Hill, M. (2003) Educating language teachers through distance learning: The need for culturally-appropriate DL methodology. *Open Learning: The Journal of Open, Distance and e-Learning, 18*(1), 9–27.

Forrester, G., Motteram, G., Parkinson, G., & Slaoutid, D. (2005) Going the distance: Students' experiences of induction to distance learning in higher education. *Journal of Further and Higher Education, 29*(4), 293–306.

Garton, S., & Richards, K. (2007) Is distance education for teacher second best? *The Teacher Trainer, 21*(3), 5–8.

Garton, S., & Edge, J. (2012) Why be an online learner in TESOL? (this volume)

Hall, D., & Knox, J. (2009) Issues in the education of TESOL teachers by distance education. *Distance Education, 30*(1), 63–85.

Hyland, F. (2001) Providing effective support: Investigating feedback to distance language learners, *Open Learning: The Journal of Open, Distance and e-Learning, 16*(3), 233–247.

King, K. P. (2002) Identifying success in online teacher education and professional development. *The Internet and Higher Education, 5,* 231–246.

Motteram, G., & Forrester, G. (2005) Becoming an online distance learner: What can be learned from students' experiences of induction to distance programmes? *Distance Education, 26*(3), 281–298.

Nunan, D. (2002) Teaching MA TESOL courses online: Challenges and rewards. *TESOL Quarterly, 36*(4), 621–624.

Parvan, F., Paulus, T. M., Yalcin, S., & Chang, C. (2003) Online learning: Patterns of engagement and interaction among in-service teachers. *Language Learning and Technology, 7*(3), 119–140.

Rovai, A. P., & Barnum, K. T. (2003) On-line course effectiveness: An analysis of student interactions and perceptions of learning. *Journal of Distance Education/Revue de l'Éducation à Distance, 18*(1), 57 –73.

Salmon, G. (2000) *E-moderating. The key to teaching and learning online.* London: Kogan Page.

Tam, M. (2000) Constructivism, instructional design, and technology: Implications for transforming distance learning. *Educational Technology & Society, 3*(2), 50–60.

Widdowson, H. G. (1990) *Aspects of Language.* Oxford: Oxford University Press.

Wilson, M. S. (2001) Cultural considerations in online instruction and learning. *Distance Education, 22,* 1, 52–64.

PART II

Teaching in Online Distance TESOL

7

CREATING COMMUNITIES OF PRACTICE

Active Collaboration Between Students

Datta Kaur Khalsa

Introduction

> This online collaboration is the antidote to the isolation of online courses
>
> (TESOL online student, 2011)

> I used to love working alone, but after this (online) collaborative experience (it has) changed my view completely. It was informative, interesting, enjoyable, enlightening, and delightful working with partner(s)...
>
> (TESOL online student, 2011)

> As we were working online, we could see how the work was coming along at any time...we sent affirming messages and encouraged one another ... a completely positive experience.
>
> (TESOL online student, 2011)

Communities of practice (CoP) are meeting places where learning is central. When communities of practice are supported in online classrooms, student connections as well as learning motivation and engagement increase, and the interactions begin to influence the individual and group ideas. Ideally the collaboration can enhance innovation and learning implementation beyond simply acquiring ideas from others. The resulting thought and action has the potential to broaden learning and efficacy, while also providing opportunities for expanded community impact. In communities of practice, sharing of personal and educational information and active, unified efforts for local community service and world change are often the fuel for bonding and sustainability (Khalsa, 2005a; Resnick, 2002; Wenger, White,

& Smith, 2009). This chapter will describe benefits, characteristics and practices for creating and maintaining interactive communities of practice in the online TESOL classroom. Provided here is a research-based framework, which will inform the work of online TESOL educators and students as they seek to actively participate, support and maintain a community of practice in their online classroom.

Background

Online education is a formalized intersection of learning, community and technology. Since online education has grown to a stunning 5.6 million students in 2009 (Allen & Seaman, 2010b), and then a year later, grown by almost 1 million more students (Allen & Seaman, 2010a), college presidents predict that 10 years from today they will they see the majority of their students taking classes online (Taylor, Parker, Lenhart, & Patten, 2011). TESOL students are included in these numbers and are part of the growing population, who appreciate the convenience and unique learning opportunities provided by technology tools applied to online education.

Current availability of technology has provided students with learning tools, which are more expansive and empowering than any tools used in the past. The proliferation of Web 2.0 technology, mobile devices, and friendship networks extend traditional relationships and afford convenient means for local and global connections. The popularity of interactive technology tools and the increased familiarity with blogs, wikis, chat rooms and videoconferencing boost opportunities, which support extensions of human relationships with distinctive knowledge-building and community-building (Lenhart, Madden, & Hitlin, 2005; Preece, 2000; Wenger, White, & Smith, 2009). By capitalizing on the popularity and prolific use of technology to build communities of practice, online TESOL education can amplify student learning and efficacy (U.S. Department of Education 2010; 2011). Interactive pedagogy, which supports technology integration, authentic interaction, virtual teamwork and community-based learning, enhances the sharing of ideas, perspectives, languages and cultures across time zones (Dheram, 2007; Dippold, 2009; Grabe & Grabe, 2004; Kennewell, Tanner, Jones, & Beauchamp, 2008; Muir, 2006). To implement such processes in the online classroom, however, it is helpful to understand the associated link between theory and pedagogy.

Impact of Theory

There are a number of theories that help instructors and students understand the impact of interactive, online communities of practice. These include Social Learning Theory (Bandura, 1971, 1986; Rotter, 1982; Vygotsky, 1978), Emergent Interactive Model (Bandura, 1986, 1999) and Identity Theories (Hall, 1990; Hofstede, 2001; Hoppe, 2004; Voronov & Singer, 2002; Wenger, 2004). Each theory enhances the broader picture of coexistence in complex social learning systems and development of self-identity in a global community. These theories also describe the influence of socio-cultural constructs and the relationship of culture, identity and community in a collaborative culture, adding understanding to virtual learning possibilities.

Wenger (2004) claims that Social Learning Theory started with the work of communities of practice, "groups of people, who share a concern or a passion for something they do and learn how to do it better as they interact regularly" (Wenger, 1998, p. 6) and expanded into the blending of social theory with learning theory. *Social Learning Theory*, also called Social Cognitive Theory (Bandura, 1971, 1986), explains how thoughts, feelings and behavior are affected by the actual or implied presence of others. Simply stated, people observe, imitate and learn socially. The social and cultural context of the individuals and how they perceive and interpret information from others is the basis of the Social Learning Theory.

The sociostructural influences, including roles, rules and social practices, regulate thought and behavior. Individuals exist and act within a broad network of environmental structures: imposed, selected and constructed (Bandura, 2001). Cognitive skills, attitudes and behavior impact the environment and the environment impacts these personal factors (Huitt, 2002, 2004). When boundaries of physical time and place are broadened online, the definition of learning, community and environment are also expanded to what exists today—digital habitats—where millions are learning together in a community of practice (Wenger, White, & Smith, 2009).

New Meaning for an Age-Old Word, Community

Communities of practice supported by technology, renegotiate the meaning of community while supporting life-long learning. This unique condition of learning is becoming a key factor in redefining traditional culture and, with transnational borders fading, perceived collective agency is becoming fortified. With a common concern, goal or passion as a unifying factor, online participants or students adapt their behavior patterns to accommodate the diversity of participants or team members, as may be the case in online virtual teamwork. Such a collaborative culture encourages working together as a team with cooperation and communication between members of a group for their mutual benefit (Heaton, 2001; Rheingold, 1998; Wenger, 2004). "The new computing includes consideration of relationships, collaborations and partnerships, which encourage finding win-win deals in which both sides benefit" (Schneidermann, 2003, p. 135). The shift in thinking and procedures begins with a new meaning for an age-old word, community, and, as a result, social inclusion has a broader meaning for students and instructors. The interactions or shared practices, which take place in online communities of practice, are affected by personal factors, environmental factors and overt behavior (Wenger, 2004).

Identity in Digital Habitats

As there is a shift in the definition and thinking about community, the personal and environmental factors related to identity are also no longer static as stereotypical pictures and influence of culture shift (Fernández–Ballesteros, Diez-Nicolas, Caprara, Barbaranelli, Bandura, 2002). *Identity* is defined for use here as a reflection of self through interaction with others (Hall, 1990; Hofstede, 2001; Jandt, 1995). No one has only one identity, but in the urge to see oneself as unique, often small differences become magnified, until they become defining characteristics (Lawler, Thye, & Jeongkoo, 2009). Since a virtual identity occurs through computer-mediated communication in situations that lack face-to-face contact, it is formed primarily through interactions with strangers and often involves acculturation. This type of acculturation accepts another's cultural patterns of behavior (Heusinkveld, 1997) with an awareness and interaction of personal cultural dimensions in a virtual time, space and workplace (English-Lueck, Darrah, & Saveri, 2002). Acculturation of identity is part of the collaboration process and condition of learning in an online community of practice or virtual teamwork and has influence on the interaction's success.

Conditions of Learning: Shared Identity

For community success, virtual identity must be negotiated collectively and conform to social rules and roles. Socio-cultural constructs, which relate to shared, ethnic, geographic and collective behaviors and patterns, are now highly influenced by blurred traditional boundaries and virtual interaction—stretching beyond traditional, more localized circumstances. With the unique opportunity to create communities of practice (CoP) in the online classroom, TESOL students can unite their individual identity to generate a collective, virtual identity. Now the traditional constructs are being altered to embody the collective, virtual identity of the community of practice with its own set of socio-structural influences—roles, rules and social practices. Singh & Doherty (2004) describe these interactions as "global university contact zones." Jund (2010) describes the "culture talk" of his international online university students, as a space where they systematically establish competing discourses, hold multiple identities and display contradictory aspects of a culture in a global, educational setting. However certain processes empower these unique human relationships and can induce creativity, cohesion, sustainability and responsiveness while others may stifle and diminish results (Khalsa, 2010).

Conditions of Learning: Empowering Human Relationships

The use of technology as a communication and learning tool heightens students' ability to fulfill basic needs of connection, recognition and power. If instructors integrate small and large group online discussion to help facilitate team-based projects then the role of online communities of practice take on a new meaning—one that holds seeds of empowerment and may eventually blossom into outlets for personal and social change. In the online TESOL classroom, the planning, discourse and activities can reinforce attributes so that students are willing to embrace possibilities in their lives, possibilities that may strengthen their local and global community.

A competent TESOL instructor can recognize, plan and shape the educational environment so that it can be a source of strength, pride and sensitivity in a confusing world. One of the first steps is to recognize personal and cultural student individuality. From Day One instructors can either invite students to speak freely and create an environment that supports empowering interaction or they can contribute to silencing discourse. Similarly, TESOL instructors can inspire imagination and spark understanding of personal, group and community power, or they can support silos of learning, which include isolated, forced responsiveness and missed opportunities for expansive learning within a broader community. Instructor qualities of openness, welcome, flexibility and equality contribute to cultivation of a space of discourse, dialogue, development of a collective identity and democratic understanding.

Conditions of Learning: Real People and Real People Needs

Democratic ideals are based on voice, discourse, social interaction, thoughtfulness and consciousness. Freire's (1995) emphasis was on dialogue as a cooperative activity. He then expected the praxis to deepen understanding, develop consciousness and have the power to transform reality (Taylor, 1993). Emergent use of technology to support communities of practice and virtual teamwork can result in authentic acts of socialization, language learning and community action—practiced in a convenient, technology-supported environment.

Kabeer (2005) speaks about how empowerment from within can change how people see their self. Rowlands (1995) states that "the core of the empowerment process involves … development of self- confidence and self- esteem, and a sense of agency … a sense of self within a wider context" (p. 102). TESOL communities of practice have the capability to increase, not only a student's language skills, but also a student's self-awareness and self-worth. Enhanced self-worth can help motivation and skills for effective virtual communication in a diversified, collaborative culture (Jund, 2010). Today, we are fortunate to have the convenience and ease of technology to stimulate critical analysis, self-reflection of language and learning in culture and society, as well as the personal role our interests and needs could have on a local or global society.

If situational discourse and activities replace isolated, artificial learning practice, then students can expand their community role and become local and global community members, advocates for change and service, possible leaders and student models while they simultaneously broaden their personal understanding of their world. Innovative, interactive and authentic community-based learning creates a new emphasis on real people and real people needs (Schneidermann, 2003). A community of practice—well-orchestrated in an online TESOL classroom—can bring understanding that is real, not isolated or theoretical, as well as understanding that is practiced, not preached.

Conditions of Learning: More Student Choices

When one acknowledges individual needs within a community of practice, students can begin to add power and meaning to personal learning, personal identity and the world in which they live (Wenger, 2004). Individuals, who are capable of collaborating with groups, learn to embrace decision-making and responsibility. More student choices in educational mediums and methods enable them to legitimize themselves, which includes extending their interpretations and perspectives of the world. Emergent use of technology, providing worldwide interactions with peers, resulting in authentic acts of socialization, learning and community action can help prepare students beyond classroom communication for a diverse world in a technological era. E-learning team interaction as roots for authentic, project-based learning is one type of interactive pedagogy that allows for student choices in learning with opportunities for genuine community-based learning. Instructor understanding and support for student engagement in such virtual collaborative activities may require new thinking, some unlearning, relearning, planned global connections, and trust in the power of the student and virtual teamwork.

Conditions of Learning: Trust in a Virtual Team Setting

Trust is often considered to be the solidifying force, the glue, which supports social capital and holds virtual networks together (Khalsa, 2005b; Preece, 2002, Putnam, 2000). Trust here relates to the belief or confidence in a person, product or organization's integrity, fairness and reliability with expectations that others will act towards the common goal and good of the team and the members. The degree of trust affects the willingness to reciprocate on the basis of words, actions and decisions of another and, therefore, the completion and quality of virtual discussions and team projects (Khalsa, 2005b). Trust can, therefore, affect reciprocity between classmates who are working on projects together. A person's ability to communicate, trust, and be trusted can have consequence on their willingness to collaborate, and engage in effective teamwork (Brown, Poole, & Rodgers, 2004). By establishing the technology tools and the discussion timeframe for students to build a firm base of trusted relationships, the end learning results could positively outweigh the presumed strain on time and effort.

Trust is one of the mechanisms that empower participants, while tones of voice and language can have an impact on trust. The instructor becomes the model for attitude and tendencies of communication, some of which can possibly stifle creativity, weaken cohesion and limit responsiveness. Through modeling cheerful, encouraging interaction with high expectations and continual notes of support, students are likely to emulate the instructor's example in their virtual team interactions, even when miscommunications occur. During virtual teamwork, they are more likely to adapt their behavior patterns to accommodate the diversity of team participants and the overall interaction will, in all probability, be supportive, while embracing unique ideas and diverse perspectives. Trust in the structure, expectations and participants are foundations for assembling innovative ideas and building individual efficacy. Alternatively, if degrees of intolerance and assertiveness exist, then over-sensitivity can lead to hindrance of debate, stifling of an individual's voice or submission to a fellow teammate.

Conditions of Learning: Guidelines for a Virtual Team Setting

E-learning team interactions require intellectual, emotional, and social support and deep appreciation for the diversified cultural experience. Efficient and effective guidelines are born from examination of multi-cultural team characteristics and challenges during a virtual team process—all with the goal of strengthening the learning, transforming the reality of self and, perhaps, adding to positive personal and community change. If instructors and students have an understanding of virtual, intercultural discourse beyond the compare/contrast mode, then they can provide support and guidelines for deepened discussions and temporary, virtual learning team projects toward the ultimate goal of full learning advantage.

Since teams are interdependent in their tasks with shared responsibilities, they must manage their relationships and are required to "share information, adapt to time constraints ... at a distance, often under trying political and cultural circumstances" (English-Lueck, Darrah, & Saveri, 2002, p. 92). To instill a base of community support and ownership, it is highly recommended that a netiquette wiki be established during the first week of an online course. If the instructor creates the wiki and invites each student to add personal netiquette "pointers," guidelines are built collectively, increasing initial expectations for interactive respect. Additionally the wiki page can be used throughout the course for reminders as needed.

Shared power and respect can also be instituted early if students are required to introduce themselves or another classmate. By discovering classmates' similarities, differences, personal interests and activities, as well as geographical locations, students uncover starting points for further conversations and relationship building. It is also important that the instructor share personal notes so as to appear genuine and approachable in a faceless environment. Alternatively, if an instructor sets an authoritative tone with too stringent discussion guidelines, dialogue and exchange of ideas, perspectives and opinions, students may be stifled for fear of reprimand, criticism or unwelcome debate.

Conditions of Learning: Issues of Power

Interpersonal interaction in a community of practice is influenced by degrees of power. Without paralinguistic cues, students often must second-guess emotions and intent of team members. Assertiveness in a virtual team involves perceptions of competition, recognition, flexibility, self-reliance and group harmony (Khalsa, 2007, 2010). If it is perceived that there exists an overly-assertive team member, then socio-cultural constructs related to status, individualism and gender can be affected. Individual identity components—such as assertiveness—can augment or alter the broader picture of the team's socio-cultural constructs. The complex interplay of invisible assumptions, values, beliefs and visible behaviors affect group behaviors.

The functions and impact of planning, discussing, and fulfilling roles and rules during virtual teamwork require nurturance, understanding and support of engagement. The decision to assign a group leader or allow "shifting leadership" during the team process depends on the audience of students and their level of knowledge, skills and dispositions. In the end individuals must display respect, trust and willingness to do their part in a timely manner with continued communication and supportive input. If teams are required to discuss and then imitate the earlier course activity of establishing netiquette guidelines and choose roles, timeframes and means of communication, which embrace individual circumstances, process effectiveness is more likely. Again modeling by the instructor with a keen eye on individual willingness, workload equality and perceived respect of each teammate will add to the success of TESOL online communities of practice.

Limitations

As with all unique practices, a person must see the benefit of participation enough to commit to the initial investment of time. The instructor who wishes to support an online TESOL community of practice—one which supports community change—will need access to technology tools and the willingness to devote extra time to set up teams, a wiki, timeframes for the process and local or global partners. Students will need to be coached and supported by an instructor, who feels confident in their facilitative abilities. Just as there is a hole in understanding if the online instructor has not themselves taken an online class, there may be a lack of understanding if an online TESOL instructor has not participated in a virtual team or observed a successful online community of practice. Authentic experience provides personal evidence and understanding of benefits and challenges. Additionally it helps the instructor portray "knowing" through trust and respect for the process and results.

Summary

Communities of practice in the online TESOL classroom can enhance student connections to the language learning content and give opportunities for stronger motivation and engagement. CoPs also give students a voice with opportunities for empowering interaction, innovation and development of a collective identity. If an instructor provides opportunities for virtual teamwork, situational discourse and community activities, which extend beyond the classroom walls, a student's sense of self has a wider context. The resulting thought and action has the potential to broaden learning and efficacy, while also providing opportunities for expanded community impact.

Communities of Practice can support active collaboration between students with an instructor's awareness of conditions of learning and guidance methods. The guidance needs to include establishing the technology tools and discussion timeframe for students to build a firm base of trusted relationships, modeling cheerful, encouraging interaction with high expectations and continual notes of support. Netiquette guidelines that acknowledge status, gender, bias and power issues can shine light on perspectives of assertiveness, competition and intimidation. Each of these has the potential to weaken group harmony, student-to-student trust, respect and accomplishment.

Instructors, who trust that the work will be high quality, and state those expectations up front, while also becoming a model for frequency and tone of communication and support are the most effective. If one is a student, discussing topics, workloads and schedules with each virtual team member towards a common understanding can establish a successful base for the community of practice. Agreed upon clarity of assignment requirements, methods, frequency of community interaction with established member roles and rules is necessary. If teams are required to compile guidelines, and supply a weekly "report" to the instructor on how well the guidelines are being implemented, trust in the process can continue. Once the structure for a community of practice is built, the unique pedagogy and community goals that accompany the learning can be well-supported and the authentic acts of socialization, language learning and community action can be expected.

Conclusion

Freire (1995) emphasized dialogue as a cooperative activity that could transform reality. Shor (1995) expanded on his lead to give students power through critical pedagogy when he wrote about how to eliminate the Siberian Syndrome and link classroom work to broader social change. Dede (2009) wrote about knowledge networking and interlinking clusters of innovators to test individual beliefs, practices and strategies. The overall intent of this writing was to provide a background, description and framework for active student collaboration in the TESOL online classroom. Virtual unification of interests, understanding and discoveries as they apply to individual and collective identity and goals is anchored in TESOL communities of practice. TESOL instructors who embrace the possibilities described by Freire, Shor and Dede and also embrace the communities of practice benefits described here can begin to implement this framework of support toward active collaboration among students on the way to powerful communities of practice.

Discussion Questions

1. Before reading the chapter, list any virtual or face-to-face communities in which you participate. Place the "reason and benefits for participation" next to each title.
2. After reading the chapter, list any community of practice of which you are a member. Place the condition(s) of learning that exists in each.
3. If you were to initiate a *TESOL* online community of practice, what would be your first three initial steps? Why?

References

Allen E., & Seaman, J. (2010a) *Class differences: Online education in the United States, 2010.* Masachusetts: Babson Research Group. November, 2010.

Allen, E., & Seaman, J. (2010b) *Learning on demand: Online education in the United States, 2009.* Masachusetts: Babson Research Group.

Bandura, A. (1971) *Social learning theory.* New York: General Learning Press.

Bandura, A. (1986) *Social foundations of thought and action.* Englewood Cliffs, NJ: Prentice-Hall.

Bandura, A. (1999) A social cognitive theory of personality. In L. Pervin & O. John (Eds), *Handbook of personality* (pp. 154–196). New York: Guilford Publications.

Bandura, A. (2001) Social cognitive theory: An agentic perspective. *Annual Review of Psychology, 52,* 1–26.

Brown, H., Poole, M., & Rodgers, T. (2004) Interpersonal traits, complementarity and trust in virtual collaboration. *Journal of Management Information Systems, 20*(4), 115–137.

Dede, C. (2009) Technologies that facilitate generating knowledge and possibly wisdom: A response to "Web 2.0 and classroom research." *Educational Researcher, 38*(4), 60–63.

Dheram, P. (2007) Empowerment through critical pedagogy. *Academic Leadership, 5*(2). Retrieved on September 23, 2011 from this website: http://www.academicleadership. org/article/print/Empowerment_through_Critical_Pedagogy

Dippold, D. (2009) Peer feedback through blogs: Student and teacher perceptions in an advanced German class. *ReCALL, 21*(1), 18–36.

English-Lueck, J., Darrah, C., & Saveri, A. (2002) Trusting strangers: Work relationships in four-high tech communities. *Information, Communication & Society, 5*(1), 90–108.

Fernández-Ballesteros, R., Díez-Nicolás, J., Caprara, G. V., Barbaranelli, C., & Bandura, A. (2002) Determinants and structural relation of perceived personal efficacy to perceived collective efficacy. *Applied Psychology: an International Review, 51,* 107–125.

Freire, P. (1995) *Pedagogy of hope. Reliving pedagogy of the oppressed,* New York: Continuum.

Grabe, M., & Grabe, C. (2004) *Integrating technology for meaningful learning.* New York, NY: Houghton Mifflin Co.

Hall, E. (1990) *Understanding cultural differences.* Yarmouth, ME: Intercultural Press.

Heaton, L. (2001) Preserving communication context: Virtual workspace and interpersonal space in Japanese CSCW. In C. Ess & F. Sudweeks (Eds), *Culture, technology, communication:*

Towards an intercultural global village (pp. 213–240). New York, NY: State University of New York Press.

Heusinkveld, P. (1997) *Pathways to culture.* Yarmouth, ME: Intercultural Press.

Hofstede, G. (2001) *Cultural consequences.* London: Sage.

Hoppe, M. H. (2004) Geert Hofstede's cultur's consequences: International differences in work-related values. *Academy of Management Executives, 18*(1), 73–74.

Huitt, W. (2002) Social cognition. *Educational Psychology Interactive.* Valdosta, GA: Valdosta State University. Retrieved at http://chiron.valdosta.edu/whuitt/col/soccog/soccog.html

Huitt, W. (2004) Observational (social) learning: An overview. *Educational Psychology Interactive.* Valdosta, GA: Valdosta State University. Retrieved at http://chiron.valdosta.edu/whuitt/col/soccog/soclrn.htmlShneirderman

Jandt, F. (1995) *Intercultural communication.* London: Sage.

Jund, A. (2010) Toward a pedagogy of intercultural understanding in teaching English for academic purposes. *TESL-EJ, 14*(1).

Kabeer, N. (2005) Gender equality and women's empowerment: A critical analysis of the third millennium development. *Goal, Gender and Development,* 13(1), 13–24.

Kennewell, S., Tanner, H., Jones, S., & Beauchamp, G. (2008) Analyzing the use of interactive technology to implement interactive teaching. *Journal of Computer Assisted Learning, 24*(1), 61–73.

Khalsa, D. K. (2005a) Support for global project-based learning: U.S. teacher motivation, online training, virtual teamwork, trust and identity. Doctoral dissertation, University of Maryland.

Khalsa, D. K. (2005b) Online learning teams: Impact of socio-cultural dimensions. *Human Computer Interaction International 2005 conference proceedings.* Englefield Cliffs, NJ: Lawrence Erlbaum.

Khalsa, D. K. (2007) Multicultural dimensions in e-learning teamwork. In A. Edmundson (Ed.), *Globalized e-Learning Cultural Challenges.* New York, NY: Idea Publishing.

Khalsa, D. K. (2010) Multicultural e-Learning Teamwork: Social and cultural characteristics and influences. In D. Pullen & D. Cole (Eds) *Multiliteracies and technology enhanced education: Social practice and the global classroom.* Hershey, PA: Information Science Reference.

Lawler, E., Thye, S., & Jeongkoo, Y. (2009) *Social commitments in a depersonalized world.* New York, NY: Russell Sage Foundation.

Lenhart, A., Madden, M., & Hitlin, P. (2005) Teens and technology: Youth are leading the transition to a fully wired and mobile nation. *Pew Internet Research,* July 27, 2005.

Muir, M. (2006) *Technology to improve learning: Strategies for middle level leaders.* Westerville, OH: National Middle School Association.

Preece, J. (2000) *Online communities: Designing usability, supporting sociability.* New York: John Wiley & Sons.

Preece, J. (Ed.), (2002) Supporting community and building social capital. Special edition of *Communications of the ACM, 45*(4), 37–39.

Putnam, R. (2000) *Bowling alone: The collapse and revival of American community.* New York, NY: Simon & Shuster.

Resnick, M. (2002) Rethinking learning in the digital age. In G. Kirkman (Ed.), *The global information technology report 2001–2002: Readiness for the networked world* (pp. 32–37). Oxford: Oxford University Press.

Rheingold, H. (1998) *The virtual community: Homesteading on the electronic frontier.* MA: Addison-Wesley.

Rotter, J. B. (1982) *The development and application of social learning theory.* New York, NY: Praeger.

Rowlands, J. (1995) Empowerment examined. *Development in Practice, 5*(2), 101–107.

Schneidermann, B. (2003) *Leonardo's laptop: Human needs and the new computing technologies.* Cambridge, MA: MIT Press.

Shor, I. (1995) *Students have power: Negotiating authority in a critical pedagogy.* Chicago: University of Chicago Press.

Singh, P., & Doherty, C. (2004) Global cultural flows and pedagogic dilemmas: Teaching in the global university contact zone. *TESOL Quarterly, 38*(1), 9–42.

Taylor, P. (1993) *The texts of Paulo Freire,* Buckingham: Open University Press.

Taylor, P., Parker, K., Lenhart, A., & Patten, E. (2011) *The digital revolution and higher education: College Presidents, public differ on value of online learning.* Washington, DC: Pew Social & Demographic Trends.

U.S. Department of Education (2010) *Transforming American education: Learning powered by technology.* Retrieved on September 23, 2011 from http://www.ed.gov/technology/netp-2010

U.S. Department of Education (2011) *Connect and inspire: Online communities of practice in education.* Retrieved on September 23, 2011 from this website: http://connectededucators.org/report/files/2011/03/0143_OCOP-Main-report.pdf

Voronov, M., & Singer, J. (2002) The myth of individualism-collectivism: A critical review. *The Journal of Social Psychology, 142*(4), 461–480.

Vygotsky, L. S. (1978) *Mind and society: The development of higher mental processes.* Cambridge, MA: Harvard University Press.

Wenger, E. (1998) *Communities of practice: learning, meaning, and identity.* New York, NY: Cambridge University Press.

Wenger, E. (2004) Learning for a small planet: A research agenda. Retrieved on September 23, 2011 from this website: http://www.ewenger.com/research/index.htm

Wenger, E., White, N., & Smith, J. D. (2009) *Digital habitats: Stewarding technology for communities.* Portland, OR: CPsquare.

8

TEACHING RESEARCH METHODS IN AN ONLINE DISTANCE COURSE

Paula Garcia McAllister

Many students in Master's programs in Teaching English as a Second Language (MA TESL) enroll in research methods courses with nervousness and apprehension. They cite reasons such as a "fear of numbers" or "discomfort with statistics" as reasons for dreading what is usually a required course in their programs. Learning research methods in an online distance course can add to students' apprehension because of the fundamental differences between online and face-to-face learning. These differences, whether real or perceived, include things like a lack of immediacy in getting questions answered, the inability to use eye-to-eye contact as a non-verbal communication of comprehension, and absence of the collaborative camaraderie and interaction of learning in a physical group setting (Lim, Dannels, & Watkins, 2008). Despite these shortcomings in online education, online courses are increasingly popular at all levels of secondary and post-secondary education. This chapter describes how a course with challenging content like Research Methods can be effectively taught to MA TESL students at an American university by providing an overview of current research on online teacher education and research methods courses, outlining the structure and basic content of the research methods course that I teach, and describing the factors that facilitate online learning.

Understanding research is much more than comprehending statistics even though this tends to be the aspect that often worries MA TESL students the most. The research conducted in TESL and Applied Linguistics can provide teachers-in-training with essential tools for deciding which instructional methods are most effective and selecting materials and resources for their students. Being conversant in research develops professionalism so that student teachers can become leaders in their schools, colleges, or school districts. It also provides them with the tools to be able to conduct their own action research or to be better prepared as researchers in a doctoral program. MA TESL students should be made aware of the benefits of understanding research for their practical and professional needs. This will move students away from the perception that research methods is a math-heavy statistics course, overly burdensome.

The past decade has seen a dramatic increase in the amount of published articles on online teaching and learning, but very few have had a specific focus on teacher education and research methods courses. Roessingh and Johnson (2005) report on their process in converting a Master's in TESL program to an online format by taking a course-by-course approach. Serving working teachers from all over the globe, course developers found that frequent discussion forums and other activities that brought student teachers together were vital in providing a context for learning. They also found that online students had expectations of "efficient, well-managed, organized, and convenient" learning (p. 112), which was achieved through the use of grading rubrics and clearly articulated expectations. Roessingh and Johnson point out that online students do not have the luxury of time to seek out learning resources; rather, they expect to have instructional tasks and tools laid out clearly before them. This resonates with Winston and Fields' (2003) recommendation that online doctoral programs adopt a format where competencies are explicitly *taught*, an idea in contrast to residential doctoral programs where research competencies are incidentally *caught* through daily interaction with professors and fellow students.

Addressing a question that is more often asked than answered, Kirtman (2009) compared an online graduate-level educational research course with a face-to-face course, both of which were taught by the researcher. Analyzing several data sources such as midterm and final exams, written assignments, and an end-of-course survey, Kirtman compared the performances of 71 online students with 69 traditional students. She found no significant differences in the writing assignment grades and a modest advantage for the traditional students on the exam scores. Survey results showed that students perceived no difference in their online courses as compared with face-to-face learning. In another interesting finding, Kirtman correlated high frequency of discussion forum entries with higher course averages, indicating that students who frequently engaged in the forums performed better in the course overall. Kirtman concludes that online learning of research methods can be just as effective as traditional, face-to-face methods as long as students are exposed to frequent interaction in discussion forums and have positive attitudes towards the online format.

Online learning is becoming more widespread at all levels of education and educators can bet that it will be increasing rather than decreasing. These days, finding a student, whether at graduate or undergraduate level, who has NOT taken an online course is rare. Despite the pervasiveness of online courses, online learning is not for every student. In a study of online students' learning experiences, Lim, Dannels, and Watkins (2008) identified three types of graduate students enrolled in online research methods courses. One type of student was well prepared for the online learning environment, partly familiar with some of the content prior to the course, and considered themselves to be independent learners. The second type was predisposed against taking a course online but was "pleasantly surprised" by the learning opportunities of the course, the instructors' abilities to effectively teach online, and their own abilities to expand their learning network and succeed in the course. These two groups were successful online learners. The last group constituted learners who had a greater need for face-to-face interaction, collective learning with peers, more immediate back-and-forth question/answer opportunities, and more attention from the instructor. This third type of student could not foster relationships with other students or with the instructor, and therefore never experienced a sense of community in the online course, which has long been seen as a factor contributing to student success in online learning (Aragon, 2003; Bibeau, 2001).

How does one build a community and foster student relationships in online courses? Tu and McIsaac (2002) explored the construct of social presence, a key factor in facilitating successful online learning and building a sense of community. Tu and McIsaac identified three dimensions of social presence: social context, online communication, and interactivity. Social context refers to students in an online course engaging in tasks on shared topics, hence building relationships among each other. Online communication refers to the degree to which students use online applications to interact with each other, including the language of communication that is acceptable and appropriate for whatever they may be engaged in. Interactivity refers to the extent to which students communicate with each other and with the instructor(s), which should be informal and immediate as a lack of immediacy can negatively impact social presence. Through qualitative and quantitative analysis of surveys, interviews, observations, emails, discussion postings, and other text generated by the course, the researchers refined the three dimensions and presented a definition of social presence as "the degree of feeling, perception, and reaction of being connected by computer-mediated communication (CMC) to another intellectual entity through a text-based encounter" (p. 140). In order to foster positive social presence, Tu and McIsaac recommend a high level of interactivity among the students, small class sizes or groupings in which students can form interpersonal relationships, clearly defined tasks that students engage in collectively, and a warm friendly demeanor on the part of all participants, including instructors, that invites cross-communication.

Building a Successful Online Research Methods Course

In the course in which I teach MA TESL students in an entirely online format, I have found that many of Tu and McIsaac's recommendations help tremendously with relieving some of the tension felt by students. In addition to their recommendations, I would like to add a few more presented here:

1. *Begin the class with introductions of each student and yourself.* Tu and McIsaac (2002) recommend using "ice breaker" activities as a way for students to get to know each other; I have found that having students write short self-introductions breaks the ice just fine. This is especially important in an online MA TESL program where students may be located all over the globe. By introducing themselves, students acquire foundational knowledge about each other's teaching contexts, something that comes up throughout the course in discussions. Furthermore, in a small program such as ours, the introductions provide an opportunity for students who have "met" each other in previous courses to greet each other and develop further those student-to-student relationships that are so important to building a classroom community and fostering successful online learning (Lim, Dannels, & Watkins, 2008).

2. *Provide multiple and varied grading opportunities.* In order to keep students engaged, provide them with weekly practice in the form of short assignments, assignments that prepare them for larger assignments, and discussion forums, all of which can be graded. I have found that just assigning exercises from the textbook helps students make connections when it's time to take exams or other performance-related activities. Types of major graded assignments include the annotated bibliography, term paper in the form of a synthesis or analytical paper, and a midterm and final exam. Smaller assignments include worksheets in which students calculate descriptive statistics, textbook exercises, discussion forums, and preliminary activities that prepare them for the larger papers and assignments. It is important to keep in mind that not all assigned work needs to be penalized for errors. Towards the end of my course, I assign a rather lengthy and challenging exercise focusing on analyzing research results that students turn in by email. I grant them the full amount of points simply for turning it in, whether their answers are correct or not. I couple this with detailed feedback on what they got wrong and how to answer correctly. This takes a lot of stress off of students who are grappling with new material.

3. *Engage students in discussion forums.* How do online discussions help students learn research methods? It has long been recognized that interaction is vital to learning in online environments (Gunawardena, Lowe, & Anderson 1997). With a pointed discussion topic or task, students are forced to prepare their responses in advance and thoughtfully reflect on the topic or task prior to posting. In our program, Master's students are located all over the globe and in myriad time zones, making synchronous discussions impossible. Asynchronous discussions, though not as spontaneous, have proven to be effective learning tools. Chou (2004) found that in asynchronous discussions, students produced a significantly higher volume of task-oriented interactions, and that students tended to generate information rather than questions. This demonstrates how students take control of their own learning: They pose their own questions, set out to answer them, then post their newly gained information in the asynchronous

discussion. The discussion forum provides a safe platform where students can present their original ideas, hypotheses, and opinions to their peers, who are also presenting their original ideas, hypotheses, and opinions. Interactive discussion forums also help improve writing skills because students need to write out their answers, which tend to be well thought-out in asynchronous discussions. Students are more reflective and try to say something original rather than just repeat what other classmates have said.

4. *Use rubrics to grade papers and other assignments.* It is important in any class, whether online or in person, to provide students with clear expectations for all assignments (Conrad & Donaldson, 2004). I provide detailed assignment prompts that include grading rubrics for my major assignments. Then, when I've graded them, I inform students about their score and which rubric categories they lost points on. For instructors, having a rubric makes the job of grading easier because it gives instructors a framework in which to critique student work. It also ensures that each student's paper is graded according to the same set of expectations, and provides a ready-made springboard for feedback.

    Discussion posts can also be evaluated on a rubric. I award points for students' original posts and for their responses to other students' posts. Other examples I have seen include specific parameters to discussion posts, such as references to academic sources that must be present in order for the student to get the points. How discussion posts are graded is something individual instructors should carefully consider for their own courses.

5. *Make use of worksheets.* The math-based worksheet has long been used in elementary and secondary schools. Such worksheets can also be quite useful for teaching basic statistical concepts like mean, median, standard deviation, and normal distribution. They are in a format that student teachers are familiar with, thus reducing anxiety, and they are easily passed from teacher to student and back in an online environment. If statistical software is available to students, assignments that include the use of developing data sets and running statistics are also quite helpful in giving students hands-on experience with statistics.

6. *Read lots of research articles.* One of the goals of the research methods course is to teach students how to read and comprehend research articles in their field. Luckily, in Applied Linguistics and TESL, most research journals are available in an online format and through Internet library resources easily accessed by students located around the world. Many students in MS TESL programs may have never read a complete research article in our field, so having students read articles in both facilitated and independent scenarios is critical for any research methods course. Having the whole class read the same research article and respond to it in a discussion forum is a good way to get novice research consumers to become familiar with the research article in a more sheltered environment. As the course progresses, students search for research articles on their own, read

them, and summarize them as graded assignments. These activities have helped my students overcome the intimidation of reading research.

7. *Don't rely on implicit learning.* When students are at a distance, it is important to have a good grasp of their ability levels. Some graduate students may need to be shown how to do literature review searches or how to write academic papers. One of my major assignments is to write a synthesis paper. I have found that even at the graduate level, students had little experience with the upper echelon of Bloom's Taxonomy (1956): application, analysis, synthesis, and evaluation. They are skilled at summarizing research articles, but when it comes to integrating several articles and making generalizations and inferences about a collection of research findings, they need to be shown how to do it. I provide students with written instructions and graphic demonstrations of how to go about analyzing and synthesizing research findings, and I have found varied but mostly successful results. MA TESL students can learn to write academically if explicitly shown how. They may not achieve success by simply observing academic writing through the reading of research articles; they achieve greater success, at least in my experience, if they are provided with explanations and demonstrations.

The seven points outlined here are meant to provide the online research methods instructor with some of the principles that have helped make my online course successful. Course evaluations have revealed that students felt challenged by the course, but were also able to become more competent in the subject area. They also felt that course requirements were clearly articulated and that grades were based on pre-determined expectations. The electronic environment poses many challenges in a teacher education program because teaching has traditionally been viewed as an interpersonal, and thus face-to-face, activity. The tremendous increase in online learning is changing how we view education and how we approach teaching and learning. With respect to research methods in particular, I would like to address one additional aspect that should not be neglected: the importance of teaching research ethics.

Research Ethics in TESL Programs

A foundation in research ethics should be an integral part of any research methods course (Kardas & Spatz, 2007; Landrum & Smith, 2007). Graduate students need to understand why ethics is important in research and what safeguards have been put in place to protect research participants and researchers, such as informed consent. These safeguards have been developed in response to harmful and dangerous research that took place mainly in biomedical fields at a time when there were no universally accepted codes of ethics or federally mandated guidelines. In many of these cases from the past, such as the Tuskegee Syphilis Study (1991) or the Stanford Prison Experiment (Zimbardo, 1973), just to name a few of the more widely known studies, the researchers had good intentions. That is, they did not consider that their research would be detrimental or cause harm because they believed so strongly that the results would benefit many others.

Unethical practices of the past have given rise to the regulations we have today, but MA TESL students may not be familiar with today's standards. TESL researchers do not do things as invasive as the things that biomedical or clinical researchers do, but they still need to consider the effects that research activities may have on research participants. Areas of research ethics that relate specifically to language learning and applied linguistics research include cultural sensitivity and privacy issues among different language groups, falsification and fabrication of research findings, ensuring voluntary participation in research, participant understanding of research expectations, and a strict adherence to confidentiality. MA TESL researchers should be sensitive to the needs and potential vulnerabilities of language learners of all ages and cultural backgrounds. Furthermore, MA TESL researchers need to consider how our research affects the entire community in which the research is conducted. MA TESL students have the potential to conduct research in all parts of the world. Do they know whether human subjects research is regulated in their locale? If so, how is it regulated and who falls under the umbrella of protection? For instance, in some countries only medical research is regulated; there may be no protections for educational or social and behavioral research participants. MA TESL researchers who subscribe to a code of ethics serve as positive models in the global research arena.

Final Remarks

The research methods course is usually the most anxiety-causing class in a MA TESL program. Providing this course in an online environment may add a level of concern for students and online instructors. Interactive discussions, activity worksheets, and clearly stated expectations can help alleviate student concerns. Explicit teaching of writing, library searches, electronic spreadsheet programs, and other graduate-level competencies add to the rigor of a research methods course and increase student success. MA TESL students also need a solid grounding in the ethical conduct of research in order to protect their own students as potential research participants and to protect themselves as TESL professionals. By considering the recommendations provided by recent research on online courses and building virtual classroom communities and incorporating some of the suggestions that I have made in this chapter, the development and execution of an online research methods course will hopefully result in success for MA TESL students.

Discussion Questions

1. As McAllister (this text) mentions, learners should be taught how to read and apprehend research materials explicitly, not implicitly. McAllister also mentions

that it is important to have a realization of students' ability levels. How can you discern a way of identifying student ability levels without being in a face-to-face classroom?

2. You are teaching an MA TESL online research and statistics class for the first time (or if you are currently teaching a research and statistics class, reflect on the first class you ever taught). One of your students sends you an email before class starts, asking you information about how the course is generally run. While reading the email you sense a great feeling of apprehension on the student's behalf. After reading this chapter, what are some things you could mention about the class that would give the student a better "feeling" about the course? How would you ease his/hers pre-class jitters?

References

Aragon, S. R. (2003) Creating social presence in online environments. *New Directions for Adult and Continuing Education, 100*, 57–68.

Bibeau, S. (2001) Social presence, isolation, and connectedness in online teaching and learning: From the literature to real life. *Journal of Instructional Delivery Systems, 15*(3), 35–39.

Bloom, B. S. (1956) *Taxonomy of educational objectives: The classification of educational goals.* New York, NY: Longman.

Chou, C. (2004) A model of learner-centered computer-mediated interaction for collaborative distance learning. *International Journal on e-Learning, 3*, 11–19.

Conrad, R. M., & Donaldson, J. A. (2004) *Engaging the online learner: Activities and resources for creative instruction.* San Francisco: Jossey-Bass.

Dabbagh, N., & A., Kitsantas. (2004) Supporting self-regulation in student-centered web-based learning environments. *International Journal on e-Learning 3*, 40–48.

Garrison, D. R., & Anderson, T. (2003) *e-Learning in the 21st century.* London: Routledge Falmer.

Gunawardena, C. N., Lowe, C. A., & Anderson, T. (1997) Analysis of a global online debate and the development of an interaction analysis model for examining social construction of knowledge in computer conferencing. *Journal of Educational Computing Research, 17*(4), 397–431.

Kardas, E. P., & Spatz, C. (2007) Teaching ethics in research methods classes. In D. S. Dunn, R. A. Smith, and B. C. Beins (Eds.), *Best practices for teaching statistics and research methods in the Behavioral Sciences* (pp. 159–171). Mahwah, NJ: Lawrence Erlbaum.

Kirtman, L. (2009) Online versus in-class courses: An examination of differences in learning outcomes. *Issues in Teacher Education, 18*(2), 103–116.

Landrum, R. E., & Smith, R. A. (2007) Creating syllabi for statistics and research methods courses. In D. S. Dunn, R. A. Smith, and B. C. Beins (Eds.), *Best practices for teaching statistics and research methods in the Behavioral Sciences* (pp. 45–57). Mahwah, NJ: Lawrence Erlbaum.

Lim, J. H., Dannels, S. A., & Watkins, R. (2008) Qualitative investigation of doctoral students' learning experiences in online research methods courses. *Quarterly Review of Distance Education, 9*(3), 223–236.

Roessingh, H., & Johnson, C. (2005) Online teaching and learning in TESL professional development. *Quarterly Review of Distance Education, 6*(2), 107–115.

Thomas, S. B., & Quinn, S. C. (1991) The Tuskegee Syphilis Study, 1932 to 1972: Implications for HIV education and AIDS risk education programs in the Black community. *American Journal of Public Health, 81,* 1498–1505.

Tu, C., & McIsaac, M. (2002) The relationship of social presence and interaction in online classes. *American Journal of Distance Education, 16*(3), 131–150.

Winston, B. E., & Fields, D. L. (2003) Developing dissertation skills of doctoral students in an internet-based distance education curriculum: A case study. *American Journal of Distance Education, 17*(3), 161–172.

Zimbardo, P. G. (1973) On the ethics of intervention in human psychological research: With special reference to the Stanford Prison Experiment. *Cognition, 2,* 243–256.

9

BUILDING AN ONLINE COMMUNITY OF INQUIRY WITH PARTICIPANT-MODERATED DISCUSSIONS

Joan Kang Shin and Beverly Bickel

Introduction

> Eventually, online courses and specially TEYL is not only a platform to learn but it is also means of experience exchange and a melting pot for different ways and flavors of teaching across cultures.
>
> (Online course participant from Lebanon, Fall 2011)

In spite of the vast diversity of our human cultures and languages, teachers around the world share a common problem. We are often isolated, so busy with our own students in our own classrooms that we may not have sufficient time to interact with colleagues to consider teaching dilemmas and possible approaches that might generate from collegial conversations. This chapter will explore one approach to encouraging discussions among international English teachers in online courses, thereby addressing this fundamental obstacle to teacher professional development.

University of Maryland, Baltimore County (UMBC) has been offering online professional development courses to international English teachers and conducting research on the courses since 2004, beginning with a single methodology course for bi-national centers in Latin America and then becoming one of the first five U.S. universities to offer a course for the U.S. Department of State E-Teacher Scholarship Program. Since that time, we have expanded our offerings to English teachers online now reaching over 700 international English teachers a year. From the beginning, we have designed courses with a teaching commitment to inclusive pedagogies; a research framework based in sociocultural learning theory, specifically communities of practice and TESOL professional development literature; and an action research inquiry approach focused on communities of practice of international English teachers. Participating teachers begin the course with detailed descriptions of English language education and student profiles from their schools and region in a unique opportunity to engage each other as experts in their local and national contexts. In addition, the courses take advantage of the affordances of online education to provide participants with access to and engagement with experts in the English teaching field from various locations beyond what is available locally.

We wanted to design courses and research focused on how the English teachers in the courses were participating in online spaces; we knew that the ways in which they worked in our online classes would have to be understood from multiple perspectives that recognized the power of their previous educational experiences, and their expectations about learning and teaching. Designers and instructors would have to be aware of a host of other influences including access to the Internet, teachers' time to be students themselves, and their English language proficiency for this specialized, cross-cultural academic and professional development learning space. We focused on the discussion board as the place where an inclusive community of learners could best be developed and expressed. Using a community of inquiry approach (Garrison, Anderson, & Archer, 2000), we explored how cognitive presence and critical thinking could be expanded and deepened through the addition of a starter-wrapper technique (Hara, Bonk, & Angeli, 2000) on the discussion board and how teaching presence could better be distributed to participants, especially the starters and wrappers who led each week's discussions (Shin & Bickel, 2008).

A central dilemma began to emerge. Instructors were asked to focus on increasing the cognitive presence of the group as a whole through the identification of problems, exploration of different perspectives, integration of various opinions and sources of knowledge, and finally the resolution or application to real world situations (Garrison, Anderson, & Archer, 2000). This work required significant instructor interaction on the discussion board. Simultaneously, we asked them to distribute teaching presence, specifically to the starters and wrappers who would be responsible to increase participant engagement and leadership through facilitating discourse. Not infrequently, instructors found themselves having to decide whether to intervene more directly and frequently on the discussion board in order to move the discussion to deeper and more integrated levels, or to remain silent in order to allow the week's starters and wrappers to manage discussions. We discovered that some instructors engaged actively and directly with individual students pushing them to think more critically, questioning, asking them to integrate knowledge of texts, and even modeling academic discourses as a corrective to what instructors perceived to be off-topic exchanges, individual experienced-based stories or unfocused social exchanges. Other instructors chose to privilege the distribution of teaching presence and remained more in the background of the discussions, allowing participant leaders to struggle with the discussion leadership tasks. Instructors take a variety of approaches to managing this dynamic tension, and this chapter will explore those approaches and discuss implications for communities of inquiry.

In this chapter, we want to explore that central teaching dilemma and discuss how it has appeared most recently across multiple courses through instructors' descriptions of their differing approaches to the participant-led discussions and the observed relationship between instructor modeling and starter and wrapper leadership as evidenced on discussion boards. The chapter will provide background and context for the program and research frameworks; describe some initial research using the community of inquiry model; describe the starter-wrapper approach to participant-led discussions; discuss some central teaching dilemmas in several recent courses; provide some conclusions and recommendations for participant-led, online teaching and future research; and offer questions for consideration and discussion.

Background and Contexts

Program Background

This chapter describes a seven-year-old non-credit, online TESOL professional development program being offered at UMBC through Continuing and Professional Studies. UMBC's online TESOL PD program, begun in 2004, worked in consortium with the University of Oregon, bringing together approximately 700 English teaching professionals from over 100 countries each year through the E-Teacher Scholarship Program. UMBC offers additional online TESOL PD courses through various U.S. Department of State funded programs centers and other organizations. The courses developed through UMBC's flagship E-Teacher program are described below:[1]

> The E-Teacher Scholarship Program offers English teaching professionals living outside the United States the opportunity to take one of seven innovative, online graduate level classes through the University of Maryland, Baltimore County, and the University of Oregon. The courses explore major areas of the academic specialty of Teaching English as a Foreign Language (TEFL). In addition to specific knowledge of each of the seven major areas of TEFL, each course:
> - introduces participants to the most recent TEFL methods and techniques;
> - engages participants in an innovative distance-learning program, employing the latest in modern technology;
> - provides participants with direct access to U.S. experts.

The online courses in UMBC's program were designed to provide English teaching professionals around the world with non-credit training for teaching English as a foreign language (EFL) and access to U.S. English teaching experts in the hopes of improving English language teaching in the participants' countries. Because the courses are designed to be at the graduate level, they were structured as seminars with the goal of building a learning community among participants that would enhance their understanding of the theories and practices of teaching EFL to young learners and delve deeply and critically into the major theoretical and practical issues surrounding the teaching of EFL in different countries around the world. Because the participants, who were nominated by the U.S. Department of State, Office of English Language Programs, are spread out across every time zone, the only way for everyone to interact as a group was asynchronously. Therefore, the site for building this online learning community was in the course's asynchronous discussion board.

In addition, one of the goals of the program that is not stated on the website but is an integral part of the program is to develop participants' leadership skills within the course and beyond. During the course, participants moderate their own discussions and collaboratively consider teaching problems and possible solutions to resolve them with each other. Every course ends with a final action or training plan assignment in which participants describe how they will disseminate the knowledge and skills learned in their online course to other English teaching professionals in their local, regional or national contexts. Thus participants leave the course equipped to disseminate their learning to their teaching colleagues.

This approach to collaborative knowledge production in the online courses requires three fundamental affordances: participating teachers having time and space to talk with each other, teachers having access to the Internet and ability to use specific courseware, and course instructors making transparent an inclusive pedagogy, specifically on the participant-moderated discussion board. This central space in the courses allows for peer-to-peer engagement and collaborations around co-constructing meanings of texts. Teachers are invited to participate in dynamic discussions led by colleagues around teaching dilemmas and domain knowledge controversies. Instructors ask participants to apply course concepts to the practices and dilemmas of their local contexts, often revealing limitations in ideas advanced from British, U.S., or Australian English teaching texts and experts. Participants work together to interpret "official knowledge" and discuss ways that suggested approaches might be discarded or transformed for use in particular local and regional contexts.

Research Frameworks

Online TESOL professional development work that focuses on the theories and practices of English language education informs our courses and research. We strive to develop each course into a community of practice (CoP) in which each participant may move fluidly between novice learner and master roles, challenging everyone to reconsider learning and teaching as a shared social process (Lave & Wenger, 1991). The participant-led discussion board is the central location and mechanism of a community that "differs from a mere collection of people by the strength and depth of the culture it is able to establish and which in turn supports group activity and cohesion" (Riel & Polin, 2004, p. 18). Drawing on Wenger's subsequent work (1998), we expect a community of practice to be a place of distributed work, doing the work of posing teaching problems and considering possible solutions, discussing cultural models for education, discussing research about teaching and learning English, and exploring application of new learning to local contexts (Shin & Bickel, 2008).

Committed to designing courses based in inclusive pedagogies (Adams, 1992; Darder, 1996; hooks, 1994; hooks, 2003; Tuitt, 2003), program leaders drew upon literature on TESOL professional development that emphasizes teachers' active engagement in their own professional development, reflective practices and the power of collaborative action research on teaching practices (Crookes, 2003; Cummins, 2001; Echevarria, Vogt & Short, 2008; England, 1998; Freeman & Johnson, 1998; and Richards, 1998) and situates its work within a critical understanding of global English teaching (Holliday, 2005). The program encompasses TESOL domain knowledge about teaching and learning English that is the base content of each course. Participants in the courses are experienced international English teachers who come to the courses with significant domain knowledge and field expertise and position themselves simultaneously as teachers and students. Thus the knowledge base of each class begins with TESOL domain knowledge structured into weekly modules, but we invite participants to deepen and extend the collective and dynamic knowledge of each course module. Instructors ask participants to critically read course texts; work together to understand, interpret, critique and extend texts; and explain to each other the relevance of concepts from the texts to their local teaching contexts. Instructors in the courses must constantly be aware of and manage this tension between what Lave and Wenger (1991) described as the reification of knowledge and the participation of diverse people in constructing knowledge using diverse sources. This tension can be productive and animating for a community as members establish shared domain or content knowledge while continually deepening the complexity of that knowledge based on its diversity and as members do the work of critically interrogating their teaching decisions within local contexts—what activity theorists call the mediating components of an educational system (Morgan, 2011)—and creatively applying shared knowledge to new situations (Polin, 2008).

We conceptualize each online professional development course as a community of practice. The courses create an online pedagogical space that provides participants who are geographically dispersed the opportunity to communicate with each other to share ideas and experiences and encouraged them to impart their new knowledge and skills to other professionals in their local context (Shin & Bickel, 2008). When learning occurs as a result of meaningful dialogue among members of a community through sustained social discourse and engagement in the acquisition and construction of new knowledge a community of practice is formed (Lave & Wenger, 1991).

The guiding framework for our work with participant-led discussion boards in a graduate-level course is drawn from Garrison, Anderson, and Archer (2000) and their community of inquiry model. Whether online or face-to-face, a graduate-level seminar consistent with socio-cultural theories of education should form a "community of inquiry" where all participants, including instructors, are deepening their understanding of course content and constructing new knowledge through social interaction (Garrison et al., 2000). The community of inquiry results in a meaningful educational experience at the intersection of the three key elements: teaching presence, social presence, and cognitive presence.

Teaching presence describes the various types of actions taken by the instructor, which include course organization and design, direct instruction of content, and facilitation of interaction among participants in the course. The facilitation of interaction among participants sets the climate for *social presence*, which describes how the participants connect with each other on a social and emotional level within a community of inquiry. Finally, through the social interaction among participants, *cognitive presence* measures how much participants in a community of inquiry construct meaning through critical interaction with each other and course content.

Preliminary Study Using Community of Inquiry Model

Initial research (Shin, 2008; Shin & Bickel, 2008) compared two implementations of one online TESOL methodology course called Teaching English to Young Learners (one of the continuing online courses offered in the E-Teacher Scholarship Program). The main purpose of the study was to see if student-moderated discussions that encourage participants to determine their own discussion topics and facilitate their own discussions using the starter-wrapper strategy would affect the levels of social and cognitive presence. During the first course, offered in the Fall semester of 2004, only the instructor determined the topics and conducted the discussions by responding promptly and encouraging participation by asking challenging questions and posing problems related to the course content. Despite the success of the course as reported by the participants, it was still uncertain whether or not a true learning community had been facilitated through interaction among participants. In fact, without an analysis of the messages on the discussion board, it was not clear if there was quality interaction among participants or just "serial monologues" that Henri (1992) defined as messages posted by individual participants to share their experiences without connecting to each other's messages. Although each participant expressed their satisfaction with sharing ideas with others, there was not necessarily any development of new ideas constructed through social interaction among participants. If a successful community of inquiry is created among instructors and participants, then participants should be constructing new knowledge and finding solutions to problems posed in the course.

Analyzing a sample from two discussion forums from the 2004 course showed that the majority of participants' posts were in phase two, the exploration phase; participants spent the majority of their interaction sharing information and playing with ideas. However they did not often engage each other much on the integration of ideas or the application of them. The lack of messages in the application phase showed that there was little construction of new knowledge or resolution of problems posed. Therefore, according to the analysis of the discussion board in the Fall 2004 course, a strong critical community of inquiry was not built. These results matched Pawan, Paulus, Yalcin, & Chang's (2003) and Garrison et al.'s (2001) studies that also found that the discussions reaching the exploration phase were most common, particularly when the instructor did not define discussion board strategies.

Increasing Social and Cognitive Presence Through the Starter-Wrapper Approach

In order to build a more successful learning community in the online course that creates a true critical community of inquiry in the second implementation of the course, an instructional intervention was developed based on studies by Arnold and Ducate (2006), Celentin (2007), and Pawan et al. (2003), which were all studies of online foreign language teacher education using the community of inquiry model. In the second year of the course, the instructor structured the discussion board more carefully with a word limit for posts (150–250 words) and a learner centered approach to the discussion using a form of the starter-wrapper technique (Hara, Bonk, & Angeli, 2000), which assigned two students to moderate the discussion by initiating topics, posing questions, and summarizing what was learned. In addition, the instructor modeled the technique during the first week as shown here in the discussion board instructions in the course materials.

Discussion Board Instructions
Here is where the real learning begins through interaction with each other! You will post at least three messages per discussion in each weekly unit. When you participate in the discussions, you should consider the content in the unit and what you are writing in your reflective essay. Your discussion board posts will be graded for quality of content (see Discussion Board Rubric). Always interact with each other meaningfully in each post and use the content in the unit to support your ideas.

Discussion Board Moderators
In each weekly unit, two participants will be responsible for managing the Discussion Board. The two roles are called starter and wrapper. These two people will moderate the discussion by asking questions that challenge, connect, and extend information posted to the discussion board.

Starter: This person will start the discussion by asking motivating questions and/or posing relevant problems related to the topics of the unit (reflective essay/discussion prompt). He/she should post some starter questions to the discussion board by Friday. He/she will also keep the discussion going by getting participants to share ideas, explore the question(s), and think critically about the topics or problems posed. He/she should continue to pose questions and respond to participants through Monday.

Wrapper: This person will encourage participants to find solutions and real-life applications to the problems posed by using motivating questions (like the starter). He/she should start moderating the discussion by Monday. He/she will integrate the ideas shared by the group and try to conclude the unit by highlighting all new ideas, solutions, and applications constructed through the discussion. He/she will continue the discussion through Thursday.

Your instructor will be the starter and wrapper for the first unit.

Starter: Messages will be posted in blue.

Wrapper: Messages will be posted in green.

Suggestion: Good discussion board posts are 150–250 words. Please try to stay within this word limit. Happy posting!

Results from an analysis of the first two years of two similar courses showed increased quantity of messages (from 603 to 1,105; per participant from nine to 22 for three units), increase in length and complexity of discussion threads, decreased serial monologues (46% to 27%), increased cognitive presence, and increased social presence (interactive and cohesive indicators).

Based on this preliminary study of the first two years of TEYL courses, program leaders decided that the starter-wrapper technique was instrumental in encouraging increased interaction as well as social and cognitive presence. Therefore, by year three all instructors began using this technique. Although no formal training has been given on the starter-wrapper technique, instructors were given the instructions above and access to previous courses where they can see models of other instructors' use of starter-wrapper, including their modeling in the first unit. In addition to the instructions, instructors are given a rubric to use to give feedback on participants' weekly messages that requires interaction with unit content and colleagues' ideas. See appendix for an example of the rubric co-constructed by instructors of the program.[2]

Differing Approaches to the Discussion Boards and Teaching Dilemmas

As the program has expanded to include 10 part-time instructors, who live in various places in the United States and around the world and may each be teaching multiple courses, the instructors' challenge has become how to most effectively use the starter-wrapper approach when they do not have much time to consider the research behind this pedagogical approach, few significant training opportunities, and limited contact with other online instructors. As a course begins and before instructors know the participants, instructors must immediately model the starter and wrapper leadership roles. They do not yet understand much about the participants: their English language proficiency for reading graduate level academic texts, integrating ideas from multiple sources, or synthesizing ideas in academic writing; their background knowledge or domain content knowledge; their Internet access; or the time participants expect to be able to be online working on the course. In light of these challenges, instructors find their own ways to use the starter-wrapper approach and work through a central dilemma of balancing the goal of increasing cognitive presence while distributing teaching presence on the discussion board.

In fact, the instructions for starters and wrappers were originally designed purposefully to encourage participant-moderators to help course participants to increase their cognitive presence in the course. According to the instructions written by Shin (2008), the starter encourages phases 1 and 2, and the wrapper leads participants through phases 3 and 4. See coding for cognitive presence in Table 9.1.

These instructions for starter-wrapper also encourage distributing teaching presence as defined by Anderson, Rourke, Garrison, & Archer (2001), and both starter and wrapper roles include aspects of direct instruction and facilitating discourse. Although each instructor receives the same set of instructions, he/she has a unique interpretation of how to model the two leadership roles; some instructors take a more facilitative role while others tend to give more direct instruction. An analysis of instructor approaches to modeling and continuing engagement with discussions from seven years of courses demonstrate three basic approaches to instruction within discussions: direct, participatory, and facilitating.

The three different approaches can be illustrated with data from three instructors from Fall 2011. We observed differences in the quantity of messages posted by the instructors in relation to the number of overall posts.

While the numeric differences are evident, differences in instructor approaches are not solely based on quantity. Some differences in the quality of the instructors' approaches are described below and could be examined more deeply in future research that might investigate the impact of these differing instructional approaches on learners' participation and content knowledge.

Deciding How to Model the Starter-Wrapper Technique

Once instructors start teaching they must model the starter-wrapper roles in the first unit with a group of participants they do not yet know, with the particular challenge of not yet understanding their English language proficiency or Internet access. Instructors must be cognizant that in this first week, their modeling will

TABLE 9.1 Starter-wrapper instructions coded with cognitive and teaching presence.

Instructions	Cognitive presence	Teaching
Starter: This person will start the discussion by asking motivating questions and/or posing relevant problems related to the topics of the unit. He/she should post some starter questions to the discussion board by Friday.	Phase 1: Triggering event	Direct instruction: Presenting content/ questions
He/she will also keep the discussion going by getting participants to share ideas, explore the question(s), and think critically about the topics or problems posed. He/she should continue to pose questions and respond to participants through Monday.	Phase 2: Exploration	Facilitating discourse: Encouraging, acknowledging, or reinforcing student contributions, drawing participants in, prompting discussion
Wrapper: This person will encourage participants to find solutions and real-life applications to the problems posed by using motivating questions (like the starter).	Phase 4: Resolution	Facilitating discourse: Encouraging, acknowledging, or reinforcing student contributions, drawing participants in, prompting discussion, seeking to reach consensus, identifying areas of agreement
He/she should start moderating the discussion by Monday. He/she will integrate the ideas shared by the group and try to	Phase 3: Integration	
conclude the unit by highlighting all new ideas, solutions, and applications constructed through the discussion. He/she will continue the discussion through Thursday.	Phase 4: Resolution	Direct instruction: Summarizing discussion

likely be used by participants assigned into discussion leadership roles, especially related to online communication features such as greetings, signing off, and length of post as well as how much time and space is dedicated to presentation of content versus facilitation of discussion. During the first unit, instructors varied significantly in how they modeled starting, moderating, and ending discussions for participants.

TABLE 9.2 Types of online discussion board instructors.

Type of approach	Characteristics
Direct approach	• Teacher-centered/content-centered • Often gives direct instruction on discussion board • Always visible on discussion board
Participatory approach	• Learner-centered • Participates as an equal member of community (shares ideas, offers information) • Always visible on the discussion board
Facilitating approach	• Learner-centered • Does not give direct instruction on discussion board • Not often visible on discussion board after modeling starter-wrapper roles

TABLE 9.3 Quantity of instructor messages on discussion board.

	# messages in 10 weeks	# messages by instructor	% total messages	Average posts per week
Instructor #1 Direct approach	2,621	371	14.2%	32
Instructor #2 Participatory approach	973	94	9.7%	8.75
Instructor #3 Facilitating approach	1,074	31	2.9%	3.9

The average posts per week with teacher-participants as the starters and wrappers. Does not include other discussions, such as the first unit with instructor modeling.

Some instructors gave specific discussion board prompts in addition to the discussion board instructions. Notice how Instructor #1 injects knowledge from one of the unit readings and poses numerous questions in order to prompt the discussion.

> Unit 1:TEFL in the 21st Century
> Discussion Board Prompt
> Many teachers use cultural content in their classrooms, believing that such a focus will motivate their students. Since English is no longer connected to the culture of Inner Circle countries (McKay, 2002), whose culture should you teach? Do you agree that a language cannot be taught without knowledge of a target culture? What are some advantages and disadvantages of using different cultural materials? Consider how the choice of cultural content is affected by the contexts where English is taught and where the teacher is considered to be the main source of information. Do you agree that non–native speakers are in an optimal position to lead their students into the realm of EIL? Use examples from your context to support your point of view.

Subsequent discussion prompts posted by Instructor #1 also cited one of the weekly readings or lectures and included related questions. Then Instructor #1 modeled the starter role in week one by posting three new starter questions on three separate threads. The model of the wrapper role was similar to the starter posts described above, except Instructor #1 concluded the discussion by posting a 13-page document with 5,799 words that included the questions posed, summary of areas of consensus, participant responses copied and pasted into the document, and concluding comments. She reported that her wrapper summary was "more exaggerated than normal … it was intended to add more content since their prior knowledge of EIL is/was limited" and that this was communicated with participant wrappers.

When modeling in the first unit, Instructor #2 gave an initial prompt in the discussion board instructions for participants.

> Week 1 Discussion Board
> Describe the assessment and testing of EFL students that takes place in your teaching context. What types of tests or assessments are commonly used? Describe these using the vocabulary from this unit. Feel free to also comment on anything that surprised you or that you learned from the presentation and the reading this week.

Instructor #2 used the prompt to encourage participants to share information about the unit topic from their local context. This instructor focuses on the teacher-participants and their teaching contexts, which may include as many as 20–25 countries in a class of 25 participants. This approach differs from the approach of Instructor #1 whose prompt focuses first on evoking comprehension of readings and then requesting local examples as support. Throughout the following nine units, Instructor #2 did not designate a discussion board prompt, but posted these instructions: "The starter will provide the prompts for this DB by Friday, midnight EST." Thus course participants were responsible for the prompts.

Like Instructor #2, Instructor #3 did not give a specific prompt with each weekly discussion forum. Instead, she modeled the development of starter questions based on the unit materials.

> "Starter Questions—Set 1"
> Dear participants,
> Welcome to Unit 1.
> As you read and listen to the lecture, reflect on what you are reading and hearing, and post your responses to some of the questions to the Discussion Board.
> • When is English introduced in your country?
> • Was the age for starting English lowered recently?
> • Why do you think so many countries are starting compulsory English education earlier and earlier?

The questions focused on the learner and prompted participants to share information about their local context and then share their opinion on the state of English education. There were two more sets of starter questions, which were in the same format, a bulleted list of three questions. Then Instructor #3 started the wrapper role by summarizing the discussion with main ideas from the discussion in a 635-word post followed by three additional questions for participants to answer for the second half of the week, which used the same length and format of the starter post.

When modeling how to start a discussion, Instructor #1 was more academically oriented and content-centered and focused on having participants display comprehension of the text, whereas Instructors #2 and #3 had a more discussion-centered approach that prompted participants to share information about their local context in relation to the unit topics.

Considering Whether and How to Intervene in Discussions

Once participants take over the starter and wrapper roles in the second week, the central dilemma considered in this chapter begins to emerge in which instructors are challenged to decide where and how to intervene in the discussions based on their judgments about the relative importance of distributing teaching presence or directly intervening to instruct with course content. Instructor #1 participated most actively, providing direct instruction by injecting knowledge from the readings and other sources independently of the amount of participation from the starters and wrapper. Her average number of posts per week was 32, which is more than the starters and wrappers who averaged 22.5 posts per week. Instructor #1 describes her own approach after being asked "To what extent do you as the instructor interact on the discussion board? How do you make those decisions about when and how to interact?"

> I facilitate the DB in the following ways: 1) ALWAYS welcome the starter(s) and wrapper(s) as soon as they post and usually comment about the question they have posed and convey how much the question fits in with the unit topic, materials, handouts, etc. OR make a subtle suggestion that a question be re-guided or expanded. 2) WAIT a day or two to give colleagues a chance to establish collaboration UNLESS a question is not getting responses, then I will offer a bridging perspective or consideration from the original moderator post. 3) JUMP-IN when great quality ideas relative to the topic are posted as well as ask for clarification from a colleague when their response lacks clarity by asking Can you please clarify what you mean by...or what do you mean when you say.... 4) ADD content (usually application type handouts) and links when knowledge base is very low of unit topic. 5) Generally, allow the moderators to take charge while I act as a guide.

As Instructor #1 describes, her approach is more teacher-centered and uses more direct instruction by adding content as well redirecting the discussion. This can be seen often in responses that instruct. A typical message was approximately 400 words and followed a similar format to the excerpted message below.

> Dear {participant name} and all colleagues,
> Did you mean "some vocabulary cannot be learned if students have no knowledge of the target language" culture? Furthermore, what culture do you think should be taught in the English language classroom?
> Let's refer to the McKay article, *Culture in Teaching English as an International Language* (pp. 88–93) from your unit required readings.
> McKay states "…"
> From our lecture, we have learned…
> The fundamental idea here is…
> She (McKay) also states that…
> Questions: The following questions are a further extension of ideas. Take a look at them and then refer back to the article pages for additional review. Pick one or two questions to comment about. Also, please indicate in your response which question you are referring to. (Series of 4 questions follow)

This type of message from Instructor #1 was over the word limit set for participants of 150–250 words (with her longest posts ranging from 295 to 700 words) partially because it contained references to readings, lectures or other unit materials.

Instructor #2 averaged 8.75 posts per week, considerably fewer messages than Instructor #1. He describes his approach to using the discussion board below.

> My general approach is to let the students "control" the discussion, but to offer my own perspectives and offer questions that I hope will guide them more towards the topic at hand or in a more academic direction. I have little trouble with students engaging in discussion, but I do struggle with keeping them on task and making sure that the discussion is at a desired academic level. So, I tend to refer to the readings and ask probing questions that require them to use the course materials and their understanding of it as they answer. Grading also helps. I like to remind participants of the items on the discussion board rubric and that they must demonstrate critical understanding, not only of their colleagues' posts, but of the course content.

Instructor #2 usually acknowledges students' contributions and describes his own experiences.

> I like your description of "Feedback Day." It is similar to what I have done, with midterm and end-of-semester conferences with students. I have found that

the learners get more out of the feedback if I ask them to prepare something to share with me beforehand. It is usually a worksheet for which they have to answer a few questions about their own perspective on their progress in the course. This makes sure that the conference is more than a handshake and delivery of grades!

Instructor #2 often shared his own experiences as a way of reinforcing the ideas expressed by participants. This approach seems similar to other participants' messages and confirms his own description that he lets the students "control" the discussion.

Instructor #3 participated in the discussions the least; in two discussions she posted zero times. In those discussions, the starters and wrappers were very active, posting from 12 to 35 times each. In a forum in which the wrapper posted only five times, Instructor #3 intervened, adding five messages that quoted participants' posts.

> Hi everyone.
> I think I'd really like to be a young learner listening to stories in your classes. You all have such great ideas for making the story come alive to your students. Chen told us…
> Irina added that…
> Ibrahim uses …
> There is a lot of good advice here. Keep posting everyone.

Having noticed a lack of participation from the wrapper, she added posts to summarize the discussion and encourage more participation. This is congruent with her description of her approach to handling the discussion board.

> I don't do a lot. One of the reasons is I fear that the focus of the discussion will shift from participant to other participants to participants to me and that's not the purpose, I don't think. It is hard to decide when to interact and when to let things go. If I saw something that seems really out of kilter, I'd comment, however.

Regardless of the differences in instructor approach to participant-led discussions using the starter-wrapper technique, teacher-participants in all courses consistently rate the courses highly for both content and delivery. There is no evident difference in participants' satisfaction regardless of the instructors' approach whether direct, participatory, or facilitating. Further examination of the quality of the instructor and participant posts is needed and is the work of future research that would investigate the impact of these different instructional approaches on the participation and content knowledge of learners.

Implications and Recommendations

Over the past seven years, E–Teacher leaders and researchers have read and analyzed thousands of posts and other evidence to understand participant learning. This chapter focused specifically on describing the variety of approaches taken by a growing number of instructors as they moderated discussions and modeled how to moderate discussion for participants who became starters and wrappers of weekly discussions. There is clearly no one right way to approach a participant-moderated discussion within an online English teacher professional development course. Instructors must balance multiple and sometimes conflicting considerations as they make decisions about whether, how and when to increase or diminish their teaching presence (direct instruction and facilitating discourse) in participant-led discussions. Instructors are also juggling the diverse expectations of participants from around the world, each of whom is an experienced teacher with opinions about the role of instructors and effective teaching and learning, which may be contradictory at times or conflicting with expectations about directed teaching versus participation. Unfortunately, many of the instructors, are working in the same relative isolation from other instructors as the teacher-participants in the courses report—they are all teachers with little time for their own professional development or participation in their own communities of practice. Thus, we offer the following recommendations for creating more collaborative opportunities for instructors to be involved in professional development and their own investigations of teaching dilemmas.

Instructors and participating teachers in courses could be involved in action research on their online or local face-to-face (f2f) classes that investigate the relationship of teacher talk to student talk. For online instructors, relevant data is often available through course software and discussion board texts while f2f teachers could record a class or ask colleagues to observe and do simple tallies of how often teachers and students talk and to whom. Once quantity is understood, the more complex and important task is to look at the quality of teacher and student talk. For the online instructors, this involves specifically the relationship between instructor modeling and starter-wrapper approaches. Given sufficient time and support, instructors could be involved in qualitative analysis of threaded posts using the four phases (triggering event, exploration, integration, application) of the Practical Inquiry Model (Garrison et al., 2001). In the most recent course offerings, program leadership staff have trained instructors, some of whom are overseas, in using a common assessment rubric of cognitive presence, but there has not been sufficient time for discussion about the course goals of increasing cognitive presence while distributing teaching presence.

Orientation for instructors should include more time for such discussions, and that could help equip instructors to involve course participants in similar metacognitive discussions. We recognize that such discussions are complicated by contextual conditions of the courses: participants' Internet access and time for participation in the course, their English proficiency, their experience with professional development contexts or discussions, and the tension between developing domain knowledge and participation in constructing locally-relevant knowledge. Nevertheless, we recommend to ourselves and readers that there be reflective assignments that challenge participants to consider the possible applications of increasing cognitive presence of students in their own settings, and even considerations of distributing teaching presence among students.

As the UMBC E-Teacher program expanded the number of online teacher professional development courses, it also needed additional instructors. As we considered the central dilemma addressed in this chapter related to the dynamic tension between domain knowledge presented by instructors and course materials and the participating English teachers' collaborative participation in deepening and applying knowledge to diverse local contexts, we understood more deeply the need for a more structured community of practice among the online instructors. We recommend that in addition to orienting materials on the conceptual framework and expectations of the courses, instructors have mentoring and participation opportunities, as well as online spaces, for discussion of teaching dilemmas and collaborative action research on their practice.

Sponsors of many teacher professional development courses have a goal of dissemination of participants' learning. We recommend considering an explicit assignment or discussion of dissemination for purposes of strategy and idea sharing among participants and dissemination documentation for program stakeholders. In a final reflection essay, this participant from Lebanon, in the Fall 2011, wrote,

> To sum up I can say that this course gave me high morale and nice reputation among other Lebanese teachers. Even the main principal of (Makassed) schools felt the great improvement in my teaching and coordination style. He asked me to train and support teachers in their teaching career and to provide them with any technique I have already learnt from my course online ... I'm working now on training teachers through different workshops and what's worth to mention here is that all the workshops that I'm going to conduct this year will be based on all the topics that were mentioned in this course. In this way you can make sure that about 65 teachers and about 3200 students will benefit from this course. I'm also trying to join an English center in our area to train more and more teachers.

Regardless of the particular instructional approach to online discussions, it is clear that throughout the courses offered during the past seven years, participants value highly the opportunity to talk with and learn from their teaching colleagues who are working in diverse contexts around the world. This work will benefit from additional research on the quality of participating teachers' experience vis-à-vis the variety of instructional approaches to participant-led discussions and our goal of increasing cognitive presence and distributing teaching presence. Each individual's knowledge and skills, sense of identity as a teacher and a learner, and a variety of other contextual components must be included in any assessment and analysis. Course evaluations have consistently rated discussions among the participating teachers as the most important contribution to participants' learning. As a Fall 2011 participant wrote,

> We have been working hard throughout the past 3 months to achieve and submit our assignments for the course that we took on ourselves to continue till the last moment. We really enjoyed working with a lot of people from all over the world. We had the chance every week to talk, discuss, and above all share knowledge and experience.

Discussion Questions

1. Think about the three different instructor approaches to discussion board moderation—direct, participatory, and facilitating. Which one do you think would be most effective? What other considerations might be relevant: type of course and its content, background of participants, or type of discussion task? Explain.
2. How do you as a teacher online or in a classroom manage the tension between teaching domain or content knowledge and invite students to participate in deepening and extending knowledge?
3. What are your biggest online TESOL teaching dilemmas? What kind of community of practice would be more helpful to you: a community of other teachers teaching in the same course and context or a community of teachers from diverse courses and contexts? Explain.
4. In what ways might cultural differences affect your approach to online discussion board moderation? How can an instructor facilitate different communication practices and prevent intercultural misunderstandings on the discussion board?

Notes

1   As stated on the U.S. Department of State's webpage: http://exchanges.state.gov/englishteaching/eteacher.html
2   This rubric was designed by Joan Kang Shin, Teresa Valais, and John Mark King for use in TESOL Professional Training Programs at the University of Maryland, Baltimore County.

References

Adams, M. (1992) Cultural inclusion in the American college classroom. In N.V. N. Chism & L. L. B. Border (Eds), *New directions for teaching and learning: Teaching for diversity* (pp. 5–17). San Francisco, CA: Jossey-Bass Publishers.

Anderson, T., Rourke, L., Garrison, D. R., & Archer, W. (2001) Assessing teaching presence in a computer conferencing context. *Journal of Asynchronous Learning Networks, 5*(2), 1–17.

Arnold, N., & Ducate, L. (2006) Future foreign language teachers' social and cognitive collaboration in an online environment. *Language Learning & Technology, 10*(1), pp. 42–66.

Celentin, P. (2007) Online training: analysis of interaction and knowledge building patterns among foreign language teachers. *Journal of Distance Education, 21*(3), 39–58.

Crookes, G. (2003) *A practicum in TESOL: Professional development through teaching practice.* Cambridge: Cambridge University Press.

Cummins, J. (2001) Empowering minority students: A framework for intervention. *Harvard Educational Review, 71*(4), 649–676.

Darder, A. (1996) Creating the conditions for cultural democracy in the classroom. In C. Turner, M. Garcia, A. Nora, & L. I. Rendon (Eds), *Racial and ethnic diversity in higher education* (pp. 134–149). Needham Heights, MA: Simon & Schuster.

Echevarría, J., Vogt, M., & Short, D. (2008) *Making content comprehensible for English Learners: The SIOP Model.* New York: Pearson.

England, L. (1998) Promoting effective professional development in English language teaching (ELT). *English Teaching Forum, 36*(2), 1–9.

Freeman, D., & Johnson, K. E. (1998) Reconceptualizing the knowledge base of language teacher education. *TESOL Quarterly, 32*(3), 397–417.

Garrison, D. R., Anderson, T., & Archer, W. (2000) Critical inquiry in a text-based environment: computer conferencing in higher education. *The Internet and Higher Education, 2*(2–3), 87–105.

Garrison, D. R., Anderson, T., & Archer, W. (2001) Critical thinking, cognitive presence, and computer conferencing in distance education. *American Journal of Distance Education, 15*(1), 7–23.

Hara, N., Bonk, C. J., & Angeli, C. (2000) Content analysis of online discussion in an applied psychology course. *Instructional Science, 28*(2), 115–152.

Henri, F. (1992) Computer conferencing and content analysis. In A. R. Kaye (Eds), *Collaborative learning through computer conferencing: The Najaden papers* (pp. 115–136). New York: Springer.

Holliday, A. (2005) *The struggle to teach English as an international language.* Oxford: Oxford University Press.

hooks, b. (1994) *Teaching to transgress: Education as the practice of freedom.* New York, NY: Routledge.

hooks, b. (2003) *Teaching community: A pedagogy of hope.* New York: Routledge.

Lave, J., & Wenger, E. (1991) *Situated learning. Legitimate peripheral participation.* Cambridge: Cambridge University Press.

Morgan, T. (2011) Online classroom or community-in-the-making? Instructor conceptualizations and teaching presence in international online contexts. *Journal of Distance Education, 24*(1).

Pawan, F., Paulus, T. M., Yalcin, S., & Chang, F. S. (2003) Online learning: patterns of engagement and interaction among in-service teachers. *Language Learning & Technology, 7*(3), 119–140.

Polin, L. (2008) Graduate professional education from a community practice perspective: The role of social and technical networking. In C. Kimble, P. Hildreth, & I. Bourdon (Eds), *Communities of practice: Creating learning environments for educators* (pp. 267–285) Charlotte, NC: Information Age Publishing, Inc.

Richards, J. C. (1998) *Beyond training: perspectives on language teacher education.* Cambridge: Cambridge University Press.

Riel, M., & Polin, L. (2004) Online learning communities: Common ground and critical differences in designing technical environments. In S. Barab, R. Kling, & J. H. Gray (Eds), *Designing for virtual communities in the service of learning* (pp. 16–50). Cambridge: Cambridge University Press.

Shin, J. K. (2008) Building an effective international community of inquiry for EFL professionals in an asynchronous online discussion board. (Doctoral dissertation). Retrieved from ProQuest Dissertations and Theses. (UMI No. 3311374).

Shin, J. K., & Bickel, B. (2008) Distributing teaching presence: Engaging teachers of English to young learners in an international virtual community of inquiry. In C. Kimble, P. Hildreth, & I. Bourdon (Eds), *Communities of practice: Creating learning environments for educators* (pp. 149–178). Charlotte, NC: Information Age Publishing, Inc.

Tuitt, F. (2003) Afterword: Realizing a more inclusive pedagogy. In F. Tuitt & A. Howell (Eds), *Race and higher education: Rethinking pedagogy in diverse college classrooms.* Cambridge, MA: Harvard Education Press.

Wenger, Étienne (1998) *Communities of practice: Learning, meaning, and identity.* Cambridge: Cambridge University Press.

Appendix

Discussion Board Rubric: 10 points per weekly discussion

Total possible points = Quantity of posts + Quality of posts		
0–10pts Reflects 0–3 posts with various levels of quality	6pts Posted 3 messages of required length	4pts Posts reflect high level of critical analysis of course unit content and of others' ideas. Posts made contributions that incorporated new perspectives on course content and others' ideas to further the discussion.
	4pts Posted 2 messages of required length	3pts Posts reflect some analysis of course unit content and of others' ideas. Posts made valid contributions to group discussions.
		2pts Posts reflected analysis of course unit content, but did not reflect analysis of others' ideas.
	2pts Posted 1 message of required length	1pt Posts did not reflect analysis of course unit content, but reflected some analysis of others' ideas.
	0pts Posted no messages of required length	0 points Posts did not reflect analysis of course unit content or others' ideas

10

DEVELOPING COMMUNITIES OF PRACTICE AT A DISTANCE

Steve Mann and Jerry Talandis, Jr.

This chapter presents practitioner research from two cases where online communities have been established to support teacher-learners (TLs) taking part in university teacher education programs based in the UK. The first case, based at Aston University, considers how a web-based archive helped reinforce and extend the value of a *majordomo* email discussion list and shows how the site encouraged TLs to make greater use of the resource. The second case, based at University of Warwick, features an initiative using a *Ning*-based online group. Ning is a commercial service enabling *communities of practice* (CofP) to create public or private social networks that allow members to set up individual blogs, engage in forum discussions, create special interest groups, communicate via synchronous chat, and share photos and videos. This case considers how Ning facilitated aspects of design, interaction, and support.

Overall, the chapter aims to share two experiences of setting up and sustaining online CofP and considers what can be learned through a comparative evaluation, focusing primarily on issues of set-up, design, development, types of interaction, usability, and sustainability while integrating perspectives from both tutors and TLs. The community of practice framework (Lave & Wenger, 1991) will be drawn upon to evaluate these two initiatives. According to this framework, such communities provide opportunities for the construction and re-construction of knowledge and experience. Since the collective process of negotiating and articulating new understandings is essentially a sociocultural one (Johnson, 2006), the community "creates the social fabric of learning" (Wenger et al., 2002, p. 28). In particular, the relationship between social, cognitive, and mutual engagement and shared repertoire is examined when considering distinctive features of online distance communities. CofP can be viewed from three dimensions (Wenger, 1998):

- joint enterprise (common purposes and goals)
- mutual engagement (the relationships that bind a group together)
- shared repertoire (communal resources developed through sharing of practice).

There has been a great deal of useful research into professional development through online CofP (e.g. Zhao & Rop, 2001; Gunawardena et al., 2009). Wenger (1998) defines CofP as groups of people who share a common interest for doing something and learning how to do it better as they interact, where learning is both situated in and supported through interactions with both peers and tutors. Membership of the Aston and Warwick online communities was based on TLs' respective involvement in their Masters programs, but each community developed embedded elements of inquiry, learning, and interest.

Review

This section teases out issues and overlap between CofP and other related types of community (*inquiry*, *interest*, and *learning*), drawing primarily upon Garrison, Anderson, and Archer's (2001) work on the relationship between *social*, *cognitive*, and *teaching presence*.

The Relationship Between Social, Cognitive and Teaching Presence

Social presence is "the degree to which participants are able to project themselves affectively" within the online environment (Garrison, 1997, p. 6). Rourke et al. (2001) have argued that social presence is a pre-requisite for cognitive presence as it makes the group interactions appealing, engaging, and thus intrinsically rewarding. Maintaining social presence is important for sustaining online engagement and involved discussion in text-based asynchronous threaded talk (Garrison & Anderson, 2003). *Cognitive presence* is a measure of how learners are able to construct and articulate meaning. For our purposes, cognitive presence involves the mapping of interactive features such as questioning, relating, narrating, reflecting, connecting, developing opinions, challenging, problematizing, and being critical. *Teaching presence* covers aspects of both design and ongoing facilitation and is concerned with the management of, involvement in, and direction of cognitive and social processes in order to arrive at effective learning outcomes (Rourke et al., 2001).

The two case studies in this paper make clear features of their design that helped sustain and promote interaction and also point to significant aspects of social and cognitive presence. A number of studies have looked at the issue of sustaining online communities (see Riverin & Stacey, 2008) and they agree that maintaining either cognitive or social presence is difficult. Why is this the case? Evidence suggests that when involvement is not officially required, then "participants lacked the time and motivation to become involved in the online courses" (Riverin & Stacey, 2008, p. 54). For various reasons, this was found to be true in both featured groups, where involvement was encouraged but not required.

Issues

Levels of Participation and Engagement

A primary issue regarding participation within an online CofP is the participant's understanding of the benefits of involvement. Gray (2004) found that motivations to participate included an opportunity to learn new skills and work practices, establish social and professional connections with colleagues, and help reduce inherent job geographical isolation.

Another factor influencing levels of engagement is the presence of leadership that takes responsibility for set-up, management, and making sure communication flows in a friendly, clear, and productive manner (Bacon, 2009). Active leadership is instrumental in helping online communities reach their potential. As Gray (2004) notes, "the presence of an online moderator helped the community evolve from a forum for sharing information to a CofP where knowledge was constructed through shared learning" (p. 29).

Given the limits TLs face when becoming involved in an online community, it is important to distinguish between levels of activity and assess the balance between active and peripheral participation. With most online communities, it is common for lurkers, those members who do not actively contribute, to outnumber regular posters (Sutton, 2001). Although increasing the number of actively contributing members is desirable, peripheral participation should be recognized as a normal aspect of community engagement (Gray, 2004): "All participation, even at the periphery, is considered legitimate learning, and it is through participation that we learn not only *how to do* but *how to be*" (p. 23).

Cognitive Overload

Kirsh (2000) has written about *cognitive overload*, a situation caused by too much information supply. The sheer quantity of information being delivered through various types of technology is an important factor influencing the sustainability of online communities (Riverin & Stacey, 2008). Considering potential cognitive demands on participants is important when forming the aims of a community and designing the tools through which members will interact. Failure to do so can result in an increase in stress and detrimentally affect participation levels. Gray's (2004) discussion on inactive members points to several questions worth considering in relation to cognitive overload: Is there a sufficient amount of interest to sustain an online community? Are potential participants familiar with the technologies involved and do they understand how these tools can assist their work? Finally, are leaders committed to doing what it takes to properly manage and nurture community interaction?

The Aston MSc Discussion List Archive

The *Aston University English Academic Subject Group Discussion List Archive* (DLA) was a website created in 2004 that enabled course participants (CPs) direct access to past messages sent through the *Aston MSc email discussion list* (ADL). The site was based on the premise that access to an interactive, searchable database of selected academically-oriented discussions could benefit and further establish a viable MSc community. This section will describe and clarify the DLA's role in supporting situated learning on the program by examining how CPs used the site and how a permanent record of ADL discourse supported situated development. Analysis of quantitative and qualitative data collected over a 12-month period indicated CPs at various stages of completion used the site in different ways, much like a reference book, primarily for interpersonal and course content support.

Background

The Aston MSc is a graduate degree program conducted at a distance and based on the concept of *situated learning*, where study focuses on real-world teaching experiences rather than decontextualized knowledge. Personal and professional development is enhanced through explorations of local contexts. CPs are encouraged to interact, cooperate, and collaborate through a network of supportive collegial relationships. In the early days of the program, over 80% of CPs worked in lock-step study groups that met occasionally on a face-to-face basis or via email. However, as the program phased into a modular-based system in the late 1990s, this natural source of support was lost since CPs were no longer working in lock-step groups. To compensate, an automated listserv based on *Majordomo* software was established in 1997 to provide more opportunities for peer interaction outside each participant's local context. After a slow start, the ADL became a key element in the program's support network.

Subscribers to the ADL received all messages sent to the list. Likewise, posting messages enabled all other subscribers to receive them. Membership was voluntary, with the ability to unsubscribe at anytime. CPs were encouraged to use the list in various ways, such as sharing struggles on the program, reflecting on classroom teaching experiences, or discussing interesting issues.

Overall, the ADL was a well-received feature of the Aston MSc. CPs remarked that participating in email discussions helped them feel they belonged to a learning community. Occasionally interaction led to the formation and development of friendships that continued off-line, which ironically may have contributed toward a decrease in overall levels of participation (Moore & Chae, 2007). Nevertheless, tutors were impressed with the friendly yet strong academic flavour of the discussions. Through facilitating peer interaction, the ADL played a role in supporting situated learning on the program in accordance to constructivist principles of learning by helping CPs articulate, examine, test, share, and extend newly formed knowledge structures.

The Problem

Despite the overall success of the ADL, a major problem was the inability of Majordomo to automatically archive contributions. As a result, all discussions had a very short shelf life, benefiting only those subscribing at the time they took place. While it was technically possible to download old discussion threads from a server, the resulting raw, unformatted text was very difficult to read, let alone search in an efficient manner.

As a written form of communication, email carries with it the primary advantage of writing, namely qualities of permanence and objectivity (Freenburg, 1989). On the ADL, this advantage was wasted, as years' worth of interesting and useful discourse remained virtually unavailable. This situation inhibited interaction on the list in several ways. First, it contributed to a sense that the ADL was an underused, unvalued resource frequented by a small core of regulars. Riverin and Stacey (2008) show how regulars can dominate norms of communication and thus mitigate against active contribution from new members. In addition, demotivation, confusion and frustration could easily set in for new members, especially if they joined during a quiet period (because they would have no way of knowing that hundreds of interesting discussions had previously taken place). Finally, without access to previous interactions, current discussions lacked context, while opportunities to revisit relevant issues and questions were lost. In short, the inability to access and build upon the learning community's previous discourse meant the ADL could not reach its fullest potential as a situated learning resource.

Developing the Site

CPs recognized the benefits of having direct, easy access to an archive of past ADL contributions, as evidenced by the practice of collecting and saving pertinent discussions on their own. The idea of creating a resource, such as a website, that cataloged interesting and useful academic discussions in an organized and searchable manner had community support. However, due to the immense size of the undertaking, little concrete action had ever been taken.

In the summer of 2003, a community request for saved discussions met with a favorable response. From these contributions, a simple, static website of ADL contributions was constructed. As an *ADL greatest hits* collection, the resulting site featured a searchable database of discussion threads organized into module categories.

CPs responded enthusiastically to the site's design, ease of use, and interpersonal and course content support benefits.

To enable further research into how the site was used, it underwent a major upgrade in the spring of 2005 by adding many more pages, improving the organization and design, and inserting code to track user statistics via a web metrics service. To encourage private as well as public interactivity with archived content, a series of seven *guided tour reflective tasks* were created. In each task, learners were first asked to reflect on their current state of practice. For example, in Task 1 (*Developing your approach to masters-level study*), CPs were asked to consider how to go about various aspects of study, such as assignments, time management, and information retrieval strategies. Next, they were directed to a number of discussion threads that corresponded to these issues. Finally, CPs were encouraged to share their reflections on DL and reinvigorate list usage by providing fresh takes on relevant, popular themes of discussion. New iterations of previously discussed topics could then be archived, and over time add to the depth, breath, and quality of the community's collective experience.

Evaluating the DLA

Research into the DLA's efficacy was guided by three questions:

1. What was the reaction to the DLA, and how did this feedback lead toward the development of the site?
2. How did CPs use the site as a collective?
3. How did individual CPs at various stages on the MSc make use of the site?

These questions were selected to investigate how CPs used the DLA and to highlight how the interaction with archived ADL content supported situated learning on the MSc. The first research question looked at overall reactions. Amongst predominantly positive feedback, users responded most favorably to the site's design and ease of use. Other comments pointed out several potential benefits, such as enhanced interpersonal and course content support. Overall, CPs felt the DLA was a useful and welcome additional resource.

The second research question focused on a quantitative analysis of site usage statistics. Findings suggested visitors used the site much like a reference book, browsing various topics on occasion for predominantly short visits of 20 minutes or less. Statistics indicated a group of 35 or so users frequented the site once or twice per month.

The third research question focused on specific usage experiences from the perspectives of CPs at various stages on the MSc. In the first case, a potential MSc applicant claimed that reading archived discussions strongly influenced her decision to apply. While certainly a best case scenario, this data pointed out how ADL discourse provided potential applicants with a unique insider's view of what studying on the program could be like, a perspective that facilitated decision making in one way or another. In another case, a new CP doing the opening *Foundation* module remarked that browsing through the DLA helped prepare her for masters level study by providing course content support and clarifying expectations. In both situations, the ability to vicariously learn from *near-peer role models* (Murphey, 1996) helped calm nerves and build self-confidence in moving from peripheral participation to full engagement. Course veterans, those beyond the Foundation module, claimed practical benefits from reading archived content, such as accessing online resources and generating assignment ideas. From the data gathered, it appeared that reading past discussions was useful for stimulating creative thinking at the beginning stages of research. Finally, there was no evidence that the site had any significant impact on ADL participation, despite the carefully crafted reflective tasks designed to encourage it.

The Ning Group at University of Warwick

Introduction and Background

This section of the chapter considers the experiences of establishing a Ning-based support group. Ning is a freely available *Java*-based platform that enables a group to establish and build a social/academic network. During this project, it was used primarily by former MA TLs. However, current MA TLs were included so that opportunities for the two groups to collaborate and share teaching experiences could be explored. The Ning initiative was supported by research funding secured through *Teaching and Learning Enhancement Funding* (TALEF).

The University's Centre for Applied Linguistics runs a suite of MA programs in the area of English language teaching. These suites include specialisms in ESP (English for Specific Purposes), EYL (English for Young Learners), ICT and Multimedia, and Testing and Assessment. The group featured here were teachers enrolled in the MA in English Language Studies and Methods (ELSM) program who had completed a Masters for TLs with less than two years experience. Many of these ELSM TLs came straight from completing undergraduate studies in their home countries and had limited or no experience. In CofP terms, during the MA program, they had been working from a position of peripheral participation through quasi-authentic practices such as micro-teaching, as well as peer-teaching action research. Upon returning to their countries, they often take up their first teaching job.

The design of the MA program itself has been reported on elsewhere (Ushioda et al., 2011), but it is worth stressing a few important features here. The MA aims to develop TLs' autonomy as learners of teaching. This involves the development of reflection and awareness-raising, as well as peer-teaching. It highlights the overlapping concerns of practitioner research, reflective practice, and action research in ongoing teacher development (Mann, 2005). When TLs graduate from this program, they should be in a position to develop their teaching in appropriate ways as they begin to teach or return to their teaching context.

The tutors involved in coordinating the MA program made the decision to use Ning in an effort to help achieve several important goals:

- Set up and maintain an online community of learning.
- Encourage graduate teachers to stay in touch and re-engage former TLs with each other, partly because novice teachers often find themselves isolated and can struggle to come to terms with the realities of teaching (Mann, 2008). Current TLs and those who had applied and been accepted onto the program were also included.
- Foster former TLs in their efforts to reflect on their practice.
- Integrate into the MA program examples from former TLs' continuing reflective practice.

Features of Ning significant in evaluating its contribution were:

- Individual profile pages and blogs; community members blogged their teaching experiences, problems and insights, as well as uploaded photos.
- Forums; interest groups were based on current topics (e.g., increasing student participation, using group work and tasks) and threaded asynchronous discussion developed along these lines.
- Synchronous chat; tutors and TLs could see who was online.
- Video content; posted by both tutors and TLs.
- Online conferences; such as the one involving tutors and TLs on the theme of "Teaching in difficult circumstances and large classes."

Outcomes and Evaluation

The overall evaluation of the tutor team was that Ning was relatively easy to set up and use. Tutors and TLs commented favorably on both functionality and the visual feel of the pages, noting that it looked and felt rather like Facebook.

TLs appreciated being able to have their own profile page and being able to leave comments and read other TLs' blogs. Some difficulties were experienced in accessing threaded discussions. For example, it could be time-consuming checking through both the central discussion and sub-group forums.

Levels of Involvement

Feedback from individuals was overwhelmingly positive, although this does not necessarily equate to high levels of involvement (e.g. through posting messages or videos).

Generally speaking, the majority of those who joined were passive, with only around 30% making significant involvement. It is interesting to compare the number of views in the forums with the actual contributions. If we look at the thread *Difficult circumstances/large classes*, there are 27 contributions but 1,883 views.

Topic areas that emerged through the process were inevitably linked to concerns developed during the on-campus MA where TLs had been engaged in a process of micro-teaching and action research (Brown, Smith, & Ushioda, 2007). An important element of the MA was the promotion of reflective practice (through the use of reflective talk, group discussion, I-statements, and repertory grid techniques). Discussions and forums provided evidence that TLs had continued to work and reflect on issues that arose in the MA.

Posting Videos

One of the most important features of Ning was that both tutors and TLs could upload videos. Twelve tutor videos featured current news and activities from the school. Others featured Dick Allwright (Exploratory practice), Jane and Dave Willis (TBL), and Fauzia Shamim (Appropriate methodology for large classes). All videos received positive comments. Although there were only 12 TL videos posted, these provided the basis for a great deal of comment and discussions, especially where they highlighted action research initiatives, such as setting up a self-access center.

Closing Comments

This kind of online community can help support TLs when they return to distance beyond their MA studies. Outcomes in terms of reflection and enhanced autonomy are detailed in Ushioda et al. (2011), where Ning functions as an:

> interim space or site for teacher learning—one that is established by and is directly connected with beginning teachers' former academic learning base, yet has the potential to be shaped and exploited by those teachers themselves in ways that meet their needs and can help to sustain their ongoing professional development.
>
> (p. 121)

The experience of using Ning was a positive one in creating a new virtual space for further interaction, support, and engagement when former participants return to distance. One of the interesting outcomes of the project was that a handful of teachers set up Ning groups of their own.

Ning is a tool that encourages interaction and support between participants at distance. The inherently social view of learning that lies behind versions of CofP recognizes that learning is at least partly an outcome of interaction.

Getting a Ning group set up and working is easy. Anyone can join, and it needs just one tutor to act as host. The role of the network creator is to approve members and approve requests to create sub-groups. Invited individuals can then create member accounts that are approved by the host. Individual members can customize their profile (e.g. RSS feeds and widgets).

Evaluation

This section looks across the experiences of setting up and sustaining both the DLA and Ning projects. Taken together, we consider both common issues and also differences in the way these CofP developed. Since a full and comprehensive analysis is beyond the scope of this chapter, only the most relevant themes will be highlighted. After reviewing key aspects of each MA program and its corresponding community space, discussion will examine levels of participation, tutor involvement, types of interaction, and conclude with a look at issues effecting the long-term sustainability of online communities.

The Aston and Warwick MA Programs

While both programs are based in the UK, there are obvious differences in the nature of each one. The Aston MSc is a classic distance group, with course participants spread throughout the globe, each working at their own pace through the program. Opportunities for face-to-face gatherings and instruction exist, but are rare and not mandatory. The Warwick MA is essentially a face-to-face program that includes blended elements. The Ning project is an additional and subsequent initiative designed to renew contact and engagement and further promote reflective practice with recent graduates. The Ning participants are at distance from the university and are now embedded and working in their teaching contexts. Both programs eschew the traditional view that distance-learning TLs are somehow removed from the center (viewing the center of learning as being the teacher's context of practice). A key rationale of both programs is to encourage teacher learners to theorize their practice rather than learn and apply theories to practice.

While each program has established online communities with the shared goal of supporting situated learning, the form and implementation of each contains several major differences. Warwick TLs made use of Ning, a fully featured social networking service that provided users with a rich variety of easy-to-use multi-media resources for interaction. Aston CPs, on the other hand, used a simple email-based listserv discussion list that limited participation to asynchronous text-only interaction, highlights of which were made accessible via the DLA website. As can be expected, these different approaches to forming the online medium through which interaction took place (a complete space vs. an enhancement to an already existing one) resulted in differences in levels and types of user engagement.

Levels of Participation and Tutor Involvement

In both programs, participation in the online community space was voluntary, albeit strongly encouraged. Given research showing that busy teachers are much less willing to participate unless compelled to do so (Gray, 2004; Riverin & Stacey, 2008), it is most likely that the voluntary nature of each program's online community curtailed participation to some degree. The balance of active vs. passive participation skewed heavily towards the former, where the majority of contributions were made by a few enthusiastic members who took it upon themselves to initiate and lead discussions or champion various topics of interest. For example, on the DLA, the vast majority of archived discussions within the *Grammar & Lexis* module category resulted from the spirited debates of roughly a half-dozen or so participants and a couple of tutors. Likewise, the *Difficult circumstances/large classes* thread from the Ning discussion forum echoed this situation, with over 1,800 page views but only 27 actual contributions. Although small numbers of people were relied upon to generate most of the activity, evidence suggests that both the Ning platform and the DLA website made most of their impact at the peripheries of each community. Both projects expanded involvement by facilitating connections between past, current, and future members. They enhanced the process of legitimate peripheral participation (Wenger, 1998) and the movement towards more established and central status. The sites did this primarily through providing access to resources and ideas, enabling the enculturation of newcomers and novices into the community, and allowing for an overall greater degree of vicarious learning.

Tutor involvement played an important role within both communities, mainly by encouraging participation and increasing the depth and breadth of interaction. For example, on Ning the Warwick tutors were able upload videos and presentations that were effective in generating a great deal of reflective interaction. Likewise, when Aston tutors became involved in asynchronous email-based discussions, participants beyond the core group of regulars tended to contribute. In addition, messages were crafted with greater care, resulting in more sustained and a perceived higher level of discussion. Leadership from the Warwick tutors played an especially critical role in keeping things focused and moving as evidenced by the severe drop off in community activity when funding for regular involvement ended. Aston tutors varied in their interactional involvement. The contributions of those tutors who did participate were felt by CPs to be extremely helpful, welcomed, and valued. Nevertheless, tutor involvement was not essential to the continuation of community interaction.

Types of Interaction

Each project was characterized by a different balance between social, cognitive, and teaching presence. On Ning, the interaction tended to be more social, which was unsurprising since the service bills itself as a social network and consists of numerous features that make communication and sharing of information easier. As a result, the social dimension of networking became the primary driver for most Warwick TLs. In contrast, archived discussions from the Aston group were predominantly academic and cognitive in nature, consisting more of drafted statements of opinion and reflection than social exchange.

Regarding longevity, the DLA community lasted much longer than the Ning one, partly because participants had more instrumental motivation (e.g. assignments, tasks, dissertations) than the more intrinsic social motivation of the Ning group. The DLA project generated much longer texts than the Ning project and, because of this, there was also evidence that at least a minority (and perhaps more) experienced the kind of cognitive overload Jones, Ravid, and Rafaeli (2002) have identified as resulting from excessively lengthy messages and a feeling that a handful of participants dominate. The Majordomo e-mail delivery system the Aston program used meant that messages could arrive at inconvenient times, thus mitigating against immediate engagement. The DLA project at least allowed TLs to access interaction at leisure through a web-based interface. The Ning site also allowed access at times convenient for the user. Of course, this did not necessarily mean greater use, as the majority was still sporadic in accessing the site.

Sustainability

For teachers wishing to transform their practices, entering into a personally transformative experience that takes place over time is beneficial (Henderson, 2006). Participants in both the Ning and DLA projects felt that the platforms had been positive in such a process of development. However, there is also evidence that many TLs established relationships or initiated discussions online but then took these offline (and therefore less visible).

There are other important issues concerning the long-term sustainability of online CofP. According to Henderson (2006), a key element in promoting and supporting sustainability is community cohesion. In particular, "participants valued social interaction as a way of negotiating mutuality of engagement, reported accountability to joint enterprise despite issues of critical mass, and shared repertoire as a way of negotiating community membership" (p. 1).

Factors regarding usability, communication, and leadership influenced the cohesion of the Warwick and Aston online communities. Technology employed to service an online CofP needs to be well-designed, easy to set up, and intuitive to use. Tutors responsible for creating and managing the online space are well advised to solicit user feedback when determining how the online space will grow. Through such co-creation, members experience more investment in the community and are therefore more likely to stick with it for the long run. The same goes for other forms of interactive technologies, be they podcasts, blogs, or instant chat. If the perceived value of such resources is not high enough, chances are these unused tools will simply add to a community's cognitive overload instead of helping diffuse it. A key reason for the DLA's success was that the idea for its creation came from the grassroots of the community. The site grew and developed according to the input and orientations of its users.

Conclusion

Garrison, Anderson, and Archer (2001) see interaction as supporting or triggering cognitive presence. This is a process through which meanings are created, adapted, tweaked, and confirmed through the ongoing discourse. The essence of a community of learners is that they share knowledge in productive and varied ways. Distance learning is enhanced by interactive online spaces that support cognitive presence through deliberately creating a varied and supportive environment where knowledge-sharing, articulation, and exploration can occur.

Riverin and Stacey (2008) are optimistic about the value and role of online communities. However, despite stated benefits, they argue that the "complexities of forming and supporting online communities will need to be addressed if they are to be sustained" (p. 55). This chapter has considered the experience of two online communities. From looking across the two cases, there are some common suggestions related to such forming and supporting. Designers of online communities need to:

- Balance the cognitive and social needs of the community with the needs of individual members.
- Avoid information overload by maintaining a welcoming and encouraging interactional context for newcomers.
- Ensure that an element of social presence contributes to a welcoming feel to the online environment. New TLs need to be encouraged and valued. Participants need to be aware that social elements (friendly bonding and banter) and initial enthusiasm can give way over time to a more rigid environment where new members may be reluctant to become visible (Riverin & Stacey, 2008) as inflexibility amongst older members can undermine the trust new participants need in order to actively contribute.
  - Make sure tutors provide some social and cognitive presence.
  - Encourage some participants to become champions or catalysts in the development of the online community. This might also involve promoting the notion that the site is a source of potential research in its own right.
- Embrace appropriate new tools to help sustain engagement and involvement (e.g. podcasts, RSS feeds, Wikis) in line with feedback from community members.
- Make sure that TLs have access to previous threads (the community's *interactional history*).

Discussion Questions

1. Why is it important for online language teacher education to provide opportunities for interaction?
2. How can online communities be sustained over time?

Acknowledgments

Steve Mann: Thanks to Ema Ushioda, Richard Smith, and Peter Brown for their contribution to the Ning project. Richard led the team, Ema led the evaluation, and Peter made sure that the social engagement was rewarding for all. I am grateful for detailed conversations about CofP with Helen Hou based at the University of Ulster. I would also like to thank all the distance learning MSc course participants at Aston University that I worked with from 1994 until 2005.

Jerry Talandis, Jr.: My gratitude goes out to all the Aston tutors and course participants for their help with the DLA project. In particular I would like to thank David Anderson for all his helpful insights and feedback. Finally, I am also grateful to my family for their continued patience and support.

References

Bacon, J. (2009) *The Art of community*. San Francisco, CA: O'Reilly Media, Inc.

Brown, P., Smith, R., & Ushioda, E. (2007) Responding to resistance. In A. Barfield& S. H. Brown (Eds), *Reconstructing autonomy in language education: Inquiry and innovation* (pp. 71–83). Basingstoke: Palgrave Macmillan.

Freenburg, A. (1989) The written world: On the theory and practice of computer conferencing. In R. Mason & A. Kaye (Eds), *Mindweave: Communication, computers and distance education* (pp. 22–39). Oxford: Pergamon Press.

Garrison, D. R. (1997) Computer conferencing: The post industrial age of distance education. *Open Learning, 12*(2), 3–11.

Garrison, D. R., & Anderson, T. (2003) *E-learning in the 21st Century: A framework for research and practice*. London: Routledge Falmer.

Garrison, D. R., Anderson, T., & Archer, W. (2001) Critical thinking, cognitive presence, and computer conferencing in distance education. *American Journal of Distance Education, 15*(1), 7–23.

Gray, B. (2004) Informal learning in an online community of practice. *Journal of Distance Education, 19*(1), 20–35.

Gunawardena, C. N., Hermans, M., Sanchez, D., Richmond, C., Bohley, M., & Tuttle, R. (2009) A theoretical framework for building online communities of practice with social networking tools. *Educational Media International, 46*(1), 3–16.

Henderson, M. (2006) Sustaining the professional development of teachers through a model of community of practice. Paper presented at the Australian Association for Research in Education Conference 2006. Adelaide, Australia.

Johnson, K. (2006) The sociocultural turn and its challenges for second language teacher education. *TESOL Quarterly, 40*(1), 235–257.

Jones, Q., Ravid, G., & Rafaeli S. (2002) An empirical exploration of mass interaction system dynamics: Individual information overload and usenet discourse. In *Proceedings of the 35th Annual Hawaii International Conference on System Sciences*, IEEE, Big Island, HI.

Kirsh, D. (2000) A few thoughts on cognitive overload. *Intellectica, 1*(30), 19–51.

Lave, J., & Wenger, E. (1991) *Situated learning: Legitimate peripheral participation*. Cambridge: Cambridge University Press.

Mann, S. J. (2005) State-of-the-art: The language teacher's development. *Language Teaching, 38*(3), 103–118.

Mann, S. J. (2008) Teacher's use of metaphor in making sense of their first year of teaching. In T. S. C. Farrell (Ed.), *Novice language teachers*. (pp. 11–28). London: Equinox.

Moore, J. A., & Chae, B. (2007) Beginning teachers' use of online resources and communities. *Technology, Pedagogy, and Education, 16*(2), 215–224.

Murphey, T. (1996) Near peer role models. *Teacher Talking to Teacher: Newsletter of the JALT Teacher Education SIG, 4*(3), 21–23.

Riverin, S., & Stacey, E. (2008) Sustaining an online community of practice: A case study. *Journal of Distance Education, 22*(2), 45–58.

Rourke, L., Anderson, T., Garrison, D. R., & Archer, W. (2001) Methodological issues in the content analysis of computer conference transcripts. *International Journal of Artificial Intelligence in Education, 12*, 8–22.

Sutton, L. (2001) The principle of vicarious interaction in computer-mediated communications. *International Journal of Educational Telecommunications, 7*(3), 223–242.

Ushioda, E., Smith, R., Mann, S. J., & Brown, P. (2011) Promoting teacher–learner autonomy through and beyond initial language teacher education. *Language Teaching, 44*(1), 118–121.

Wenger, E. (1998) Communities of practice: Learning as a social system. *Systems Thinker, 9*(5).

Wenger, E., McDermott, R., & Snyder, W. (2002) *Cultivating communities of practice: A guide to managing knowledge*. Cambridge, MA: Harvard Business School Press.

Zhao, Y., & Rop, S. (2001) A critical review of the literature on electronic networks as reflective discourse communities for inservice teachers. Paper presented at the Annual Meeting of the American Education Research Association, New Orleans, LA.

11

INVESTIGATING ASSESSMENT IN ONLINE DISCUSSIONS

A Case Study of Peer Assessment in an LTED Course

David R. Hall and John S. Knox

Introduction

Online discussions have become a staple in tertiary education, and particularly so in distance education. This is also the case in language-teacher education by distance (LTED), and there are now studies looking at the role of online discussions in LTED programs from a range of perspectives, citing such positive aspects as high-quality interaction, communal learning, and flexibility (e.g. Arnold & Ducate, 2006; Biesenbach-Lucas, 2003; Kamhi-Stein, 2000; Salleh, 2002). The ubiquity and importance of online discussions in LTED programs raises questions about their role in the curriculum, and their relation to other aspects of the curriculum such as content and objectives. Of particular relevance for this chapter are questions about the relation between online discussions and assessment.

> First, should they be assessed as part of the formal grading of a program? Second, if discussions are to be assessed, then what exactly should we assess (e.g. control of subject matter, quality of argumentation, facilitation of learning among the group, amount of reading, task response, enthusiasm of participation, number of contributions)? Third, how should they be assessed?
>
> (Hall & Knox, 2009a, p. 221)

In this chapter, we present a case study of one offering of an LTED course which attempted to address these questions (see also Hall & Knox, 2004). The course involved both distance and on-campus students participating in online discussions, and assessing their peers' contributions.

Before outlining this course, the issues that emerged for us as teachers, and the learners' reactions, we contextualize the case study by looking more broadly at the question of assessment in LTED courses, examining data collected in two surveys: one of LTED providers, and one of LTED students.[1] Several of the issues raised by providers and learners in the survey responses are consistent with the case study findings, and demonstrate the importance of assessment to all stakeholders in language-teacher education by distance.

Assessment in LTED Programs: Views From the "Inside"

In this part of the chapter, we discuss issues of assessment in LTED as seen from the perspective of participants: providers and learners. These data come from two surveys. The first was an international survey of LTED providers: 138 teachers and administrators from 116 LTED programs were invited to participate, and there were 24 responses from 23 institutions (see Hall & Knox, 2009b for reporting of other results, and for the full survey). The second was an international survey of students from three LTED programs, each on a different continent. We had 137 responses from former and current LTED students living in 32 different countries.

The survey of institutional providers asked about plagiarism, but did not have any open-ended questions about assessment more generally. Due to the focus of this chapter, the topic of plagiarism is not considered here. The student survey had two Likert-scale questions regarding assessment methods, and then one open-ended question asking for any relevant comments on assessment. Qualitative responses from both surveys which discussed assessment in LTED were collated and categorized according to the themes that were identified in the responses (Ryan & Bernard, 2003). A number of the themes are discussed here.

Issues in dealing with technology were mentioned by a number of providers and a small number of students, and a number of providers also mentioned that assessment of teaching and practical knowledge is difficult by distance—"but not impossible" as one respondent noted. Of the other themes identified in the data, three are discussed in more depth below: situated learning and assessment, quality and type of assessment methods, and the assessment of online discussions.

One of the key benefits of LTED is situated learning: the ability of students to remain in their teaching context (wherever in the world it may be) and study in the program of their choice. There were three comments in the provider survey responses on the relation between situated learning and assessment, and two from the relevant item on the student survey. We believe, however, that this is an important factor in assessment in LTED programs, since there should always be a strong connection between teaching and assessment.

Two providers cited the relation between situated learning and assessment as an advantage of LTED programs.

Students are at the chalk face every day, so tasks can build on that (in the materials and in assignments).

Students can tailor the focus of practical assignments to reflect their own teaching contexts and development needs—not forced to base assignments on the same contexts as their classmates.

One student response also touched on this theme.

[My university's] focus on assignments, small scale research projects, and thesis allowed me to acquire knowledge and integrate it into my unique, localized, and specific teaching circumstances. Thus [this] approach was far more relevant more [sic] "generic" examinations. It was an extremely relevant and useful way of learning, more so than other [sic] I have ever experienced.

Another student went further, raising issues of validity in assessment which are considered later in this chapter in relation to the peer assessment case study.

In the end, so much depends on the teaching context that there seems to be no better assessment than the teacher's self-assessment.

For the current chapter, this theme is particularly relevant, due to the nature of the online discussion tasks assessed in the case study, which required the students to consider the course content in relation to their own context (see Table 11.1).

While providers were slightly more likely than students to comment on the relation between situated learning and assessment, the students were more likely to comment on the nature of the assessment methods (15 students commented on this, whereas none of the providers did). This is likely to be attributable to the nature of the questionnaire item on the student survey, which had asked them to identify the validity and pedagogical usefulness of various assessment methods, and then to add further comments (recalling that the provider survey had no open-ended item on assessment). Nonetheless, the comments from the students on the nature of assessment methods, overall, showed a sophisticated appreciation of the nature of assessment, and in many cases of what they expected from their LTED program.

I was happy to be assessed on my ability to write the 5000 word assignments and the dissertation—that is as it should be at this level. One friend at another institution never really got past 500 word contributions—that's not even an ICELT assignment!

I found assignments, research projects and the dissertation to be the most useful in terms of developing my own thinking.

As might be expected, not all respondents agreed on what assessment methods should be employed, nor which were most valuable.

> Assessment is of the participants [sic] ability to write a good essay. The MA is in Teaching. Strange.

> I haven't found that the assessment has helped me to better understand the content OVERALL. As I wanted to take this course to increase my overall understanding of the field, I would have rathered [sic] assessment opportunities which assisted this, rather than just narrowly focussed essays. Or if a combination of both types of assessment were available/applied, than [sic] this would have been more helpful.

Preferences for, and opinions about assessment depend on a range of factors, including students' backgrounds and their purposes for study.

> I don't like small-scale research projects because I signed on to a COURSEWORK Masters, not a RESEARCH Masters. Not that I'm averse to research—I've completed research degrees in other fields—but I signed onto a coursework degree because I want to learn the basics and explore the issues first. These half-arsed research projects take time that I could spend reading the literature and learning things in greater detail. I do agree, however, that "learning by doing" is a good way to do things, but every time I do one of these mini-research projects I feel like I'm being asked to do something before I fully understand the fundamentals.

One thing to be taken from these comments is that it will not be possible to please all the students all of the time. For LTED providers, another implication of these comments (and other similar ones) is that a whole-of-program perspective is important when considering assessment in order to avoid over-reliance on a small number of assessment methods, some of which may be well-suited, or even necessary for particular units in a whole program, but may be substituted for other methods in other units.

One provider and seven students commented on online discussions in relation to assessment. In order to contextualize these comments, we first wish to present the quantitative data from the student survey on online discussion postings as an assessment method.

Items on the survey asked students about the validity and pedagogical usefulness of online discussion postings as an assessment method, and the results are shown in Figure 11.1 and Figure 11.2.

Figure 11.1 shows that a majority of students who had experienced online discussions as an assessment method (64 of 116 respondents) considered this a valid form of assessment. Of the 52 respondents to this item who did not indicate they

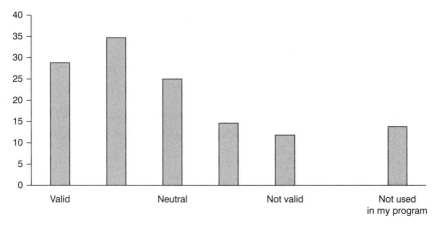

FIGURE 11.1 Student responses re the validity of online discussion postings as a form of assessment

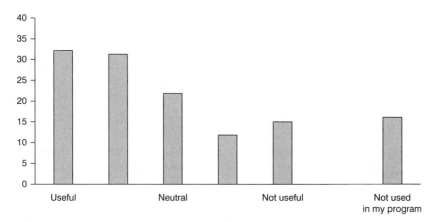

FIGURE 11.2 Student responses re the pedagogical usefulness of online discussion postings as a form of assessment

thought it was valid, 25 were "neutral," and 27 indicated they did not see online discussions as a valid form of assessment.

Similar to Figure 11.1, Figure 11.2 shows that a majority of students who had experienced online discussions as an assessment method (63 of 112 respondents) considered this a pedagogically useful form of assessment. Of the 49 respondents to this item who did not indicate they thought it was valid, 22 were "neutral," and 27 indicated they did not see online discussions as a pedagogically useful form of assessment.[2]

The first thing to note from this is that there is a variety of opinion among the respondents, and while a majority do value online discussions as an assessment method, there are many who are neutral or who do not value this kind of assessment.

Second, the qualitative comments that follow, which are mostly negative, do not appear to be a representative indication of all respondents' opinions of assessment and online discussions in LTED.

Turning now to the qualitative data, a number of students commented on their dissatisfaction with the nature of interaction on online discussions.

> I have found the on-line discussions can be frustrating, sometimes because of lack of student interest, at other times because they can be dominated by one or two overbearing students.

One student questioned the point of this form of assessment on a number of grounds: validity (are they assessable?), reliability (what are the criteria?), and pedagogical value.

> I am far from persuaded of the value of online discussions as anything assessable (and was so even before my instructor's admission that they were just for "general slather"). What are the criteria by which contributions are assessed? What is the pedagogocal [sic] aim of such discussions anyway?

One provider discussed the pedagogical benefits of online discussions, mentioning in passing that they are sometimes assessed, and sometimes not.

> The discussions on Blackboard—we do both student-led and instructor-led discussions breaking students into small groups to address key issues; instructors provide input/feedback (sometimes graded not always) and students really do "dig down" into the material in those discussions. Students have opportunities to put out what they think about an issue, get peer feedback on how well they communicated their understanding (and sometimes corrections on their understanding from their profs). They then revise their words and poof! They learn! It's great to see that.

This comment is a good illustration of why many teachers and students value online discussions, and also shows the value of feedback from teachers and from peers. But, together with the previous student comment, the seemingly random approach to assessment of online discussions (to assess or not to assess) raises a question of communication between teacher and learners, and points to the value of making explicit the pedagogical purpose of the discussions and their assessment where they are assessed.

Another student pointed out the value of feedback in online discussions, but from a different perspective. Online discussions can be very valuable as part of an overall assessment regime, and their absence may be symptomatic of a more fundamental problem in curriculum design.

> If the online discussion boards weren't used much and/or the tutor didn't make an effort to establish a connection with distance students, I felt very much on my own, with only 2 opportunities (assessment of assignments) to get any feedback/connection at all, once in the middle and once at the end. Which means actually during the module there is only ONE chance for feedback/discussion.

These data demonstrate that online discussions can play a very important role in assessment in LTED programs, and that many learners see their value, but that many learners are also unconvinced of their value, especially as a formal assessment instrument.

Overall, we take three conclusions from the data discussed in this section. First, that the value of situated learning to LTED should be recognized and used in assessment, and students' contexts should be drawn on as part of assessment in LTED programs.[3] Second, that a variety of assessment methods should be used across any given program, and that online discussions are one valuable choice available to LTED curriculum designers. And third, that the purpose and rationale of assessment methods in LTED programs should be communicated clearly to learners.

In the following section, we present a case study of an LTED curriculum innovation involving peer assessment of online discussions.

Case Study: Peer Assessment of Online Discussions in an LTED Course

In 2002, when we implemented the curriculum discussed below, we had none of the data discussed above. Nonetheless, our decision to implement a peer-assessment component in our curriculum development unit was in response to similar issues we had identified in our own teaching, and our experience of using online discussions in our programs.

Background and Procedures

The course we taught, "Innovation in language teaching," was relatively new: in its second year at the time we introduced our own innovation. The unit introduced students to curriculum innovation, and the content covered recent trends in TESOL curriculum, the social and institutional context of curriculum development and implementation, case-studies of teacher-led curriculum innovations, and curriculum evaluation.

The course assessment included two major assignments: an essay analyzing and comparing two innovations, worth 45%; and a choice of a critical analysis of a textbook, a logframe, or a proposal for a curriculum innovation, also worth 45%.

The remaining 10% was for a third assignment—participation in four online discussions—which was peer assessed.

Distance students received course notes and the set text, and participated in the online discussions. On-campus students also participated in the online discussions, and online discussion groups (see below) were arranged to include both on-campus and distance students. Online discussions that included on-campus and distance students made for unique opportunities for interaction. For instance, Korean teachers of English living and studying in Australia were able to communicate with Australian teachers of English living and studying in Korea.

We had already made online discussions compulsory in this course, as past experience had shown us that unless they were compulsory, participation was relatively limited (cf. Manathunga, 2002, p. 6; Salmon, 2000, p. 121). Other strategies we "designed into" the discussions to increase participation, and to make them worthwhile included having set times for participation (from Monday to Friday of specified weeks in the semester), providing specific tasks related to the content of that part of the unit, dividing students into groups of approximately eight to keep the reading load manageable, and building in a requirement for students to respond to others' postings (see Table 11.1). The requirement to respond to other student's postings was managed, in this case, by assigning "group leaders" in each discussion group, for each of the second, third and fourth discussion tasks. Group leaders (2–3 per discussion) were required to respond to the task, and then the other students in the group were required to respond to one of the group leader's postings.

Students received the assessment task and criteria as shown in Figure 11.3.

Teacher Perspectives

We had decided to implement peer assessment for a number of reasons. We had both introduced innovations in other curricular contexts (e.g. Hall & Kenny, 1988; Knox, 2007), and had found them a worthwhile and rewarding educational experience for students. In a course on curriculum innovation, we felt that introducing peer assessment in the online discussions would provide the students first-hand experience of innovation, thereby encouraging "critical reflection on curriculum issues such as assessment, student and teacher roles, and the costs and benefits to different stakeholders of introducing curriculum innovations" (Hall & Knox, 2004, p. 7).

As experienced language teachers, we felt our students would be ready to take on the responsibility of peer assessment, even if they were reluctant to do so. Online discussions were relatively new at the time, and we had been exploring different ways of awarding "participation" marks, none of which we had found to be completely satisfactory. Further, student feedback from previous semesters had raised questions about the value of assessing discussions—some students were in favor, some were against. Because peer assessment would involve the discussion participants in

- Participate in the online discussions.
- In the week following the last online discussion:
1 give each student in your discussion group a score out of 10 (see below for details)
2 write a short comment for each student (*absolute* maximum of 20 words per student)
3 submit the marks and comments via the private mail function on the website using the message subject heading, "peer assessment".

Marks should be awarded based on the Macquarie University Grading System (see below) and the following four criteria:

- participation
- quality
- relevance
- clarity

(Note that the criterion of clarity does not imply an assessment of English-language ability *per se*, but of the ability to express and communicate concepts and arguments. You should also be mindful that conventions of online writing are more flexible than those of formal academic discourse, and may not include standard punctuation, spelling, capitalization and so on.)

Macquarie University's grading system

HD (85-100) High Distinction: denotes performance which meets all unit objectives in such an exceptional way and with such marked excellence that it deserves the highest level of recognition.

D (75-84) Distinction: denotes performance which clearly deserves a very high level of recognition as an excellent achievement in the unit.

Cr (65-74) Credit: denotes performance which is substantially better than would normally be expected of competent students in the unit.

P (50-64) Pass: denotes performance which satisfies unit objectives.

PC (45-49) Conceded Pass: denotes performance which meets unit objectives only marginally.

F (0-44) Fail: denotes that a candidate has failed to complete a unit satisfactorily.

FIGURE 11.3 Peer assessment task and grading criteria

TABLE 11.1 Overview of discussion tasks and their relation to course content.

Course content relevant to online discussion	Week of task	Online discussion task
—	Week 2	Introduce yourself to the list. Include some or all of the following information: • name • nationality • current country of residence • language(s) spoken • language learning experience • language teaching experience • current professional situation. Maximum 150 words. Please "sign" all contributions with the name you prefer to be called by.
Weeks 1–3	Week 4	Part 1 of the unit deals with the various directions that language teaching has taken in recent years. How have any of these changes impacted on the classrooms of your own experience? What problems or successes have you observed? Maximum 150 words. Please "sign" all contributions with the name you prefer to be called by.
Weeks 4–6	Week 6	Examine a newspaper or magazine in any language you are familiar with. Look for and make notes on stories where language is an important factor. In view of the theme of this part of the unit, we ask you to look in particular for examples where attitudes to language play an important role. The apparent "unnewsworthiness" of underlying language issues may mean that language is not highlighted at all, or is marginalized even where it is a key issue. You may find it helpful to look at Chapter 9 of *Using Functional Grammar* (Butt et al., 2000), at the section on news stories (pp. 228–232). Maximum 150 words. Please "sign" all contributions with the name you prefer to be called by.

Weeks 7–9	Week 9	Read Chapter 18 of the LING938 unit reader. Notice Hall's use of the word "authentic."
		• Is the division between authentic materials and authentic learner response one which you feel might be valid in your own situation?
		• Are there any ways in which you could involve your own learners more in the selection of material for study purposes?
		Maximum 150 words. Please "sign" all contributions with the name you prefer to be called by.
Weeks 1–9	End Week 10	Submit peer assessment.

decisions about the value of contributions, we believed that it might provide more valid assessment, since discussions are by definition collaborative and co-constructed events.

As indicated in Table 11.1, there were four discussions. The first discussion was primarily social in orientation, so for that discussion we kept everyone in the same group. For the remaining three discussions, we split the students into eight groups. In some groups, discussion proceeded as we had anticipated, but there were also problems. Some students had enrolled late in the course and did not receive materials in time to join the second discussion. A small number of students withdrew from the course, and others participated little, or sometimes, in some discussions not at all. Due to the way the discussions had been set up, problems occurred when group leaders did not respond to the discussion task, leaving other students waiting for the leaders' posts to respond to, sometimes requiring tutors to intervene (e.g. allowing students to respond directly to the task).

The complexity, and volume of work involved in organizing eight separate discussion groups and dealing with queries and some learners' understandable confusion was at times much greater than we anticipated. We had four teaching staff (the two authors of this chapter, and two tutors located in Japan). Each of us took two groups per discussion, and we swapped groups for each discussion (to give us all a chance to interact with a greater number of students, and to give the students access to more than one staff member). In some ways this was a good idea, but it added to the complexity of an already complex innovation.

Student Perspectives

We conducted an evaluation of the course, which included surveying the students. The survey included questions on the online discussions and on the peer assessment component. There was a response rate of approximately 33%, of which roughly half came from on-campus students, and roughly half from distance students. A number of issues emerged from student comments on the survey, and also in comments from students provided by email, and some of these are discussed below.

As noted above, a number of students enrolled (and therefore received their materials) late. This led in some cases to delays in these students participating in the online discussions; in other cases students simply posted contributions late. This caused some dissatisfaction with the discussions on the part of some students.

> There should be a penalty on grades for submitting the discussions late.

More problematic for some was the impact of late contributions on peer assessment.

> Evaluating people who are late to the discussion for one reason or another complicated things.

> I hope these grades are ok. I wasn't exactly sure what to do about the grades for latecomers.

Lateness was not the only factor that caused students problems in assessing their peers.

> I found the non-adherence to word limit very off-putting, many contributions rambled and I lost interest.

> Not valid because of lack of responses from members of the group.

> I'm not entirely sure how I'm supposed to complete this, when many of the members of my discussion group have yet to contribute anything beyond an introduction. My group borders on being a NON-discussion group.

These were problems we had not foreseen; in retrospect, we had expected that 10% was a sufficient portion of a grade to motivate all students to participate. As already mentioned above, this exposed a flaw in our design of this aspect of the curriculum, as students had to rely on their peers not just for assessment, but also in order to participate effectively. This was also due, in part, to the role of "team leaders" in the discussion groups.

A number of students had a negative reaction to what they saw as an imposition on their time.

> Even though there are just about 10 students in a group, the job of doing peer assessment is huge.

> The discussions took a lot of time and commitment—I felt I HAD to log on every evening to keep up—especially as a "leader."

This was not only limited to the online discussions themselves, but the learning curve to be able to use the required technology.

> I'm sure all the relevant information is there—but there's so much on the websites and there are too many websites. It's not clear how to get to each one and why there are different passwords etc (linguistics general, [course], Macquarie home page, personal page, library home page). All very confusing— again very time consuming.

A key issue commented on by a number of students in the evaluation, and also in the submission of their assessment of their peers, was the use of the grading criteria (see Figure 11.3). We had given careful consideration to what the grading criteria should be like, and had decided to keep them relatively minimal for several reasons including avoidance of influencing the discussion as far as possible.

In some cases, students expressed uncertainty as to how the criteria should be interpreted and applied:

> a checklist (more analytical) would have helped in the assessment here.

> I'm still not convinced I've done this properly ... I'm not sure whether this is the way you want the scores to be awarded.

> We were asked to give our comments based on the Macquarie University Grading System, but this system refers to concepts like: would normally be expected of competent students in this unit.

> I have no idea what a competent student in this unit can produce ...

In other cases, comments from students appeared to indicate that they used different criteria from those specified:

> I'm not quite sure how to go about doing the peer assessment. I can only assess on participation and if all 4 discussions were completed.

> My peer assessment is based on three areas: number of participation (3) + relevance (3) + words limitation (3) + substantiality (1) = 10.

It is clear that the issue of criteria is a particularly challenging one if peer assessment is to be implemented in LTED contexts. Training with assessment criteria is challenging and time consuming, and is unlikely to be feasible in most LTED contexts. This could be an argument for limiting peer assessment to qualitative feedback (i.e. not assigning grades), but even in such cases the development and application of criteria is important, and as Brown, Bull, & Pendlebury (1997) argue:

> peer- and self-assessment are primarily tools of learning. But to demonstrate that these tools are valuable it is necessary to incorporate some peer- and self-assessment into the system of summative assessment otherwise most students will use them indifferently.
>
> (p. 173)

A number of our students, however, were not convinced by the kind of arguments put here by Brown et al., and the following comment is representative of a number of communications we had with on-campus and distance students.

> I would prefer not to do the peer assessment component. I feel that I'm not knowledgable enough to assess my peers for this course. I would prefer the lecturers to assess us. I feel that they would know more on how to assess us fairly.

One of our decisions in designing the innovation was to use groups in order to keep the reading load manageable for students. Due to the constraints of the learning management system we were using at the time, we also decided to keep all discussions that a student was *not* a member of invisible to that student. The cost of giving all students access to read all discussions would have been a confusing mess of discussions on students' screens, and (we anticipated) either great disorder in who contributed where (making the peer assessment effectively impossible), and/or a small mountain of enquiries from confused students. But not all students were satisfied with the approach we took.

> No groups online. People could choose postings they were interested in and find like-minded people more easily. They wouldn't have to be restricted by the output of people in their groups.
>
> the discussion groups should be larger—begin with at least 20 so that a balanced and varied discussion is possible.

The decision to include on-campus and distance students in the same groups also drew some criticism.

> Mixing distance and on-campus students in discussion groups has caused many obstacles. Distance students have different needs, questions, etc than on-campus students.

There was informal feedback about this kind of grouping, however, that was very positive, and many students were positive about the discussions and the peer assessment.

> It was a very worthwhile exercise to review all the contributions again after all were submitted and the discussions seemed a lot easier to follow. I certainly made some notes whilst reading this morning that I will refer to in the future.
>
> I have enjoyed participating in online discussion. It is my first experience of working in a discussion group in quite this manner. I feel like I am just starting to function effectively in this communicative environment.

The feedback from learners indicated that many of them found various aspects of the innovation challenging, and also that some students were quite dissatisfied with aspects of the innovation. Some of this may be a result of specific aspects of the design of this particular curriculum, and others are likely to be a reaction against online discussions and/or peer assessment more generally.

Conclusion

Overall, though the innovation involved a massive amount of extra work for us, and many students were dissatisfied with various aspects of the course, we believe that it was worthwhile. Markee (2001) argues that most curriculum innovations fail over time, but this statement depends on what is meant by "succeed" or "fail"; we would question whether these are even appropriate terms to use.

As teacher educators, we had a cohort of language teachers who, whether they enjoyed every aspect of the course or not, have experienced first-hand from the learner's perspective what peer assessment can be, and have been forced to confront questions of what role online discussions have in a curriculum, what contribution they can make to learning, and how they might be assessed. Our students, studying both on-campus and by distance, were brought together, across distance and across learning modes, to participate in a learning experience where they had a real stake in their own outcome, and those of their peers. From our perspective, this in itself is a success, as it provided these students with an educational experience that is likely to stay with them beyond many of the other things they did as part of their studies.

Our own experience of the innovation questioned an assumption we took into it about how online discussions can be assessed validly. Issues of student participation, logistics, task design, and assessment criteria showed us that the validity of peer assessment in online discussions (both as an exercise in assessment and pedagogy) depended very much on individuals' response to a range of factors, often beyond our control.

But ceding control is what peer assessment is about; and questioning assumptions is what online discussions should be about.

Discussion Questions

1. The authors of this chapter found that their students—all experienced language teachers—were uncomfortable assessing their peers. Why do you think many students find the practice of assessing their peers uncomfortable? Do you believe that peer assessment is a fair expectation in the education of (trainee) language teachers? Are there any ways that language-teacher educators could take advantage of the affordances of distance education to make peer assessment more attractive to students studying by distance?
2. Peer assessment tasks are often different from formal assessment tasks, but not necessarily. The key difference in peer assessment is that the person doing the assessment is different. In a course moderated by distance, does it increase the validity of the assessment regime to include judges who are also experiencing the course by distance? Why or why not?
3. Should online discussions be assessed? Why or why not? If "yes," how should they be assessed?

Notes

1   The survey of students was conducted together with Fiona Copland, Liz England, and Sue Garton.
2   It is not clear why the total number of respondents differed between the two items, but the numbers are reported faithfully here.
3   Survey responses from providers on the topic of plagiarism, informal discussions with colleagues, and our own experience indicate that many LTED programs already do this.

References

Arnold, N., & Ducate, L. (2006) Future foreign language teachers' social and cognitive collaboration in an online environment. *Language Learning and Technology, 10*(1), 42–66.

Biesenbach-Lucas, S. (2003) Asynchronous discussion groups in teacher training classes: Perceptions of native and non-native students. *Journal of Asynchronous Learning Networks,* 7(3), 24–46.

Brown, B., Bull, J., & Pendlebury, M. (1997) *Assessing student learning in higher education.* London: Routledge.

Butt, D., Spinks, S., & Yallop, C. (2000) *Using functional grammar; an explorer's guide.* Sydney: NCELTR Publications

Hall, D. R., & Kenny, B. (1988) An approach to a truly communicative methodology: The AIT pre-sessional course. *English for Specific Purposes, 7,* 19–32.

Hall, D. R., & Knox, J. S. (2004) Peer assessment in distance learning. *IATEFL's Testing, Evaluation and Assessment SIG Newsletter,* 6–13.

Hall, D. R., & Knox, J. S. (2009a) Language teacher education by distance. In A. Burns & J. C. Richards (Eds.), *Cambridge guide to second language teacher education* (pp. 218–229). Cambridge: Cambridge University Press.

Hall, D. R., & Knox, J. S. (2009b) Issues in the education of TESOL teachers by distance education. *Distance Education, 30*(1), 63–85.

Kamhi-Stein, L. D. (2000) Looking to the future of TESOL teacher education: Web-based bulletin board discussions in a methods course. *TESOL Quarterly, 34*(3), 423–455.

Knox, J. S. (2007) Foreign eyes on Thailand: An ESP project for EFL learners. In A. Burns & H. de Silva Joyce (Eds.), *Planning and teaching creatively within a required curriculum for adults* (pp. 119–142). Alexandria, VA: TESOL, Inc.

Manathunga, C. (2002) Designing online learning modules: An Australian example in teacher education. *International Journal of Instructional Media, 29*(2), 185–195.

Markee, N. (2001) The diffusion of innovation in language teaching. In D. R. Hall & A. Hewings (Eds.), *Innovation in English language teaching: A reader* (pp. 118–126). London: Routledge.

Ryan, G. W., & Bernard, H. R. (2003) Techniques to identify themes. *Field Methods, 15*(1), 85–109.

Salleh, N. S. M. (2002) Practical teaching programme online: Overcoming communication issues. *Internet and Higher Education, 4,* 193–201.

Salmon, G. (2000) *E-moderating: The key to teaching and learning online.* London: Kogan Page.

PART III

Administration of Online Distance TESOL Programs

12

ADMINISTRATION OF ONLINE DISTANCE EDUCATION

Academic Services in Support of ESOL E-Learners

Leslie Opp-Beckman

This chapter identifies some of the issues which are specific to e-learning services in an academic context and offers ideas for identifying and delivering such services to an English for Speakers of Other Languages (ESOL) population—both learners and teachers of English—with a focus on remote e-learners who are not on a traditional campus or physical school site. Academic e-services may include but are not necessarily limited to application; registration; technical information; privacy and confidentiality; orientation; the formation of study buddies or study cohorts; tracking and record-keeping; retention and persistence; appeal processes; and, academic support tools. This chapter will provide an overview of the following key concepts and practices.

- Understand the support services that your population requires in order to be successful participants in your e-learning environment, from start to finish and beyond.
- Stay abreast of trends in the development of support systems and tools for delivering e-learning and its associated services.
- Keep in mind that the e-learning process is dynamic and recursive and that services must take this into account over time.
- Be a keen judge and make judicious allocation of budget, institutional capacity and resources that may be available to support both your learners and you (your instructional and administrative needs).

Definitions

New terms and new definitions emerge daily on the Internet. The following are definitions of some of the terms that are central to this chapter.

E-learning (E-Learner, Event, Environment)

As of this writing, there was surprisingly no entry or definition for "e-learning" in the widely recognized Merriam Webster Online Dictionary (Merriam Webster, 2011). The American Society for Training and Development (ASTD, 2010), however, defines e-learning as "a wide set of applications and processes, such as Web-based learning, computer-based learning, virtual classrooms, and digital collaboration. It includes the delivery of content via Internet, intranet/extranet (LAN/WAN), audio- and videotape, satellite broadcast, interactive TV, CD-ROM, and more." This will be the basis for references in this chapter to e-learning and for those who engage in such practices ("e-learners") for periodic events (e.g., online courses, short-term single or multiple sessions, etc.) and in a variety of electronic ("e") environments.

Support Systems and Services

Merriam Webster *does* define a "support system" as "a network of people who provide an individual with practical or emotional support" (Merriam Webster, 2011) to which, in an e-learning context, I feel we must add some components of computer-based or technical support as well. Entities such as Google Apps (Google Apps, 2011), for example, publish lengthy descriptions of how and when e-support systems and services may be made available—some for free and some at varying levels of cost, some through interaction with a human and some without—depending on the nature of the agreement with the user or e-learner.

In this chapter, e-learning support systems and services will refer to a blend of human and computer-based options that are integrated into an academic, e-learning context. In some cases for example, the e-learner may receive an automated response upon completing a web-based form or be able to find the answer to a course-related question independently, using resources already available through a course-related website. In other cases, the learner may consult on a more personal basis through email, chat, phone, or in person with alumni, peers, a course instructor or administrative personnel. Factors such as an individual's amount of previous e-learning experience, level of confidence, and personal preference may in part determine the path a learner seeks to acquire support and gain access to help in an e-learning environment (Cheng & Tsai, 2011).

Tools

The Merriam Webster Online Dictionary (Merriam Webster, 2011) also provides as follows a range of appropriate definitions for the ways in which the concept of "tools" may be expressed in an e-learning context. The brackets are mine.

1. a [handheld] device that aids in accomplishing a task

2. *a*: something (as an instrument or apparatus) used in performing an operation or necessary in the practice of a vocation or profession <a scholar's books are his *tools*>

b: an element of a computer program (as a graphics application) that activates and controls a particular function

c: a means to an end

3. one that is used or manipulated by another [can be a positive concept as in <acts as a *tool* for change>]

4. plural : natural ability <has all the *tools* to be a great [educator]>.

Support Services and Systems

Adult ESOL Learners in "Developing" Countries

Research and resources for e-learning support services have emerged and multiplied in recent years (Amelung, Kreiger, & Rosner, 2011; Kim, Song, & Yoon, 2011; Stella & Gnanam, 2004) as online learning has gained popularity and access to it has become increasingly ubiquitous (Eynon & Helsper, 2011; Leppisaari, Vainio, Herrington, & Im, 2011; Wang & Wu, 2011). As with traditional or "legacy" face-to-face institutional learning environments, courses and programs can and should be evaluated using criteria and measures that take into account such aspects as: learners' course-related needs both before the class begins and after it finishes, retention rates and documented reasons for attrition, learner satisfaction, and learning outcomes. Such "best practice" guides, however, often seem to be geared to audiences in high resource locations (Guerlac, 2011; Jia, Wang, Ran, et al, 2011; Mishra & Mishra, 2011).

Although such findings and recommendations may have global application for e-learner populations worldwide, this chapter will focus in particular on English for Speakers of Other language (ESOL) adult learners in e-learning environments in low resource or "developing" countries (World Bank, 2011; World Trade Organization, 2011) with an emphasis on support services that are especially relevant for them. I will draw on the past 15 years of experience developing and delivering e-learning programs with colleagues at the University of Oregon (UO), in institutions in the United States and worldwide. In such cases, the learners are aged 17–70 and typically "remote" in the sense that they do not have access to the physical campus or institution which is providing the e-learning event. The prospect of a "digital native" (Prensky, 2001) population may yet be many years in the future for them and they are often acting as "early adopters" and "change agents" in their local contexts (Rogers, 1995), struggling with a range of challenges that those of us teaching in "developed" countries may not typically encounter in our daily lives (e.g., regular lack of electricity, unstable access to Internet, aging or unstable hardware, lack of antivirus protection, pervasive economic hardship, climatic disturbances [e.g., drought, earthquakes, tsunami], socio-political barriers, medical barriers such as untreated eye conditions or endemic malaria, the demands of a large family, agricultural or religious calendars that require them to be absent from the course, and so on).

E-learner Priorities for Support Services

In surveys and email correspondence with incoming e-learners, participants who have had to withdraw from our e-learning courses, and alumni who have successfully completed the courses, our 3,000+ adult e-learners from over 100 countries worldwide have ranked in terms of importance the following support services for e-learning.

1. Timely and courteous communication with the instructor(s) and support staff from the time they first establish contact with UO, throughout the course, and during follow up as needed after it ends.
2. Stimulating and courteous dialogue pertaining to course topics and local challenges—may be synchronous and/or asynchronous—with instructors, guest moderators or speakers, tutors and peers (not necessarily in that order of importance).
3. Interesting and relevant course content with downloadable files for use after the course ends.
4. Ease of use of course tools with 24/7 access to grades.
5. Reliable delivery of certificates and records (e.g., letters of recommendation, transcripts).

Support Systems Designed Around E-Learner Needs

Taking into account the above learner-centered priorities, and moving from a macro to micro level, the following are some of the support systems and strategies we have implemented, using a blend of human and computer-based options.

At a program level, we use Gantt charts to regulate workload, flow and schedule of weekly tasks. To maintain continuous communication, we use email accounts that are assigned to teams of support staff according to the task (e.g., registration@uoregon.edu for communication and tasks related to registration, instead of a person's personal email address). In this way work-related tasks can be covered even when some employees are out.

Examples of computer-based services that save both e-learners and support staff time include the following.

• Online registration forms which feed into our in-house database records and give e-learners immediate feedback that can be corrective (e.g., they have omitted required information or skipped steps) or confirmatory (e.g., they agree to share information about grades with sponsors, agree to the spelling of names on the certificate at the end of the course, have completed all steps on the form, etc.). This has resulted in significantly improved satisfaction levels compared to trying to collect similar information via email.

- Needs analysis surveys prior to the start of the course with text boxes for open-ended responses to allow individuals to provide further details as needed. This allows instructors to better anticipate and meet learners' needs.
- Course information on websites and/or learning management systems so that e-learners can have easy access as needed.
- Online gradebooks for confidential, individual access throughout the duration of the course.
- Testing-as-learning activities with automated feedback.
- Midterm and/or end-of-term course evaluations with signed vs. unsigned options plus text boxes for open-ended responses to allow for further feedback as desired.
- Web-based contact forms to request information, transcripts, etc., via email.

In other cases, personal communication through email, chat, phone, or in person with alumni, peers, a course instructor or administrative personnel can better serve the purpose. The following examples of "early intervention" in particular have had a positive impact on retention rates, increased program stability, and led to higher levels of satisfaction for all parties.

- Alums: With more than 3,000 people now in our e-learner alumni network, when a new participant is struggling or has seemingly left a course, we have had good success contacting local alumni and asking if they would be willing to lend a hand. In many cases, this extra bit of assistance from "an old hand" can get the new person through a temporary set-back. It has the added advantage of potentially establishing or strengthening local networking as well.
- Sponsors: Nearly all of our e-learners engage in online studies with us voluntarily and are sponsored through government and/or non-government agencies. Local sponsors are strong allies in supporting their participants and also often help make contact by email, phone or in person to offer encouragement, assist with technical difficulties, and bridge communication gaps.
- Mentors: Institutions which have local people who can act as mentors can be of invaluable assistance when formally or informally linked with e-learners (e.g., alumni who are now local leaders or course co-facilitators, English Language Fellows[1] or similar visiting scholars who are assigned to the local school, etc.).
- Peers: We actively encourage sponsors to enroll e-learners in pairs or cohorts to encourage local collaboration and capacity building. As with alumni, in cases when an individual is experiencing difficulties, we have had very good success

with "virtual shoulder tapping" by requesting help from local partners to assist "lost" or temporarily missing individuals and find solutions for getting them successfully re-engaged in the course.

- Local professional networks: Partnerships with local professional networks and programs such as TESOL affiliates,[2] the English Opens Doors Program[3] in Chile, the Model Schools Network[4] in Gaza, the Royal Thai Distance Learning Foundation[5], and the Teach Women English program in Lebanon[6] have proved to be very successful in creating short-term ESOL language learning and teacher training projects with what we hope will be positive, long-term results.

To sum up, we try to strike a reasonable balance of using computers to handle processes that can be done efficiently and accurately around the clock at everyone's convenience in tandem with person-to-person interactions that help keep alive the "human" element that is the stated number one priority of our e-learners.

Challenges

From an administrative standpoint, some challenges specific to e-learning and for which we've had to develop solutions include the following.

- Instructor workload for developing and delivering courses.
- Instructor absence, planned and unplanned.
- Archiving and protection of digital course content.
- Archiving and protection of digital student records, including FERPA[7] compliance.
- Processes for the handling of complaints.
- Processes for handling violations of Acceptable Use Policies for computing resources and Student Conduct Code for intellectual property.

Tools

The most valuable tools in our e-learning programs are the people which comprise them. We strive to create e-learning instructional and administrative teams based on a combination of servant leadership (Greenleaf, Spears, Covey, & Senge, 2002)— which places a high value on person-to-person interactions and the importance of making sure that other people's (i.e. our e-learners') highest priority needs are being served—and tribal leadership (Logan, King, & Fischer-Wright, 2008) and its emphasis on building and empowering "natural" groups of teams within an organization. Our goal is to use this team approach in all program phases (proposal generating, program development and delivery, administration, support, evaluation, etc.). In this way, the needs of the program and its constituents are served even when individuals are absent or unavailable.

It is also important to engage in regular program planning and review using tools which are based on recognized standards from sources such as International Teachers of English to Speakers of Other languages (TESOL) (Healey et al., 2011), the International Society for Technology in Education (ISTE), the American Council for Teachers of Foreign Languages (ACTFL) in partnership with the National Council for Accreditation of Teacher Education (NCATE) (ACTFL, 2002).

As for the software tools that we use to design, develop, deliver, assess and determine new and existing program directions, they vary according to what the needs analysis shows us, the budget permits, and what is available. Basic categories of tools include the following. For more details, see the next chapter.

- Communication (email, audioconferencing, videoconferencing, etc.).
- Databases.
- Website development and content management.
- Spreadsheets and gradebook software.
- Graphics.
- Surveys and testing.
- Word processing and collaborative authoring.
- Social networking.
- Task-specific tools such as journaling and blogging.
- Content-specific tools such as games, simulations and interactive environments.

Capacity and Budget

The planning and allocation of budget is critical to the success, sustainability and replicability of an e-learning program. It is important to have a thorough understanding of the institutional capacity on both the side of the institution that is delivering the content and the local setting where the content is being received.

In crafting budgets for e-learning courses and programs, it's important to build in funding to account for the personnel, tools, time and supporting resources (e.g., equipment, supplies, software, books, postage, outside contracted services, etc.) for the following. Using institutionally-approved budget templates to make sure all costs are accounted for can be very helpful. Funding categories should account for the following:

- Course development and updates over time.
- Instructor salaries and any associated overhead costs.
- Administrative and staff support costs plus any associated overhead costs.
- Instructor and staff development (mentoring of new people on the team, ongoing professional development, etc.).
- Any other costs related to the e-learners themselves (e.g., certificates, postage, faxing, e-texts, licenses for sites or software, etc.).

- Formative and summative observation and assessment processes,
- Audit costs.
- Data storage and back-up.
- Core infrastructure (e.g., buildings or rooms with electricity and temperature control, adequate bandwidth, securely and properly configured networks, degree of access to good quality computers with working virus protection, etc.).
- Marketing, outreach and maintaining contact with alumni.

It's been our experience that, careful budgeting in combination with high quality programming and the team and cross-training approach described previously, enable us to continuously cover personnel needs and offer e-learners the support and services they need.

Discussion Questions

1. What strategies and tools should administrators consider to support long-term stability and managed growth in e-learning programs?
2. What other challenges have you faced in your endeavors to deliver academic e-learning courses or events? What creative solutions have you found? At what point do you "cut your losses" and move on?
3. In what ways do you imagine the future profile for e-learners for ESOL in developing countries may change in five years? Ten years?
4. Do you see an increase or decrease in future e-learning services, support systems and tools in your institution? Why?

Notes

1 Information on the English Language Fellows program through the U.S. Department of State is available: http://exchanges.state.gov/englishteaching/el-fellow.html
2 For more on TESOL affiliates, see: http://www.tesol.org/s_tesol/seccss.asp?CID=160&DID=1630
3 For more information on the English Opens Doors Program, see: http://www.centro devoluntarios.cl/
4 For more information on the USAID/AMIDEAST Model Schools Network program for Palestinians, see:http://www.amideastorg/msn/about-msn/model-schools-network -msn-program
5 For more information on Thai-UO programs, see: http://thaiuo.uoregon.edu
6 For more information on TWE and the related *Women Teaching Women English* open access materials, see: http://aei.uoregon.edu/wtwe/
7 Information on the Family Educational Rights and Privacy Act (FERPA) for students is available: http://ed.gov/policy/gen/guid/fpco/ferpa/students.html

References

Amelung, M., Krieger, K., & Rosner, D. (2011) E-assessment as a service. *IEEE Transactions on Learning Technologies, 4*(2), 162–174.

American Council for Teachers of Foreign Languages (ACTFL) (2002) *ACTFL program standards for the preparation of foreign language teachers*. Retrieved from http://www.actfl. org/files/public/ACTFLNCATEStandardsRevised713.pdf

American Society for Training and Development (ASTD) (2010) E-learning glossary. Retrieved from http://www.astd.org/LC/glossary.htm

Cheng, K. H., & Tsai, C.C. (2011) An investigation of Taiwan university students' perceptions of online academic help seeking, and their web-based learning self-efficacy. *Internet and Higher Education, 14*(3), 150–157.

Eynon, R., & Helsper, E. (2011) Adults learning online: Digital choice and/or digital exclusion? *New Media & Society, 13*(4), 534–551.

Google Apps Technical Support Services (2011) Google apps technical support services guidelines. Retrieved from http://www.google.com/apps/intl/en/terms/tssg.html

Greenleaf, R. K., Spears, L. C.; Covey, S. R., & Senge, P. M. (2002) *Servant leadership: A journey into the nature of legitimate power and greatness.* New York: Paulist Press.

Guerlac, S. (2011) Humanities 2.0: E-learning in the digital world. *Representations, 116*(1), 102–127.

Healey, D., Hanson-Smith, E., Hubbard, P., Ioannou-Georgiou, S., Kessler, G., & Ware, P. (2011) *TESOL technology standards: Description, implementation, integration.* Alexandria, VA: Teachers of English to Speakers of Other Languages.

International Society for Technology in Education (ISTE) (2008) *NETS for teachers.* Available http://www.iste.org/standards/nets-for-teachers.aspx

Jia, H., Wang, M., Ran, W., Yang, S., Liao, J. , et al. (2011) Design of a performance-oriented workplace e-learning system using ontology. *Expert Systems with Applications, 38*(4), 3372–3382.

Kim, S., Song, S., & Yoon, Y. (2011) Smart learning services based on smart cloud computing. *Sensors, 11*(8), 7835–7850.

Leppisaari, I., Vainio, L., Herrington, J., & Im, Y. (2011) International e-benchmarking: Flexible peer development of authentic learning principles in higher education. *Educational Media International, 48*(3), 179–191.

Logan, D., King, J. P., & Fischer-Wright, H. (2008) *Tribal leadership.* New York: Collins.

Merriam Webster (2011) *Merriam Webster Online Dictionary.* http://www.merriam-webster. com

Mishra, A., & Mishra, D. (2011) E-learning experience at various universities: Academics perspective. *Tehnicki Vjesnik-Technical Gazette, 18*(1), 133–140.

Prensky, M. (2001) Digital natives, digital immigrants. *On the Horizon, 9*(5), 1–6. Retrieved from http://www.marcprensky.com/writing/prensky%20-%20digital%20natives,%20 digital%20immigrants%20-%20part1.pdf

Rogers, E. M. (1995) *Diffusion of Innovations.* New York: Free Press.

Stella, A., & Gnanam, A. (2004) Quality assurance in distance education: The challenges to be addressed. *Higher Education, 47*(2), 143–160.

Wang, S., & Wu, C. (2011) Application of context-aware and personalized recommendation to implement an adaptive ubiquitous learning system. *Expert Systems with Applications, 38*(9), 10831–10838.

World Bank (2011) How we classify countries. Retrieved from http://data.worldbank.org/ about/country-classifications

World Trade Organization (2011) Who are the developing countries in the WTO? Retrieved from http://www.wto.org/english/tratop_e/devel_e/d1who_e.htm

13

REWARDS AND CHALLENGES OF ONLINE PROGRAM ADMINISTRATION

David R. Hall and John S. Knox

Some institutions provide dedicated open and distance learning environments, and many around the world are devoted exclusively to distance education. Increasingly, however, and especially in the field of language teacher education, distance programs have been developed in traditional institutions as an addition to standard face-to-face programs. Establishing and maintaining a distance education operation within such an institution presents a number of difficulties and challenges, not least because most aspects of course delivery, development, assessment, record-keeping and communication conflict with systems that have been established on the assumption that students and teachers are physically present at the institution and live locally. This chapter will explore the unique features of distance learning from the administrative point of view.

The origin of almost all the administrative problems is that the needs of the distance program are non-mainstream and marginal to the main business of the larger institution. Procedures serve the needs of the administration, and exceptions and deviations are not suffered gladly, understandably in a context, common around the world, where economic pressures mean that administrative staff members are often expected to do more and more with fewer resources. Administration emerged as one of the most important topics in our surveys of distance educators and students (Hall & Knox 2009a, b), and there are some mentions of administrative issues in the literature, but there has been very little investigation of the dynamics of a distance education operation in a traditional institution. It is not always appreciated that despite the frustrations, the rewards in terms of job satisfaction for distance program administrators can be high and learner appreciation of administrators is expressed much more often than in comparable face-to-face programs.

In this chapter we will cover some of the difficulties that the committed distance teacher will almost certainly come across when working in an institution that is not primarily dedicated to flexible modes of learning. While some of these difficulties relate to distrust of distance learning and a perception of it as a second-best alternative, the more common problems involve having to deal with administrative and academic systems that were not set up to deal with the distance learner and with the unrealistic expectations, particularly with regard to cost-saving, that administrators often have about teaching by distance and managing online resources. We suggest that novice distance teachers need expertise not only in obvious areas such as instructional design but also in various aspects of management, including people skills, financial planning, management of change and innovation, strategic committee work, group dynamics and public relations. We emphasize the need for high-quality interaction between the distance learner and all of the people that go to make up the human capital of the institution, including administrators, technicians, teachers and accountants. It is ultimately up to the distance teacher to ensure that learners are receiving positive support at all points.

Many of us have become involved in distance learning through our own efforts of trying to provide flexible learning opportunities for our students. It is probably fair to say that most of the authors represented in this book originally became enthusiastic about the possibilities of distance learning through our experiences as practitioners rather than through a desire to research the area. Nonetheless we are all now interested in research, having become aware of the interesting questions about learning and teaching, and the relationship between teachers, learners and different kinds of mediated interaction. While the present chapter is primarily focused on practical aspects of distance education delivery (if delivery is not too loaded and one-sided a term), we are also all interested in pursuing research not just in order to improve practice but in improving our understanding of learning in its specific social contexts such as the online environment and the wider contexts in which online learning takes place.

In this chapter, however, we focus on an aspect that has not been covered to any great degree in the literature, but that was one of the issues that emerged from a survey of distance teacher education providers that we conducted a few years ago, and that is the relationship between the distance teacher and the institution, especially where the core business of the institution is education using the conventional traditional modalities of face-to-face lectures, tutorials and closed-room examinations.

If you work or study in a traditional institution of this kind, you will be well aware of all the different elements that go to make up the institution, in theory working together but in practice often jealously defensive of their own turf. When you are setting up any new operations, you will have to deal with all of these different elements. In our institution, for example, this would include the Postgraduate Office, the Higher Degree Research Office, the Admissions Office, the Finance Office, the Student Systems Office, the IT Group (currently called Informatics), the International Office, and, on the committee side, committees at departmental, faculty and University levels: Learning and Teaching Committees,

FIGURE 13.1 The student on campus

Standards and Quality Control Committees, Full Department Meetings, Faculty Boards, right up to the University's Academic Senate and Institute Council. This can all be frustrating, especially when committees and offices sometimes appear to be pulling in opposite directions rather than trying to find solutions to problems as they arise. On-campus students are well aware that the university consists of multiple elements with different functions (see Figure 13.1), and know that they will have to go to different offices in different buildings to find out what they need. Distance learners, however, are more likely to see the university as a single point (see Figure 13.2), giving rise to sentences such as "I wrote to the University, and they told me…"

When we first started our DL programs at Macquarie University some 20 years ago, we had some seemingly intractable problems. For example, the student record system assumed that all students lived in Sydney, and the space in the system for the correspondence address would allow only a maximum of three lines with up to 45 characters per line, and then a postcode of four digits only.

Similarly, our International Office seemed reluctant to understand that our international students would not be coming to Australia and would not need a visa and would not have to be registered as full-time students (a government requirement for students on an international student visa in Australia). So students kept getting letters (when they received letters at all) instructing them to send in their visa details and airport pick-up times.

Seemingly small problems such as these were repeated many times over, and if you had asked us when we wrote a report called *Going the Distance* (unpublished Macquarie university internal document) on the first two years of our distance learning operation what advice we would give to anyone considering starting up a distance program, we would probably have given a very short answer: *Don't*.[1]

University

FIGURE 13.2 The distance student

Things, however, have shown remarkable improvement since then, partly but not only because of technological advances. We no longer rely on mail to send fee invoices that often arrived after the deadline for payment. We have a much better student information system that acknowledges the possibility that not all of our students live in north Sydney. We have online enrollment and online delivery of materials. We have online access to the library and its journals. We record and publish online seminars by visiting speakers and department lecturers. Many things are much better.

But the battle to remind all sections of the university that there is a population of Macquarie students who never set foot in Australia, let alone Macquarie, is on-going. By and large the distance program and its participants are invisible. When the catastrophic earthquake and tsunami hit Japan early in 2011, the university showed concern for the many Japanese students studying on the Sydney campus and for the one Australian student who was visiting Japan in an academic exchange, but showed little recognition that the university actually had large numbers of students studying by distance and living and working in Japan, some in the most badly affected areas.

This lack of awareness is not surprising. In a mainstream institution, distance learning will always be marginalized, despite the fact that its modalities are being adopted increasingly to deliver learning materials to on-campus students and that in an era where governments are aiming to have an ever-increasing percentage of the population educated to degree level, flexible learning options are going to be become more and more prominent.

It seems to us that as providers of distance education, we need to engage with this lack of awareness, and that we have to take on, in addition to our other commitments to teaching, supervision, research and administration, that of public relations. As part of our role as distance learning managers, we need to manage how different sections of the institution relate to our distance learners. And it is not enough to convince people once. Institutional memory is not long, and knowledge and experience often do not survive changes of personnel. So there is a constant struggle to maintain the visibility of distance learning.

This means ensuring that brochures and publicity material and websites maintain up-to-date and accurate information, that centrally-generated communications to remote students are relevant to them and not misleading, that the Finance Office understands that arrangements through overseas banks may take a little longer, and that everyone makes allowances for different holiday seasons and different school years. It means above all trying to counter the perception that for administrators such learners present an additional administrative burden. In other words, it means constant internal public relations on behalf of distance learning operations: working on committees at all levels of the institution; pointing out the contribution of distance learners to institutional income and to institutional diversity; celebrating the international perspectives brought by distance learners; highlighting international collaborations made possible through connections first established through distance learning participants; ensuring that lessons learned through distance education can be transferred to mixed-mode teaching as increasing numbers of students compete for space on the traditional campus (space for lecture-rooms, for private study, even for car-parking) and as increasing student numbers have increasingly diverse needs for study support. In this way, your institution can become one that embraces diversity in all its forms, including flexibility of study mode.

None of this is easy, and if you are to become involved in designing programs for remote delivery, you have to bear in mind that it will increase your workload and you will need to be prepared for and committed to this. Distance teaching is not cheap teaching. It can lower costs, but not in the way that the bean-counters think, by needing fewer teaching hours. It is a considerable commitment that has to be fully acknowledged in workload calculations for both teachers and administrators. This was a very clear finding from our survey of distance education providers. We know from our own experience that those administrators who are most closely involved with distance programs—often at a departmental rather than a central university level—quickly become the most important people in the networks of communication that students interact with, becoming the "go-to" people whatever the question. Year after year, we receive glowing feedback from students about particular members of the professional staff group: "I don't think I could have got through the program without the support of x ...." The well-documented isolation that remote students feel can be assuaged or exacerbated depending on the sensitivity and empathy exhibited by the people they deal with. If distance and online operations are to be successful, we have to work towards a situation where all the stakeholders understand the importance and impact of their work, feel happy and engaged with the processes involved and where their contribution is seen to be valued. The distance teacher, in other words, in addition to all the other roles that a teacher routinely fulfills, and without necessarily being in a designated management position, needs to be a skillful and motivating manager of people.

Discussion Questions

1   The authors of this chapter argue that: "It is ultimately up to the distance teacher to ensure that learners are receiving positive support at all points."
    • Try to list "all points" of the distance student experience.
2   Is it fair to expect language-teacher educators who are teaching by distance to take responsibility at all points?

- If so, why?
- If not, who should take responsibility at different points? What should the language-teacher educator do if there is no one to take on these responsibilities?

3   Students' experience of an institution by distance is primarily mediated through documents (printed and online), and through (usually) written communication with a limited number of individuals in the institution. What can be done to make institutional structures and administration processes more transparent to distance students?

Note

1   David was involved in setting up the program and writing the report mentioned here. John was, at this time, a distance student in the program.

References

Hall, D. R., & Knox, J. S. (2009a). Language teacher education by distance. In A. Burns & Jack Richards (Eds), *Cambridge guide to second language teacher education* (pp 218–229). Cambridge: Cambridge University Press.

Hall, D. R., & Knox, J.S. (2009b). Issues in the education of TESOL teachers by distance education. *Distance Education, 30*(1), 63–85.

14

PLANNING A DISTANCE EDUCATION COURSE FOR LANGUAGE TEACHERS

What Administrators Need to Consider

Deborah Healey

Providing online courses to domestic students is often seen as a way to reach non-traditional learners as well as regular students who want more flexibility in when and where they learn. Many institutions are also looking for a wider audience internationally. As the Sloan Consortium reports in their 2010 survey of U.S. higher education, online courses in U.S. colleges and universities have expanded dramatically. In Fall 2009, there were 5.6 million students enrolled in at least one tertiary-level online course. The Consortium reports an increase of almost 1 million students between their 2009 and 2010 survey (Sloan Consortium, 2010). This growth in online education is not limited to the United States. With increasing availability of high-speed Internet worldwide, the potential for online learning has expanded dramatically. For example, the Internet World Stats website reports that as of March 2011, 44% of the world's Internet users were in Asia, and the number of users there has grown over 700% in the last decade (Internet World Stats, 2011a). China has 485 million Internet users, approximately 36% of the population (Internet World Stats, 2011b). The potential for marketing distance teacher education internationally is high.

There are a number of issues to consider before launching online courses. Many of the issues addressed here will also be relevant to hybrid courses that include both face-to-face and online elements. However, this chapter will focus on logistical issues that an administrator will need to consider when deciding to implement fully online courses for language teachers. These issues include:

- Human resources: Who will plan and prepare the courses? Who will teach the courses? Who will provide technical support both locally and to distant students? What are the differences and challenges in course preparation and

delivery with online courses? How will the courses be kept up-to-date? What are the legal aspects of online learning that need to be considered? How will quality be assessed and maintained?
- Marketing: Who is the audience? How will the right learners be attracted to the new course? What marketing mechanisms are needed to attract the target audience? How will your institution compete with what is already available?
- Technology: Is the institutional infrastructure robust enough? What course management system choices are available? How much of the course will be accessible via mobile devices, such as cell phones? What equipment and skills do course developers and instructors need? What equipment and skills do prospective students require in order to participate? How will the technologies used be kept up-to-date? How will final examinations and other end-of-course assessments be handled?

This chapter will not provide an exhaustive overview of all of the choices, but it will provide administrators with a set of questions to ask. Armed with answers, administrators can then make good decisions that will improve the chances for success in a distance education venture.

Human Resources

Planning the Course

Administrators must be attentive to pedagogy, professional development and legal issues when planning a distance education course. The failures in distance education courses have shown that a successful distance education course cannot be created simply by putting the text into PDF format and recording lectures in digital video format to post online. A charismatic face-to-face lecturer is rarely as charismatic in recorded video. The new medium requires a different, deliberately inclusive pedagogy that is truly student-centered, that builds community among learners separated in space and time and that recognizes and supports differences in learning styles and strategies (Cini & Vilic, 2004; Yang & Cornelious, 2004). Planning from a human resource (HR) perspective includes carefully selecting appropriate course developers, instructors and technical support staff. Faculty and staff should be chosen with past experience in distance education in mind.

Course developers, instructors, technical support staff and administrators need ongoing professional development to stay abreast of changes in technology and methodology. Changes in technology, such as mobile learning, are driving research and changes in best practices. Teachers of English to Speakers of Other Languages (TESOL) offers a certificate program in Principles and Practices of Online Teaching (TESOL, 2011), which is particularly appropriate for those interested in teaching language online. The annual TESOL Conference offers many related sessions, as well. The American Educational Research Association (AERA) is the primary professional organization in the United States involved with research on education and teacher education. AERA has two special interest groups (SIGs) with a strong interest in online education: Online Teaching and Learning; and Technology, Instruction, Cognition, and Learning. The Sloan Consortium, EDUCAUSE, and other internationally recognized organizations produce regular updates on pedagogy and the state of the art in distance education.

An online course has additional legal considerations that administrators need to consider. The online environment makes sharing information easy, and private student information that is not stored securely is at risk. In the United States, federal regulations require that educational institutions protect student information. Administrators should be aware of legal requirements outside the United States as well, and sensitive to student concerns about privacy. Safeguarding private information about students from conflict zones is particularly important.

Regulations in many parts of the U.S. mandate that learners in credit-bearing online courses have the equivalent amount of advising and library support as their face-to-face counterparts. This is both an HR issue and a technical issue. Advisors need to be prepared to address the needs of distant learners, some possibly in different time zones and not available during normal 8am to 5pm work hours. Language proficiency in English may also be an issue with international students. While access to digital library resources may be the same off-campus as on-campus, access to physical library resources and the expertise of reference librarians needs to be addressed. Administrators will need to initiate discussions with advising and library staff, and additional staffing may be required to achieve the level of equivalent access.

Another issue that arises especially in credit-bearing courses is finding the online equivalent of "seat time," or the number of hours that the student physically spends in a face-to-face class. This has little or no meaning in asynchronous online courses without a clear way to assess how much time the student is actually spending on coursework. In general, the decision about what counts as one credit in an online course is by a governing body. This may be a local or regional board of education or Ministry of Education, although it can also be a decision made by the senior administration of an institution of higher education. Seat time requirements will affect the number of courses and instructors needed to implement a teacher education program.

Preparing the Course

Online course developers, who may or may not be course instructors, need to be prepared for the unique aspects of online teaching and learning. These include creating a learning community, setting timelines, adapting material and paying attention to copyright requirements. Creating a sense of community is essential to success in online learning (Karayan & Crowe, 1997; Garrison, Anderson, & Archer, 2000). The informal conversations that occur when people are in the same classroom looking at each other build rapport and make pair and group work feel natural. These face-to-face interactions inside the class encourage a sense of teamwork that enables students to interact with each other more easily outside class. Students separated by space and time, however, and working online independently simply do not have the same connection to each other that they would have when sitting together with each other in a classroom. The course developer must include activities to create community, such as formal introductions and informal sharing of personal information, designated partners who serve as peer readers/peer advisers or "study buddies," and a requirement in discussions to respond to at least one other person's post.

Online learners need clear deadlines, since they will not have the informal reminders that often come in a face-to-face class. The timeline for discussions, activities and assessments should be stated from the beginning of the course (Cole & Kritzer, 2009). As in any class, best practices in an online course include clear objectives that are shared with students, lessons in a rational order supported by research and formative and summative assessments based on the content of the course (Zhu, Payette, & DeZure, 2003). With online teacher education, it is even more important to model best practices so that learners who later themselves develop their own courses or teach online will be better prepared to do so.

A common mistake in an online course is to assume that a course developer, armed with a textbook from a face-to-face course, will be able to use that the text largely as it is for online delivery without change. The online teacher will not be able to see puzzled brows as learners read material or work on tasks. All material will have to be scrutinized for clarity and perhaps annotated, especially if learners are not highly proficient English language users. Course tasks need examples and clear rubrics so that learners will have multiple ways of understanding what is expected. Similarly, a lecture that is effective face-to-face is not necessarily going to work when recorded in a studio and put online. Shorter video clips with focused activities will hold the attention of online learners more effectively. The online environment is uniquely designed for multimedia and multiple routes through material (hypertext). Course designers should provide media options and alternative paths through material whenever possible.

Copyright is a large issue in an online course. A face-to-face teacher is protected in many instances by "fair use" and by the simple fact that what the teacher does in the classroom is largely invisible to the outside world. "Fair use" also applies online. However, the provisions of fair use in the United States are eroding, and even classes completely within an institution's password-protected site may be held to strict fair use provisions. The use of commercial video is particularly curtailed, even under fair use – only 10% or three minutes, whichever is less, without explicit permission from the copyright holder (American Distance Education Consortium, 1996). Restricting video use has large implications for language teacher education, which uses authentic video extensively. The course developer should seek permission for all copyrighted material used in the course and either be prepared to pay for its use or locate a substitute. The onus will fall on the administrator to be aware of copyright provisions and ensure compliance.

Teaching the Course

Good material and good instructor preparation are essential elements for effective teaching in an online course (Zhu, et al., 2004; Cole & Kritzer, 2009, *inter alia*). Other issues for the administrator to consider with online teaching include the instructor's interactions with students, teacher evaluation and appropriate teaching load and compensation.

The instructor in an online course is responsible for making sure that the learning environment is working, encouraging community-building, checking that each learner is making appropriate progress and facilitating content learning. If the course developer has done a good job of setting up methods to create community, sequencing activities, addressing a variety of learning styles and incorporating appropriate assessment and feedback, then the instructor has a strong framework for the class. If any of those elements are missing, the instructor will need to supply them. The instructor, like the course developer, must also be attentive to copyright issues.

A well-prepared online instructor will realize that the material that students are using, their tasks and assignments and students' online interactions with each other and the teacher are at the heart of the learning. An instructor who thrives on one-on-one interactions in a face-to-face course may be dissatisfied with the loss of the personal touch in a largely asynchronous course. This sense of isolation from the students may be alleviated by using real-time interaction tools with students, such as Skype (Cole & Kritzer, 2009).

An online course thrives on interaction. Research in online teaching indicates that course discussion is important and useful, and that it is what makes online teaching more time consuming than a face-to-face class (Davidson-Shivers, 2009; Manderbach, et al., 2007; Cavanaugh, 2005). Keeping up with email communication from students is another essential part of the instructor's job. Learners who cannot understand an assignment or who cannot make a course tool work need to be able to tell the instructor. They also need to be able to trust that the instructor will respond to the problem in a timely way. The instructor should establish ground rules for response time, such as within 24–48 hours, so that students do not expect an immediate response to email at 6 o'clock on a weekend morning (which may be 4pm on a workday in some parts of the world). Many learner problems relate to technology, so the instructor needs to recognize and respond to common technical problems that do not require skilled intervention. For example, students who cannot see newly added online material might just need to refresh the screen or restart the browser. The instructor should also recognize problems that require help from technical support staff.

Teacher evaluation in a fully online course will look different from that in a face-to-face class. Class observation is frequently part of an assessment of teaching effectiveness. In a face-to-face class, the observer sets a time to arrive, looks at the teacher's plans for that time, comes in for an hour or so, takes notes and then writes a report, perhaps after a debriefing session with the classroom teacher. Unless the online class uses lectures via videoconferencing, there is unlikely to be a single hour where the observer in an online course could be guaranteed of seeing online interaction. Where the online course uses extensive asynchronous online discussion, there is plenty of opportunity to observe the interactions among learners and between the instructor and learners. The structure of the online course will determine how much of an emphasis to put on different course elements, such as asynchronous discussion, synchronous interaction and instructor response to student products (e.g., essays, sample lesson plans, worksheets). Tobin (2004) includes guidance about online teacher evaluations as well as a helpful checklist.

Student evaluations are another means of assessing teacher effectiveness. Many of the same factors are at play in online and in face-to-face classes: student comfort level, motivation and achievement; and students' sense that the course structure and activities make sense, that the teacher has helped them learn and that they have been graded fairly. As with a face-to-face course, administrators should consider the elements of the course over which the instructor may have no control, including technical issues and course content that the instructor has not chosen. It is also important to remember that there is little certainty about who has actually completed an online evaluation.

Administrators need to recognize that teaching an online course is often more demanding than teaching a face-to-face course in a classroom (Davidson-Shivers, 2009; Mandernach, Dailey-Hebert, & Donnelli-Sallee, 2007; Cavanaugh, 2005). Reading and responding to 20 five-page essays submitted online takes just as much time as reading and responding to the same number of pages printed out. A recent study by Cavanaugh (2005) noted, "The major difference in the time spent teaching online was in communicating with the student. It is probable that any significant reduction in student communication would have a negative effect on the quality of the instruction" (Cavanaugh, 2005: Concluding comments paragraph 2). Instructors may prefer to have the flexible work hours that online teaching can offer. Nonetheless, administrators who want or expect instructors to provide an effective online learning environment need to be prepared to pay appropriately for instructors' time.

Marketing

A market analysis is a key component to any new venture, and offering an online course is no exception. The first step is to define the target audience for the course. In teacher education, the audience might be pre-service teachers seeking a certificate or a degree, others using a short course to explore their real interest in becoming a teacher, current teachers looking for short professional development opportunities, or current teachers interested in advanced training for a certificate or an advanced degree. They may be working full-time all year, or they may work full-time during the school year but have more study time available in the summer months. They may be novices or experienced with the content, the specific technologies the course will use and with online learning. They may also be a mixture of all of the above, making marketing and planning more complex.

Once the target market is identified, the next step is to determine how to attract the right learners to the course. It will be easiest if the course or courses are aimed at students who are already identified, perhaps because they have taken previous face-to-face courses, they have expressed an interest in your institution or they will be sponsored by an outside group or agency, such as the U.S. Department of State or a state or regional educational agency. If the students are not known, then the administrator needs to consider carefully what marketing mechanisms might be necessary to attract a new audience. There are well over 14 billion web pages that are indexed by Google, Bing, Yahoo or other major search engines (WorldWideWebSize. com, 2011), so just having a web page will not be enough. Targeted marketing for the identified audience is needed, possibly in multiple languages. One approach is to join forces with a larger entity or group, such as the larger institution within which your program is located, a regional consortium or a professional consortium and jointly market course offerings. In many cases, effective marketing will require working with a marketing agency that has a proven record in finding an international audience for online teacher education.

Looking at the competition is another aspect of the market analysis. A web search for "teacher training online" or "online teacher education" yields a long list of others in this market. In addition to formal courses online that students pay for, the Internet is rich in free resources. One such free English language teacher training resource is the "Shaping the Way We Teach English" series of videos and supplementary material from the U.S. Department of State (Office of English Language Programs, 2007). Websites related to English language skill building, often a component of training for non-native English teachers and of interest to general English language learners, are also widely available. Many of these sites offer full courses, some free, some with audio/video, some with real-time conversation practice and all with extensive practice activities. Clearly, it is essential to offer value that distinguishes your program's offerings from others available and makes your course worth the tuition or fee charged.

Technology

Online courses are expensive to create and maintain. Most of the technical needs for the course must be thoroughly considered and decided upon at the planning stage.

The delivery stage brings additional technical demands. Technology changes rapidly, so technical needs must be reconsidered regularly.

Planning the Courses

Planning for technology in an online course includes assessing the needs and demands for basic Internet speed and capacity, the tools needed to achieve course objectives, including the possible use of a learning management system (LMS), and the ability of online students to use the technology that is selected.

The institutional infrastructure must be robust enough to support the demands of the course. Being able to handle multiple simultaneous users is a basic need. Video is a very useful tool for online teacher training. Video clips of actual teachers in classrooms convey the reality of classroom teaching, both for pre-service teachers and for current teachers. If the institution and the users do not have sufficient bandwidth (Internet capacity), a video will load slowly or not at all, the video will start and stop constantly, and the end result will be very difficult or impossible to watch. Video also takes a lot of online storage space – 5MB per minute for compressed video with modest resolution to 200MB per minute for DVD-quality video. Audio is much less resource-intensive.

Videoconferencing is one approach to present course content: a real-time lecture and an interactive discussion with course participants over a video link. This requires a very high-speed line, most likely a dedicated line, and good quality video cameras. One-way videos where learners can see but not be seen and streaming pre-recorded video lectures consume fewer Internet resources than videoconferencing during delivery, but both need a high-speed line for best results.

Class discussion is another basic element in language teacher education. Asynchronous online discussion takes relatively little space or bandwidth. Synchronous audio discussion is more resource-intensive, and having multiple simultaneous speakers is generally quite confusing when the listener cannot be certain who is speaking. A synchronous video discussion can work with a small group. The quality of the Internet connection will determine how many people can interact on video simultaneously.

A learning management system (LMS) is one way to organize course information and student record-keeping. A number of LMSs exist, including the commercial Blackboard and the open source (free) Moodle and Sakai. The institution needs a server to run the LMS and a trained team who can provide technical support for the server, course developers, instructors and students. All major LMS options for education provide user authentication (login plus password), a space for course content consisting of text and graphics, asynchronous online discussion, a way to email course participants, some options for creating and delivering tests and a grade book; other options will depend on the LMS. Possibilities include individual student blogs, journals, web pages and e-portfolios (file storage); an interactive whiteboard-style synchronous space where learners can write, annotate and draw together; audio and video streaming options; and support for multiple languages, including non-Roman languages.

The LMS chosen has to be able to provide the features that the course requires for the expected number of users. An online teacher education program will benefit from the use of all of the standard features of an LMS as well as reflective journals, e-portfolios for work samples, audio and video streaming and probably a place for synchronous interaction, such as a shared whiteboard.

Other options for course delivery include working with tools that are not hosted by the institution but rather at third-party sites such as Google, Wikispaces, WordPress, or Skype. Creating a mixture of third-party tools may work well when delivering a single course to a relatively small number of users. A non-credit-bearing course for language teachers, for example, can be effectively delivered with third-party tools. This is not a good approach for a series of courses, degree- or certificate-granting programs, a large number of enrolled students, tracking what course pages students visit and for how long or keeping confidential student data private.

Planning the technical needs for the course also must take into account the computer and Internet capacity that students are likely to have. Students may have older computers and limited or poor Internet capacity. In that case, the students may need to receive video and audio resources on CD or DVD rather than online. Using an LMS may add an additional layer that takes bandwidth, making it more difficult for students in low-resource environments to participate.

Preparing the Course

Technology-related issues in course preparation include the relationship between technical support staff and course developers, the use of design standards, provision for use of mobile devices, and the timing of updates.

Technical support staff and course developers should set up a working relationship early. The expectations of both will need to be synchronized. Course developers should know what the technology makes possible. They should also incorporate only those features that the infrastructure and course delivery system will allow. Because technology changes, the course developer will need to keep abreast of any new possibilities or limitations in the infrastructure and course delivery system. If the technical support staff knows far enough in advance what the course developer is trying to do, they can in some cases make changes to the infrastructure or the course delivery system to enable additional features. In many settings, a content specialist works with a technical specialist to create online course content. Where the content specialist knows a bit about technology and the technical specialist knows something about teaching, this collaboration can work very well.

Best practices in digital content delivery include Universal Design (UD), creating digital content that is accessible to those with physical disabilities such as limited vision, hearing and mobility. A set of UD guidelines can be found at http://www.udlcenter.org/aboutudl/udlguidelines (CAST, 2011). The institution may also have design standards related to course websites. Knowing what the standards are from the beginning eliminates the need to change later in order to conform to institutional requirements.

The use of mobile devices (cell phones, smartphones, personal digital assistants and the like) has grown dramatically around the world, reaching more people than the Internet in some developing countries. The broad use of mobile devices means that course development now should take their use into account, especially with content that may be delivered in countries with less Internet access. The course delivery system may already be able to adapt content for the smaller screen size of mobile devices. The course developer should consider the possibilities and limitations of mobile devices when planning course tasks and interactive elements.

Since advances in technology occur that affect infrastructure and course delivery systems, there must be a system in place to address the timing and frequency of updates that could dramatically affect the look and feel of a course. A change in the way the LMS looks or works may mean that help documents are out of date, that certain types of course content may not perform as expected, or that some content may become unusable. Course preparation should be seen as an ongoing process rather than as something finished the first time..

Course Delivery

Ensuring that students have information about technical requirements before they register, providing adequate technical support and training for students and instructors and assessment of online courses are all important aspects of course delivery for administrators.

Prospective students will need to know what equipment and software they will need in order to participate in the course successfully. Ideally, they will be able to test what they have before they register for the course to be sure that they will be able to go online and use the course tools. Once the class starts, students who have technical problems will need a variety of ways to contact technical support staff for help. Having only an email address for technical support is not helpful if the student is unable to go online. Students who are working at a distance already feel isolated, and when technology does not work appropriately, then help is needed quickly. With international participants, there may be an additional burden if they are unable to communicate well in English or if technical support staff cannot make themselves understood. It is very helpful to have more than one student from any language group; the less frustrated person may be able to mediate better or translate between technical support and the student.

Instructors also need reliable technical support throughout the course. Instructors will need initial training with the course delivery system, whether it is an LMS or a set of third-party tools. Instructors will need to have computers and Internet access that will be adequate to support their work, wherever they are expected to be working. This will often be from home if students are taking the class from different time zones. Like students, instructors will need quick responses from technical support when there are problems.

Assessment is a significant issue in online course delivery. Online courses that do not use interactive videoconferencing have major issues with end-of-course (summative) assessment. A video-based format may allow the instructor to see who is actually physically present during an assessment. Otherwise, there is a question of who is doing the work. If the course is non-credit and without a formal certification involved, then assessment is not a large issue and can be an online element of the course. In a course that offers credit or formal certification, there must be a way to know who is actually taking the exams. A number of institutions have proctors at distant locations. When they register for the course, students should be informed that they would need to be physically present at the proctored location for assessments. Needless to say, this can dramatically increase the hardship and cost for students who have long distances to travel.

Conclusion

Having the right people in the right place is the first step in any successful enterprise. A successful online course for language teachers requires good course development, with teaching and technology skills customized to the specific online environment being used. Effective marketing is another key element: attracting pre-service or current teachers who are interested in, prepared for and equipped with the technology needed for the course that is offered. Ongoing, continuous evaluation and a readiness to revise the course in the light of changes in technology and methodology are also necessary so that the course continues to meet the needs of the target learners. Most importantly, ongoing professional development for course developers, instructors and technical support will enable timely response to changes in technology.

California State University, Chico (2003) has developed a Rubric for Online Instruction that administrators may find useful in designing, implementing and evaluating an online teacher education course (California State University, Chico, 2003). In addition, *TESOL Technology Standards: Description, Implementation, Integration* (Healey, Hanson-Smith, Hubbard, Ioannou-Georgiou, Kessler, & Ware, 2011) includes a chapter on how the TESOL Technology Standards apply in online teaching. These standards should be considered when developing and implementing a program for language educators.

Yang & Cornelious (2004) point out that the administrator needs to serve as a "planner, motivator, promoter, and supporter in the process to ensure quality online education" (p. 855). This is a demanding role. However, a high-quality online teacher education course or program will have ongoing effects, since the learners who are served by the course will be in a position as teachers to replicate at least some of what they have experienced with their own learners. The benefit can continue long after the end of the online course.

Discussion Questions

1   Consider the different personnel required for an effective online language course: administrators, marketers, course developers, instructors, technical support staff, and perhaps in-house trainers for ongoing professional development. How many people who fit these roles are on your staff now, and how many would need to be hired or developed from within?

2   In online language courses, the course developer may or may not be the course instructor. What are the advantages and disadvantages of having the course developer be different from the course instructor in your institution? What the advantages and disadvantages of having the course developer be an instructor in an online course that you offer?

3   What teacher evaluation measures do you use now? How would they need to be adapted to work in an online environment?

References

American Distance Education Consortium (ADEC) (1996) Fair use guidelines for educational multimedia. Retrieved from http://www.adec.edu/admin/papers/fair10-17.html

California State University, Chico (2003) Rubric for online instruction. Retrieved from http://www.csuchico.edu/tlp/resources/rubric/rubric.pdf

CAST (2011) *Universal Design for learning guidelines version 2.0.* Wakefield, MA: CAST. Retrieved from http://www.udlcenter.org/aboutudl/udlguidelines

Cavanaugh, J. (2005) Teaching online – a time comparison. *Online Journal of Distance Learning Administration, 8*(1), 1–9. Retrieved from http://www.westga.edu/~distance/ojdla/spring81/cavanaugh81.htm

Cini, M. A., & Vilic, B. (2004) Faculty guidelines for online teaching. Retrieved from http://www.scribd.com/doc/8696942/Faculty-Guidelines-Rider

Cole, J. E., & Kritzer, J. B. (2009) Strategies for success: Teaching an online course. *Rural Special Education Quarterly, 28*(4), 36–40.

Davidson-Shivers, G. V. (2009), Frequency and types of instructor interactions in online instruction. *Journal of Interactive Online Learning, 8*(1). Retrieved from http://www.ncolr.org/jiol/issues/getfile.cfm?volID=8&IssueID=25&ArticleID=127

Garrison, D. R., Anderson, T., & Archer, W. (2000) Critical inquiry in a text-based environment: Computer conferencing in higher education. *The Internet and Higher Education, 2*(2–3), 87–105. Retrieved from http://communitiesofinquiry.com/files/Critical_Inquiry_model.pdf

Healey, D., Hanson-Smith, E., Hubbard, P., Ioannou-Georgiou, S., Kessler, G., & Ware, P. (2011) *TESOL technology standards: Description, implementation, integration.* Alexandria, VA: Teachers of English to Speakers of Other Languages.

Internet World Stats (2011a) World Internet users and population stats. Retrieved from http://www.internetworldstats.com/stats.htm

Internet World Stats (2011b) Usage and population statistics. Retrieved from http://www.internetworldstats.com/stats3.htm

Karayan, S. S., & Crowe, J. A. (1997) Student perceptions of electronic discussion groups, *T.H.E. Journal, 2* (9), 69–71. Retrieved from http://thejournal.com/Articles/1997/04/01/Student-Perceptions-of-Electronic-Discussion-Groups.aspx

Mandernach, B. J., Dailey-Hebert, A., & Donnelli-Sallee, E. (2007) Frequency and time investment of instructors' participation in threaded discussions in the online classroom. *Journal of Interactive Online Learning, 6*(1). Retrieved from http://www.ncolr.org/jiol/issues/getfile.cfm?volID=6&IssueID=19&ArticleID=96

Office of English Language Programs (2007) Shaping the way we teach English. Retrieved from http://oelp.uoregon.edu/shaping.html

Sloan Consortium (2010) *Class differences: online education in the United States, 2010.* Newburyport, MA: Sloan Consortium.

Teachers of English to Speakers of Other Languages (TESOL) (2011) Principles and practices of online teaching certificate program. Retrieved from http://www.tesol.org/s_tesol/sec_document.asp?CID=664&DID=2635

Tobin, T. J. (2004) Best practices for administrative evaluation of online faculty. Retrieved from http://www.westga.edu/~distance/ojdla/summer72/tobin72.html

WorldWideWebSize.com (2011) The size of the World Wide Web. Retrieved from http://www.worldwidewebsize.com/

Yang, Y. & Cornelious, L. F. (2004) Ensuring quality in online education instruction: what instructors should know? In Association for Educational Communications and Technology Conference proceedings, Chicago, IL, Oct 19-23.

Zhu, E., Payette, P., & DeZure, D. (2003) *An introduction to teaching online.* CLRT Occasional Papers, Number 18. Available at http://www.crlt.umich.edu/publinks/CRLT_no18.pdf

PART IV
Looking Ahead

15

THE FUTURE OF ONLINE TESOL

Liz England and David R. Hall

Introduction

This chapter addresses the future of online distance TESOL and makes some projections on what lies ahead for new teachers and researchers in this extraordinary and fast-growing area of professional and scholarly development. Changes in online distance TESOL are driven by many forces—economic challenges worldwide in the countries addressed in this volume, professional and scholarly innovations in face-to-face and online English language learning, teaching and program administration. For those interested in online distance TESOL, it may be a good time to take heed—to avoid the pitfalls of poor planning and to enjoy the results of excellence in online distance TESOL.

While well-aware that there is an artificial quality to prediction-making, the authors here attempt to "unpack" the issues for online distance TESOL. We draw on our own experience (spanning two decades), and on literature in other fields where research in online distance education has been conducted.

The content of all chapters in this book describes in depth and for the first time, the current issues that face online distance graduate programs in TESOL on four continents. Among those chapters, authors have identified well the rewards and challenges for learning, teaching and administration of these programs. We look now on what may be ahead for online distance TESOL. While crystal ball-gazing comes with risks, the predictions here are based on published work (little that there is available) as well as our own joint experience addressing graduate online distance TESOL on two continents (and with students located on six of those).

While the future does not necessarily have to be a reflection of the past, online teaching in general has experienced some challenges in the past several years. According to Kim and Bonk's valuable research published in 2006 (from a survey conducted in 2005), online distance TESOL may follow national trends in the United States in terms of some of the challenges facing learners, teachers and administrators of programs. In their study, results showed evidence of significant problems ahead for online distance programs in the United States. For learners, Kim and Bonk's research shows, there is a "pervasive sense of e-learning gloom, disappointment and bankruptcy and lawsuits and a myriad of other contentions" that face online distance programs in education, in general.

It is estimated that over 1 billion people are currently learning English worldwide. According to the British Council, as of the year 2000 there were 750 million English as a foreign language speakers. In addition, there were 375 million English as a Second Language speakers. The difference between the two groups amounts to English as a Foreign Language speakers using English occasionally for business or pleasure, while English as a Second Language speakers use English on a daily basis. For more detailed information on the trends behind English learning around the world, take a look at the British Council's "English Next." While some of these students will take English classes in face-to-face settings, it is very likely that many of them will be taking classes taught by teachers who have had online distance TESOL professional preparation courses. Increasing numbers of English language learners worldwide mean growth in the need for teachers; and teachers will continue to want to acquire their language teaching skills and credentials in online distance programs because those programs offer flexibility, high quality and easy access, especially for those in geographical areas where there may be limited or no face-to-face TESOL preparation courses.

How will online distance TESOL instructors be prepared in the future?

For instruction in online distance programs, myths and the accompanying institution-level problems for administering online programs include "misconceptions and myths related to the difficulty of teaching and learning online, technologies available to support online instruction, the support and compensation needed for high-quality instructors, and the needs of online students [which] create challenges for vision statement and planning documents." Equally disturbing are these *Chronicle of Higher Education* findings in 2011: there is "…a pervasive sense of e-learning gloom, disappointment bankruptcy and lawsuits, and a myriad other contentions."

As an academic discipline and profession, TESOL prides itself in quality standards setting. It is our sincere intention to provide information necessary to support and maintain TESOL's role in the world of online distance education as a leader and model for high quality standards of practice—now and for the future. Technological innovations have in the past often attracted "early adopters" who enthuse about the technical capabilities of the innovation and lose sight of what we know about good teaching and learning practice. This was an early criticism of CALL approaches and is still a temptation for technology-lovers, as pointed out by Henry and Meadows (2008—see also other references listed by them): "For those of us who love technology and gadgets it can be tempting to integrate such options into our courses just because they're there ... or because they're neat and we've become enamoured with them". As the rapidity of technological developments has increased and the variety of applications has multiplied, however, teachers and curriculum developers are now less liable to be dazzled by the software, instead looking for the contribution to learning and interaction the software can provide. Just as university teaching has long progressed beyond its traditional ex cathedra modalities to include group-work, collaborative projects, student research and countless others kinds of educational experience, so online teaching is exploring ways which go beyond the traditional reading-and-assignment models, examining issues such as what constitutes effective teaching and learning in an online environment and how the affordances of technology can be used to advantage (e.g. Stephenson, 2001; Paxton. 2003; McQuiggan, 2007; Gerber et al., 2008; Keengwe & Kidd, 2010).

The exact number of online distance TESOL programs worldwide is not known. A recent search for "online TESOL" on gradschools.com, a U.S.-based site for finding graduate education programs, yielded 72 hits (www.gradschools.com, retrieved October 10, 2011). There is little question that that number will grow for the United States and those in other countries will as well. Numbers of online language teacher education programs worldwide are large and apparently growing, though actually quantifying them is difficult, as there is no single site, as far as we can see, that lists all online programs. The problem of quantification is exacerbated by the differing terminology (TEFL, TESOL, Language Teaching, Applied Linguistics and specialist sub-groups such Teaching Business English, LSP/ESP, Teaching Young Children, etc.) and different kinds of accredited and non-accredited awards (Certificate, Diploma, Postgraduate Certificate, Masters, etc.).

The proliferation of programs and the lack of clarity about their status serve to remind us that there are no globally accepted minimum standards for TESOL qualifications, the programs that underpin them and the institutions that confer the awards. This is not to say that local criteria have not been developed in some areas, but the lack of transparency or agreement on what qualifications worldwide actually mean remains an issue that the relevant major TESOL/TEFL Associations might usefully turn their collective minds to, especially now that online learning allows access to programs everywhere.

What Are the Issues for the future of Learning Online and at a Distance?

Drawing on the work presented in this volume, the following "learning" issues for online TESOL students lie ahead:

1. Who will enroll in TESOL courses and programs online and by distance? Where will they teach? How many students will seek online distance, and not

face-to-face, courses and programs? What will their goals be for professional education?

While the British Council figures on English language learners worldwide (noted above) are of interest and may be useful in making predictions for the future of online English language learning, we found no reliable statistics on the number of students enrolled in online distance TESOL programs. However, in one study, focusing on the United States, the following information was compiled in 2010 on the number of students enrolled in online programs generally. Of those, we can only guess that some choose TESOL.

The 2010 Sloan Survey of Online Learning reveals that enrollment rose by almost 1 million students from a year earlier. The survey of more than 2,500 colleges and universities nationwide finds approximately 5.6 million students were enrolled in at least one online course in Fall 2009, the most recent term for which figures are available.

While "the proliferation of online instruction is, of course, not unique to L2 teacher education" (Kissau, 2011), teacher education has historically been particularly well-represented in distance education and, as Hall & Knox (2009, p. 64) point out, the mobility of language teachers and employer demand for higher qualifications are key factors in ensuring that TESOL professionals are a prominent group in the distance education population.

2.   What is ahead for the English language teaching market in the future? Will students of English language want to study face-to-face or online and by distance? What profiles can we identify among the millions worldwide who have in the past and will in the future most assuredly want to learn to use English as a tool for global communication? To what extent can we identify contexts, goals, ages and proficiency for those English language learners who seek online distance courses and programs of study?

As we enter the second decade of the twenty-first century, predictions about the identity and needs of English language learners of the future are little more than crystal-ball gazing. We take here some license, then, in an effort to make those predictions, knowing well that unforeseen world events—economic, political and scientific, among other factors—will have a strong impact on who those learners are and how many we may wish to take English classes—in any context, face-to-face or online.

There seems little argument that the demand for well-qualified English language teachers will continue for many years to come. The demand from the so-called BRIC countries (Brazil, Russia, India, China) (O'Neill, 2001) alone is already enormous and will continue to grow with economic expansion. Not all clients of online applied linguistics or language teacher education will be teachers of English, and it can also be expected that demand for teachers of the languages of the BRIC countries, as well as other economically important languages such as Spanish, will grow along with world trade. The future for online language teacher education, in other words, looks rosy despite the recent global financial problems, and the market for teacher-training programs is likely to continue to be buoyant.

How Will Instructors' Roles and Responsibilities Change in Online TESOL Programs of the Future?

Who are the instructors who will be available and effective, for online distance classes? What instructor skills and knowledge are needed for online distance TESOL in the future? How will instructors sustain their skills and knowledge? How will online distance instruction be evaluated?

While all TESOL instruction, whether face-to-face or online distance, requires the same knowledge base for instructors, TESOL online distance courses additionally require that instructors address the intersection among pedagogy, technology and learner needs. Effective online instruction in TESOL demands that instructors possess skills in addressing curriculum, materials, activities and tests.

In addition, success of instruction in online distance TESOL requires skills in building community (as described in Shin's and Khalsa's papers).

As is the case in all academic and professional disciplines nowadays, online distance language teacher education is increasingly more available as an instructional delivery option for prospective students. The surge in online distance language teacher education, particularly for TESOL, has already been described in Chapter 1 of this volume. And the reasons for the growth in online distance teacher education in TESOL, specifically, are obvious: the fact that our academic and professional field knows no geographical boundaries (due to the global status English enjoys worldwide now and for the foreseeable future); students can and do prepare to be ESL/EFL teachers while living on one continent, studying in a program housed on another, and planning to teach English on yet a third continent!

In fact, this scenario is far from exceptional now, in the twenty-first century.

At the same time that many students seek online delivery of their instructional programs, academic tradition demands that course content is based on research already done, models already proven and approaches derived from the past. Very little research is now available on online distance TESOL programs' efficacy and power compared to face-to-face programs.

Preparing for the future, while addressing the academic traditions of the past, makes it challenging for the most well-established and respected TESOL programs to provide the preparation students need to meet their increasingly complex and far-reaching professional and academic goals.

TESOL students prepare to teach in an unprecedented and wide range of contexts: all age groups, all proficiency levels and a staggering variety of contexts of English language study. Sometimes, online distance instructors in TESOL programs are familiar with the contexts in which students are currently living, but often they will not be. Sometimes, students in online TESOL programs are also teaching (or working at other jobs) as they pursue their TESOL degree or certificate. In other cases, online TESOL students have no idea where they will be going in the future to teach English. It may be that they will be able to land a job in their home country; or they may decide to take a position somewhere overseas. Political turmoil, natural disasters and unpredictable international relations make it more difficult than in the past for new ESL/EFL teachers to know where they may be teaching in the future.

The short of it is this: in the twenty-first century, online TESOL programs are addressing a far wider range of student expectations, needs and future plans from those that students brought to those programs in the past.

Until recently, teacher education research has focused almost exclusively on face-to-face teaching. And until now, research paradigms—both for learning English online and for teaching English online—have been unavailable. At best, when attempting to apply research done in traditional, face-to-face settings to the online distance learning setting, we can anticipate complex challenges.

The reality we face in TESOL in the twenty-first century offers extraordinary challenges—students all over the world demanding instructional delivery models that rely on projections for the future using innovations in technology to provide quality instruction—while the content of our instructional programs is based on the past—research done, models already proven and approaches derived from the past. Instructors and administrators too face challenging days ahead as we attempt to meet the needs of this very different, highly diverse student market.

TESOL faces a significant period of transition as more and more programs are providing online distance options for prospective students, in some cases relying on old models and traditions, and in other cases, lunging forward on the basis of very skimpy research to support decision-making in the design, implementation and assessment of online distance TESOL programs.

For the foreseeable future, then, instructors will be required to present concepts and principles from the past (based on research conducted in most cases in traditional face-to-face settings—Freeman, Johnson, Murray) to address the future needs of today's extraordinarily diverse teachers-in-training in online distance teacher education. This may be one of the biggest challenges of all for the future of online distance TESOL: predicting the needs and presenting material in ways that address the needs of very diverse student groups. Please see Garton and Edge's chapter for useful analysis on this subject. As Garton and Edge, note: instructors introduce new ideas, students in online distance TESOL courses and programs in the future will acquire skills in addressing their evolving approaches to their classroom practice and research interests. The trail between face-to-face-based research and applications of it to online distance TESOL remains to be explored in more depth in the future.

Two aspects are of particular significance. First, the people coming into teacher-training now are by and large of a generation that has grown up with electronic interconnectedness, for whom there is nothing particularly startling, or even innovative, about linking groups of people instantly and worldwide. For those who are familiar with the graphics and capabilities of sophisticated computer games developed at the cost of millions of dollars, there is little we can do as course designers that will be impressive; we need to focus on using the technologies available as facilitating devices for the kinds of activity that we know promote a critical engagement with learning and personal and social development. Second, many language teachers will have experience of teaching online, or will be expected to teach online in their future careers. This is true whether they work in traditional public sector formal education establishments, private language schools or in the huge (and largely under-researched and under-reported) private one-on-one language teaching industry, a burgeoning area now that technologies such as Skype make "face-to-face" tuition easily accessible (Kazar, 2011). This means that online methodologies demonstrated in our teaching materials are likely to have direct relevance to our students' own teaching, and materials and activities that provide mental stimulation and motivational interaction will have a positive influence on what the teacher-trainees will take into their own future teaching.

All aspects of instructional content and assessment of learning must change as TESOL programs increasingly embrace online formats: foundation courses in principles of TESOL, applied linguistics and cross-cultural communication; courses addressing methodology, materials development and curriculum; testing and program assessment content; statistics and research; and the variety of other content addressed in TESOL programs: English for Specific Purposes, English for Young Learners, technology applications in ESL/EFL, bilingualism, and second literacy development, to name several content areas (among others) found in many TESOL programs. To what extent are teacher educators prepared to meet this challenge of teaching in online distance TESOL? The authors make the following suggestions for TESOL practitioners, and these areas may also generate topics for doctoral programs preparing students for careers in teaching applied linguistics and TESOL online and by distance:

1. Evaluate and use online, distance pedagogical tools on the basis of what kinds of educational experience they can facilitate.
2. Ensure that learner diversity can be accommodated by taking advantage of the affordances and flexibility of online tools.
3. Design distance applied linguistics/TESOL in terms of relevant content but with a continuously developing awareness of the ways in which technology can support learning
4. Evaluate online assessment tools for how far they serve your purposes. Assessment of students in online distance TESOL may differ widely between institutions, but they may include synchronous and asynchronous testing (with students taking their examinations at a distance), physical attendance at a specific location for assessment purposes, oral assessment using media such

as Skype, and graded assignments (discussion postings, quizzes and tests online, oral presentations (e.g. video, virtual classrooms), written essays and projects, etc.). Where traditional (i.e. pre-electronic) distance learning assessment was relatively limited in the number of ways that students could be assessed, there are now very few preclusions.

5. Finally, classroom observations and practical training experiences, in particular, will require new structures, combined with e-learning knowledge, experience and skills. Capstone courses, as well as thesis requirements, will require new ways of providing students with the academic support required to complete these culminating experiences and others like them. See McNeill (2010) for a view of how Capstone courses can be used to assess the outcomes of complex learning.

Evaluation of instruction, decisions about tenure and promotion and other aspects of online distance TESOL faculty evaluation are critical questions for leaders in our field in the twenty-first century. At this time, many universities have no specified guidelines for tenure and promotion of full-time faculty teaching online courses and in many institutions there is little awareness of the procedures and workloads associated with distance learning. An informal survey of the authors of this book (representing online distance TESOL programs) reveals that specific criteria for evaluation of online distance faculty are either non-existent or vague. More worrying is the over-dependence on part-time adjunct faculty at many universities offering online distance TESOL. While held to standard solid criteria for hiring faculty for mainstream teaching and research positions (PhD, experience, record of service and publishing, to name a few), the hiring of inexpensive adjunct faculty (part-time, on-demand hiring, last-minute hiring decisions and no or very limited employment benefits) is alarming for TESOL professionals, as the practice simultaneously marginalizes and devalues the practices of online teaching and learning. Online teachers in many institutional settings need to struggle hard to establish and maintain a suitably high profile for their work, so that their efforts on behalf of their institution do not go unrecognized and unacknowledged.

Adjunct or full-time, online distance TESOL faculty must acquire, use, maintain and sustain professional skills in order to teach effectively in the online distance environment. The fast evolving and long list of technology tools the extraordinary growth in the size of the online distance TESOL market among graduate-level students worldwide (as well as its increasing diversity), and the different needs of distance students compared with their on-campus colleagues are some of the reasons for online distance TESOL instructors to design and plan for their professional development activities, including attendance at workshops and conferences where experiences can be shared.

Advocacy, leadership and reflective practice are all different in online settings when compared to face-to-face ones. Both new faculty and more experienced instructors require ongoing professional development programming to remain effective in the online distance classroom.

In addition to the two critical global issues for online distance TESOL faculty: definition and evaluation of instructional effectiveness in online distance education, and over-dependence on less expensive, part-time adjunct faculty, universities face another critical issue in terms of online distance TESOL: the traditional "big three" for faculty evaluation—teaching, service and scholarly activity—as those are applied worldwide.

Online distance TESOL faculty must be evaluated on criteria that are appropriate to what they do, including their ability to apply technological tools available to them in an increasingly diverse world of TESOL students online using a pedagogical approach that meets learners' needs.

Service, in traditional settings, includes institutional, local, regional, national and international activities that promote the profession and scholarly discipline of TESOL. In online distance settings, faculty members engage in webinars, work individually and with colleagues whom they may never have met face-to-face, in addressing the needs of the profession. Institutional service may apply to serving on a committee or other unit that was previously unknown as a part of the tenure and/or promotion process; or may involve the training of a new colleague in the technological tools (often these are institutionally supported and require that faculty work closely with Institutional Computing, Academic Support and/or Centers for Teaching and Learning to access and correct technology problems that are an inevitable component of all online distance TESOL programs).

As universities begin to realize the financial benefits of online distance TESOL, they must develop new mechanisms to assure quality instruction by providing appropriate professional development support as well as criteria for tenure and promotion (using the teaching-scholarly activity-service approach of the past and perhaps adding new categories within those three components of evaluation) for online distance faculty—full-time as well as adjunct instructors. Student performance and satisfaction as well as alumni support for the institution depend on it. And indeed, with the growing numbers of online distance students, we can anticipate in our programs of study in TESOL and other disciplines as well, our institutions' futures depend on it.

In the next section, we will address, among other issues in program leadership in online distance TESOL, the role and significance of accrediting bodies in online distance TESOL, another source of quality assurance for online distance TESOL programs worldwide.

How Will University Leadership Address Online Distance TESOL Program Needs in the Years Ahead?

Readers know and it is common knowledge that financial and human resources worldwide are in economic flux. Online programs are viewed by most universities' leaders as a way of saving money. And faculty, as well as accrediting agents, seek to assure high quality in TESOL and all instructional disciplines in online distance programs. We will end this chapter with what we intend as a starting point for discussion of an, until now, under-addressed issue: What is the role of program leadership and administration in addressing high quality in TESOL online distance education? How can online distance TESOL model ways of effective use of shrinking financial resources?

In the absence of clear and effective guidelines for faculty evaluation (as noted above), a critical gap exists for program leaders in an effort to assure quality in program and course offerings in online distance TESOL. First and foremost, a system of criteria for addressing effectiveness in online distance education will be needed in the future.

Accreditation and quality control issues will continue to be complex issues for online distance TESOL programs in the future. New accrediting bodies focus on online delivery systems for graduate education; their guidelines, competency lists and goals appear on web sites for the following groups: Distance Education and Training Council (DETC), Quality Matters (QM) and National Standards for Quality Online Education: International Association for K-12 Online Learning (iNACOL). While none of these places emphasis on quality standards for TESOL programs, specifically, these accrediting agents assess online delivery of TESOL instruction. The extent to which distance is a consideration will vary with the accrediting agent. In addition, and relevant to the issue of accreditation in TESOL online distance programs, a recent United States government ruling, reported at the American Council on Education requires U.S. universities offering online distance programs in one state to students who reside in another state to justify reasons for seeking online programs at universities located elsewhere. It is largely due to the lack of understanding of what online teaching is and what it does that misconceptions about quality may arise, and judgments such as the one just outlined, made at a political level, can seriously misjudge the seriousness and rigor of online programs. Similar distrust of distance programs, often reinforced by (true) press reports of degree-mills where domestic pets have been awarded degrees, underpins reports that some governments or education ministries go through phases of discounting degrees that have not been earned through physical attendance at the degree-awarding institution. The United Kingdom's Open University struggled to be taken seriously in its early years (see *The history of the OU* http://www8.open.ac.uk/about/main/the-ou-explained/history-the-ou), and eventually won over its critics largely through the high quality of its coursework books and readers and the acceptance by employers of its graduates.

There is no doubt that providers of online education—and distance education more generally—are of exactly the same variable quality as other educational endeavors, but generally speaking not all universities are damaged by the discovery of questionable practices at a single university, whereas a scandal in distance learning does seem to have an effect on the reputation of the whole sector, since it confirms a common prejudice. For this reason, it is our contention that quality providers would be well-advised to support each other. In a competitive world (a competitiveness that means that sharing of information is only undertaken cautiously, if at all—see Hall & Knox 2009), it may go against the marketing grain to praise the quality of other schools, but we feel that quality needs to be mutually defined, mutually assessed and jointly celebrated if we are to enhance the reputation of the field as a whole.

It seems to us inevitable that the creation of international consortia of reputable educational institutions will grow. It has already started in some fields and at some levels. Business degrees such as the MBA are often taken by attending more than one university as part of the same degree. Joint degrees and co-tutelle arrangements are increasingly common at doctoral levels. The Bologna model, now being adopted across much of Europe and elsewhere, is designed to enhance the possibilities for collaborative degrees. The European *Erasmus Mundus* scheme exists to promote collaborative degrees at masters and doctoral levels and to encourage student mobility. As a result of these and other opportunities, it is probable that worldwide consortia will be formed, much in the same way that airlines have formed groups such as One World and Star Alliance (though probably not as exclusive or monolithic).

Online learning makes such collaborative degrees much easier to achieve and much easier for potential students. There is no reason, once the good will, determination and trust are in place, that a group of providers should not furnish students with the opportunity to take a degree based on a collection of different single courses all taken through different providers. Such consortia would have to agree on quality assurance mechanisms and there would need to be detailed work on costs, student management systems, intellectual property and a host of other administrative details. At the university where one of the authors of this chapter works, there is a current proposal for an award which will involve doctoral candidates being affiliated with five different universities in five different countries, with a final certificate to be signed by each of the five universities. The legal, logistical, practical and even academic issues are considerable, and assuring the compatibility of regulations certainly presents a challenge, but it is a challenge that senior management groups at all the universities are happy to confront. In the case of TESOL and Applied Linguistics programs, the benefits for students (especially in the wide range of options that would be on offer), the profession (in the establishment of more collegial relations and eventual inter-institutional research and course development collaboration) and the institutions (especially in terms of reputation with more robust accreditation and quality assurance processes and links with other quality providers) make the consortium prospect, despite the difficulties, a very attractive way forward.

Conclusion

The future for online distance TESOL, (and all of TESOL beyond online distance programs) depends heavily on a) how programs and the institutions in which they are housed apply standards of quality in applied linguistics/TESOL and how well teachers and researchers in applied linguistics/TESOL are prepared in their online distance programs to meet the changing and evolving needs of English language learners worldwide; b) how well teacher educators are prepared to meld principles of TESOL pedagogy, technology and learner needs in online distance settings; and c) to what extent institutional (universities, in our descriptions) support and compensation address the critical and somewhat urgent needs to build high-quality online distance TESOL programs. In this book, readers will find "a place to begin" in addressing the critical issues ahead for these programs for effective online learning, teaching and program administration.

Discussion Questions

1. This chapter provides readers with some projections on the future of online TESOL. What is the most important and/or useful idea for you as you read this chapter?
2. Describe one idea that you find surprising about the future of online TESOL.
3. Based on your reading of this chapter, write one or two sentences describing online TESOL in the year, 2025. What proportion of TESOL content will be taught online? How many students will be enrolled in online TESOL programs of study leading to graduate-level degrees and/or certificates?
4. Check the web for examples of universities offering joint (collaborative) degrees. Are there more examples of these in some content areas rather than others? Are collaborations more likely to be international than national? Are they likely to involve online programs?

References

Gerber, M., Grund, S., & Grote, G. (2008) Distributed collaboration activities in a blended learning scenario and the effects on learning performance. *Journal of Computer Assisted Learning, 24*, 232–244.

Hall, D. R., & Knox, J. (2009) Issues in the education of TESOL teachers by distance education, *Distance Education, 30*(1), 63–85.

Henry, J., & Meadows, J. (2008) An absolutely riveting online course: Nine principles for excellence in web-based teaching. *Canadian Journal of Learning and Technology, 34*(1) Winter / hiver, 2008. http://www.cjlt.ca/index.php/cjlt/article/view/179/177

Kazar, O. (2011) Watch this space: an emergent industry of teaching English online via synchronous audio/video tools. Unpublished draft PhD thesis, Macquarie University.

Keengwe, J., & Kidd, T. T. (2010) Towards best practice in online learning and teaching in higher education. *MERLOT Journal of Online Learning & Teaching, 6*(2). http://jolt.merlot.org/vol6no2/keengwe_0610.htm

Kissau, S. (2011) Perceptions of self-efficacy for two types of second language methods instruction. *Computer Assisted Language Learning*, ifirst, 1–23.

McNeill, M. (2010) Technologies to support the assessment of complex learning in capstone units: Two case studies. In D. Ifenthaler, P. Isaias, J. M. Spector, S. D. Kinshuk (Eds), *Multiple perspectives on problem solving and learning in the digital age*. New York, NY: Springer.

McQuiggan, C. A. (2007) The role of faculty development in online teaching's potential to question teaching beliefs and assumptions. *Online Journal of Distance Learning Administration, X*(III).

O'Neill, J. (2001) *Building better global economic BRICs*. Global Economics Paper 66. New York: Goldman Sachs.

Paxton, P. (2003) Meeting the challenges of online learning through invitational education. *Educause in Australasia 2003 Conference Proceedings*, pp. 144–151. Adelaide: Educause in Australasia, available at http://www.caudit.edu.au/educauseaustralasia/2003/EDUCAUSE/PDF/INDEXSCR.PDF

Stephenson, O. (Ed.) (2001) *Teaching and learning on-line*. Abingdon: RoutledgeFalmer and Sterling, VA: Stylus Publishing.

CONTRIBUTORS

Anne Burns holds joint positions as Professor of Language Education, Aston University, Birmingham, a university internationally known for its high quality distance programs, and Professor of TESOL, University of New South Wales, Sydney. Her research interests include action research, teacher education, the teaching and learning of speaking, and teacher cognition. More than half of her many doctoral thesis supervisions have been undertaken through distance mode and she has recently supervised PhD research on feedback in online teacher education courses. She has published book chapters on distance education course development (e.g. Burns, A. (2003) "Grammar as fishing or poison? Developing an Australian distance-learning course in systemic functional grammar," in Lui, D. & Master, P. (Eds.), *Grammar Teaching in Teacher Education* (pp. 57–73). Alexandria: TESOL). She is the co-editor (with Jack Richards, 2009, CUP) of *The Cambridge Guide to Second Language Teacher Education* (CUP, 2009), shortlisted for the 2009 Ben Warren Prize, which includes contributions on current issues in distance/ online education. Her most recent books are *The Cambridge Guide to Pedagogy and Practice in Second Language Teaching* (co-edited with Jack C. Richards, 2012, CUP), which contains chapters on technology in the classroom, and online and blended instruction, and *Teaching Speaking: A Holistic Approach* (co-authored with Christine Goh, 2012, CUP). She has been Chair of TESOL's Standing Committee for Research, is a Member-at-Large of AILA, and in 2011 was appointed Academic Advisor to the Oxford University Press Applied Linguistics Series to succeed Henry Widdowson.

Beverly Bickel is the Interim Director and Research Assistant Professor in the Language, Literacy and Culture PhD program at the University of Maryland,

Baltimore County (UMBC). Her teaching and research focus on digital storytelling and digital literacies, globalized communication in cross-cultural contexts, critical pedagogies and online pedagogies, and how the public space of the Internet supports transformational dialogue and knowledge projects. A former ESOL instructor and Director of the UMBC English Language Center, she has worked extensively with English language teachers and learners in a variety of community and higher education settings. Working with instructors at UMBC, she initiated the digital storytelling work in the ELC and led the team that developed the first online course for international teachers of English. This work led to the team's successful proposal to become one of the first five U.S. universities to offer a course for the U.S. Department of State E-Teacher Scholarship Program. The E-Teacher program courses and other online English teacher professional development courses are now reaching 700 international English teachers a year. Dr. Bickel has collaborated with doctoral students and colleagues on research on effective pedagogical approaches for online English teacher professional development and digital storytelling for student-centered, digital literacy projects as well as community development projects.

Christopher N. Candlin is currently Senior Research Professor at Macquarie University and has had a distinguished career in the field of language education and applied linguistics research. In addition, he has guided doctoral (and other) students from countries around the world toward completion of their dissertations (both on site and online) and he continues to lead large-scale and award-winning research projects on discourse analysis and professional communication. With dozens of awards and scores of publications and presentations worldwide, he brings a wealth of knowledge, wide-ranging experience and deep understanding to this volume.

María del Carmen Contijoch-Escontria has worked as an English teacher and teacher trainer for 26 years. She is on the staff of the Foreign-Language Teaching Center at the Universidad Nacional Autónoma de México (UNAM) and graduated with honors from UNAM's master's degree program. In 2009, she obtained a doctorate in applied linguistics from Macquarie University. Her work has focused on communication between tutor and learner, emphasizing the importance of quality feedback and the relationship it fosters. Her interest in online learning began in 2000 with the design of an online diploma course for foreign language teachers. Since then, she has taken several courses related to online learning including the online education and training diploma offered by the London University Institute of Education. She has been an online tutor since 2002 teaching courses in the areas of action research, reading comprehension methodology and introduction to applied linguistics. She has published several articles in Mexican journals, books, and proceedings from international conferences. Currently she is actively involved in training new researchers as well as leading the production of an educational television series for university teachers related to the tutor's transition from the classroom to the online environment and the different competencies, strategies, and roles that he/she needs to acquire in these new digital learning scenarios.

Fiona Copland is Course Director for distance learning MSc TESOL programs at Aston University. She has held this post for three years and previously contributed to the programs as a visiting lecturer. She has worked previously in Nigeria, Hong Kong, Japan, and the United Kingdom as a teacher of English and as a teacher trainer. She holds an MA in applied linguistics and a PhD from the University of Birmingham. Her research interests include feedback processes in initial teacher training, qualitative research methods, and teaching English to young learners. She is also interested in distance learning, particularly in how the learning processes can be enhanced to improve the distance learning experience.

Julian Edge is a Senior Lecturer in Education at Manchester University, where he teaches online courses. He has previously worked with teachers in Jordan, Germany, Egypt, Singapore, Turkey, and Britain. His publications include *Action Research* (2001), *Continuing Cooperative Development* (2002), *Relocating TESOL in An Age of Empire* (2006) and most recently, *From Experience to Knowledge in ELT* (2009, co-authored with Sue Garton).

Liz England is currently Professor and Chair of an established online distance TESOL postgraduate (master's and certificate) program. Based in the United States, at Shenandoah University, she has served students for more than a decade on five continents worldwide. She has been a full-time faculty member at universities in the United States, Hong Kong, and Egypt. In addition, she has been an invited speaker on a variety of issues related to online distance teacher education in Dubai, Pakistan, and the United States. Her published papers on online distance TESOL include articles about the use of technology tools by English language teachers (*CALICO Journal*). Her chapter, "The road map to the future: Online distance TESOL," in a book, co-edited (with Coombes and Schmidt) for University of Michigan Press (2011) addresses the transition from face-to-face to online instruction for online course developers and instructors. She has given invited and refereed papers on online distance TESOL in the U.S., Dubai, and Egypt. Her publications appear as chapters in a variety of books and articles in journals, as well as in electronic volumes (*Business Ethics*, Fall 1999, *Civil Society: An Online Journal*, USIA). As the recipient of awards for her research and service, Liz has traveled to more than 20 countries worldwide to lead workshops and address English language policy issues with colleagues in the following countries: Afghanistan, Chile, the Czech Republic, the Dominican Republic, Dubai, Egypt, Guatemala, Germany, Hungary, India, Israel, Japan, Jordan, Kuwait, Mexico, Oman, Pakistan, Palestine, Russia, Saudi Arabia, Syria, Taiwan, Thailand, Turkey and Venezuela. She has presented refereed papers at TESOL and

IATEFL and for a dozen TESOL affiliates worldwide. Her plenary, *Leaders in Online TESOL*, funded by the Middle East Studies Initiative, U.S. State Department, was presented at the TESOL Arabia Teacher Leadership Academy. She is the recipient of grants from TESOL, U.S. Department of State (English Language Programs Office), Fulbright, Ministries of Education, and K-12 U.S. schools. She is also a reviewer for two Fulbright-funded programs in English language teaching. She also provides workshops for U.S. citizens traveling on Fulbright grants to teach English in overseas settings. An academic accrediting body has identified Liz England's online distance TESOL courses for excellence in online distance education.

Sue Garton is a Lecturer in TESOL at Aston University. She is involved in a range of postgraduate programs in TESOL mainly by distance learning. She has published articles on classroom interaction and teaching spoken language skills. Her most recent publications are *Professional Encounters in TESOL: Discourses of Teachers in Teaching* (edited by Keith Richards) and *From Experience to Knowledge in ELT* (co-authored with Julian Edge). Before moving to Aston, she taught English in Italy.

David R. Hall is an Associate Professor in the Faculty of Human Sciences Macquarie University. He has lived and worked in England, France, Rwanda, Iran, Malaysia, Thailand, and Australia. He is founding coordinator of postgraduate distance programs in applied linguistics at Macquarie University. He co-edits (with Christopher Candlin) *Applied Linguistics In Action* (Pearson Longman) and *Research and Practice in Applied Linguistics* (Palgrave Macmillan).

Deborah Healey is a recognized and accomplished leader in the field of online distance learning and teaching of English as a foreign/second language. She is currently Director of the English Language Institute at the University of Oregon. She is the author of many journal articles and book chapters and also designs high-quality courses for online distance learning. Among her publications is a chapter in *Information Technology in Languages for Specific Purposes* (Cambridge, 2006) and an article "A place to start in selecting software" (co-authored with Norman Johnson) in *CAELL Journal, 8*(1), 1997–1998.

Steven Humphries is an Associate Professor in TESOL and Human Development Director at the School of Education, Shenandoah University. He is an experienced online distance-language teacher educator. With four years' experience in the online context, his contribution to this volume is his first paper based on research with students in observation and curriculum development courses. He has previously worked with teachers worldwide in programs in Korea, Panama and Florida.

Datta Kaur Khalsa is currently Professor and Program Director at the University of Maryland, Baltimore County's Graduate School of Education. With a doctorate in language, literacy, and culture, she has built on dissertation research in the field of online distance education toward building a framework to support virtual teamwork, assessment, and multicultural global interaction.

John S. Knox is a Lecturer in the Department of Linguistics, Macquarie University, and teaches on postgraduate applied linguistics programs. His research interests are in multimodality, media discourse, and language teacher education. He has taught applied linguistics courses in both face-to-face and online distance formats for 10 years.

Miranda Legg is a Senior Language Instructor at the Centre for Applied English Studies (CAES) at the University of Hong Kong. She teaches English for Academic and Specific Purposes to a wide range of undergraduate and postgraduate students. She also teaches on the CAES master's in applied linguistics program. Her research interests include curriculum design, genre analysis, discourse analysis, communication across the curriculum, and language assessment. She has had considerable experience in distance education, having completed an MA in applied linguistics by distance through Macquarie University. She is currently completing a PhD by distance, also through Macquarie University.

Steve Mann is currently an Associate Professor in the Centre for Applied Linguistics at the University of Warwick. He is a course development specialist who supervises doctoral level research groups investigating teacher education. His research includes the investigation of the role of metaphor in teaching. He has taught in Hong Kong, Europe, and Japan.

Paula Garcia McAllister has taught research methods to students located all over the world in a highly interactive course with a strong focus on writing and evaluation of research. She has published several book chapters and research articles in *Language Awareness, TESL Electronic Journal, Canadian Modern Language Review* and *Bilingual Research Journal*. She has taught and lived in Morocco as well as in the United States and is currently adjunct Associate Professor on the faculty at Shenandoah University.

Florin Mihai is an Assistant Professor in TESOL at the University of Central Florida (UCF) where he teaches courses in second language research, applied linguistics, and curriculum development. His research interests include the influence of globalization on foreign language curriculum development, implications of form-focused instruction, language and content-area assessment for English language learners, and pre- and in-service teacher education. Upon the completion of UCF's IDL 6543 interactive distributed learning for technology mediated course delivery course for faculty, he has been teaching all his undergraduate and graduate classes either as M or W courses. W courses are fully web-based courses that are delivered through the Internet, whereas M classes are mixed-mode courses combining web delivery and synchronous class delivery where the web-based instruction substitutes for some face-to-face class time. In his M and W courses, he has developed and tested new, traditional, and alternative assessment instruments that address the challenges of online instruction and are based on solid evaluation principles.

David Nunan is Vice President for Academic Affairs at Anaheim University, California, and Emeritus Professor at the University of Hong Kong, Professor in Education at the University of New South Wales, and Senior Academic Advisor to Global English Corporation in San Francisco. He has published over 100 scholarly books and articles on teacher education, curriculum development, classroom-based research, and the teaching of grammar in the communicative classroom. He is past President of TESOL and Trustee of the International Research Foundation for Language Education. In 2005, he was named one of the 50 most influential Australians internationally.

Leslie Opp-Beckman is a faculty member at the University of Oregon's Linguistics Department and American English Institute where she is the Distance Education Coordinator. Working with a team of faculty and staff, she develops and helps deliver a combination of face-to-face and online distance education courses for ESOL educators. She has published, lectured, and conducted professional training workshops in the area of computer assisted language learning (CALL) for English language educators extensively across the United States and internationally. She is the author of the "Shaping the way we teach English" video-based teacher training materials and a coordinator in the E-Teacher Scholarship Program for ESOL educators worldwide. Related websites of interest include: http://www.uoregon.edu/~leslieob, http://aei.uoregon.edu/distant.html, http://umbc.uoregon.edu/eteacher/, http://oelp.uoregon.edu/shaping.html

Joan Kang Shin currently holds several positions at the University of Maryland, Baltimore County: Research Associate, English Language Center, Clinical Assistant Professor, Education Department, and Director of TESOL Professional Training Programs at the English Language Center. As Director of Programs at the English Language Center she administers, in a consortium with the University Oregon, the U.S. Department of State's E-Teacher Scholarship Program, a fully online teacher training program for EFL teachers around the world. She is also the Project Director of the U.S. Department of Education (USDOE) funded STEP T for ELLs Program (Secondary Teacher Education and Professional Training for English Language Learners) in the Education Department at UMBC. This five-year program provides online and face-to-face professional development to secondary math, science, and social studies teachers in Maryland to give effective content instruction to English language learners (ELLs). See www.umbc.edu/stept for more information. Her recent publications include her dissertation titled "Building an effective international community of inquiry for EFL professionals in an asynchronous online discussion board," a chapter in *Communities of practice: creating learning environments for educators* (edited by J. K. Shin and B. Bickel, 2008), and "Distributing teaching presence: Engaging teachers of English to young learners in an international virtual community of inquiry," in C. Kimble, P. Hildreth, and I. Bourdon (Eds.), *Communities of practice: Creating learning environments for educators.* She also conducts teacher training programs abroad.

Jerry Talandis, Jr. is currently a teacher of English at Toyo Gakuen University in Japan and has also developed technological tools for teaching English. He is a frequent presenter at JALT (TESOL affiliate in Japan) and has recently published a paper in *JALT 2007 Proceedings* entitled "Web 2.0 in the ELT classroom: An introduction."

INDEX